Lessons of a
Generation

CLIFFORD ADELMAN

Lessons of a Generation

Education and Work in the Lives of the High School Class of 1972

Jossey-Bass Publishers
San Francisco

Substantial discounts on bulk quantities of Jossey-Bass books
are available to corporations, professional associations, and other
organizations. For details and discount information, contact the
special sales department at Jossey-Bass Inc., Publishers.
(415) 433-1740; Fax (415) 433-0499.

For sales outside the United States, please contact your local Paramount
Publishing International office.

Manufactured in the United States of America. Nearly all Jossey-Bass
books and jackets are printed on recycled paper that contains at least
50 percent recycled waste, including 10 percent postconsumer waste.
Many of our materials are also printed with vegetable-based inks;
during the printing process these inks emit fewer volatile organic
compounds (VOCs) than petroleum-based inks. VOCs contribute to
the formation of smog.

The epigraph to Chapter One was excerpted from *How Societies
Remember,* by Paul Connerton. Copyright © 1989 by Cambridge University
Press. Reprinted with the permission of Cambridge University Press.

Library of Congress Cataloging-in-Publication Data

Adelman, Clifford.
    Lessons of a generation : education and work in the lives of the
high school class of 1972 / Clifford Adelman. — 1st ed.
        p.   cm.—(A joint publication in the Jossey-Bass higher and
adult education series, the Jossey-Bass social and behavioral
science series, and the Jossey-Bass education series)
    Includes bibliographical references and index.
    ISBN 1-55542-636-0
    1. High school graduates—United States—Longitudinal studies.
2. High school graduates—Employment—United States—Longitudinal
studies.   3. Educational surveys—United States. I. Title.
II. Series: Jossey-Bass higher and adult education series.
III. Series: Jossey-Bass social and behavioral science series.
IV. Series: Jossey-Bass education series.
LB1695.6.A34   1994
373.12'912'0973—dc20   94-21633
                                                            CIP

FIRST EDITION
HB Printing   10 9 8 7 6 5 4 3 2 1   *Code 9432*

Contents

Preface

As the high school class of 1972 was preparing to graduate that spring, I published a first book called *Generations* (Praeger and Penguin). It had all the clumsy hallmarks of a first book of a twenty-something, and I dread opening up to its inflated prose and amateurish research today. It tried to explode then-fashionable myths of youth culture. It tried to set its theses in a complex web of cultural attitudes, media habits, political language and behavior, and higher education. It relied on a survey of 530 people between the ages of seventeen and thirty-two, and the less said about the way in which the sample was drawn, the better. There was no real data analysis, only single-dimensional tables. All events were in the present tense: there was no past, there was no growth.

The electronic media did not care about those limitations. I was propelled onto the talk-show-book-hype circuit. NBC made sure I received my first hair styling before going into the "green room" and following heavyweight champ Joe Frazier onto the set to face curve balls from the late Frank McGee. Lonely people called in to the radio control rooms for advice on school, drugs, politics, and love. I had no choice but to respond, however embarrassed I was at the shallowness of my words.

Perhaps one must develop a past of one's own to perceive such limitations. Yes, there was much in that book that was right and that has been borne out by time. But little could I imagine how much the three million people in the high school graduation lines that spring would change the very way I thought about time, let alone the kind of historical evidence necessary for people to reflect fully on their own lives and times.

The subtitle of this book echoes across two decades. Instead of a flat snapshot of people between the ages of seventeen and thirty-two, though, the stories of this book are scenes from a movie made by a large group of people as they became thirty-two from seventeen. There are no myths to explode, rather stories to discover.

Background and Audience

Lessons of a Generation is about critical educational and occupational choices people made in what, in the craft trades, would be called the journeyman's period of becoming an adult in the United States in the last quarter of the twentieth century. To highlight those choices, it extracts from a massive archive of data some key strands of the tapestry of our recent domestic social and economic history. While its principal subjects are the 56 percent of 1972 high school graduates who continued their formal education in any way by the time they were thirty-two years old, and while higher education is at the core of its accounts, this book was not written solely for college and community college professors, administrators, or student service personnel. True, they would benefit from reading these accounts and understanding better what happens to the millions of students who pass through their institutions—and why it happens.

But the book was also written for a more general audience. It is a reflective gift to the class of 1972 itself, and to the other high school graduating classes of the same period. It says, in effect, "You have taught us, as a nation, a great deal about the way we are and how we got there. You did not know how much you taught us, and how much of the warp and woof of our history you created. These are some scenes from your spinning: may they both comfort and challenge you."

Among the high school graduates of the early 1970s are people who have become legislators, journalists, and key decision makers in other fields of our social, cultural, and economic life. I have written with them in mind, too. In fact, I was stimulated by many phone calls from such individuals that I received at the U.S. Department of Education in the late 1980s. The callers were seeking information, analysis, guidance, and—most of all—empirical evidence that would help them make better policy decisions or craft more responsible news stories or write more beneficial laws.

Fortunately, the department's National Center for Education Statistics (NCES) had the foresight to plan and execute a series of longitudinal studies of single-age cohorts of Americans. But too few people seemed to know how to use these data and render the information comprehensible and accessible to the general public. That became one of my principal jobs for the department—making the data sing.

The federal government is often seen to be an intractable environment that stifles thought and creativity and that washes all language into bland, sanitized, impersonal, and passive voices. It ain't necessarily so. A wise government knows that one of its most important obligations is to provide its constituents with information that they can turn into knowledge, and to engage the imagination of its constituents through clear and compelling communication. A wise government learns from its own information in the same way. Governments, in fact, behave with personality and are often filled with self-doubt. They aren't quite sure whether the information they routinely collect is valuable. They have to be persuaded.

I am grateful for the tolerance of the bureaucracy in the process of producing both the studies that preceded this book and the book itself. To be sure, there were some rocky moments along the way, but ultimately, the federal government is wiser than most people (including its own employees) think. To fulfill its obligations, it accepts—within boundaries—individuality, even modest eccentricity. That strategy allows for organizational learning. If nothing else arises from this book, I hope the federal government is persuaded to continue the type of data collection and studies on which I have relied.

Acknowledgments

The foremost acknowledgments are due to the Office of Educational Research and Improvement (OERI) of the U.S. Department of Education, under whose auspices I was able to carry out the data base cleaning and analyses reflected in this volume. Four of the six chapters here were originally published as monographs by OERI, as were the reference materials and taxonomy necessary for researchers to work with the NLS-72 archive. In these efforts, I am grateful for the support and encouragement of former Assistant Secretaries Chester Finn, Christopher Cross, Bruno Manno, and Diane Ravitch, as well as three directors of the Office of Research: Sally Kilgore, Milton Goldberg, and Joseph Conaty. The commissioner of NCES, Emerson Elliot, and the chief of staff of NCES, P. Ron Hall, were essential partners in persuading the bureaucracy that my reshapings of national data were constructive. The director of OERI's publications branch, Cynthia Dorfman, and my in-house federal editor, Margery Martin, provided invaluable editorial advice.

Four of my colleagues at NCES should receive special citation. Without C. Dennis Carroll's leadership and Paula Knepper's work, there would be no longitudinal studies in the U.S. Department of Education worth talking about. Without Nabeel Alsalam, I could not have learned how to put this archive together in an intelligent way. Without John Burkett's critique and eagle eye, the text would not be as persuasive.

Both the National Science Foundation and the U.S. Department of Labor's Employment and Training Administration contributed much-needed funds for computer time in the reconstruction of the data archive. Without their assistance, this project would not have been either as timely or as reliable. The staff of the Division of Computer Resources and Training and the National Institutes of Health were particularly patient and helpful over the period during which the data were being cleaned and cranked.

Dozens of people reviewed various chapters in this volume, and their comments were always insightful and provocative. They included Alexander Astin, Lena Astin, and Arthur Cohen of UCLA, Judith Eaton of the Council for the Advancement of Education,

Zelda Gamson of the University of Massachusetts, Boston, Gerald Graff of the University of Chicago, Theodore Marchese of the American Association for Higher Education, Kit Morriss of the Knight Foundation's Commission on Intercollegiate Athletics, James Palmer of Illinois State University, Jill Tarule of the University of Vermont, Jeffrey Thomas of the National Endowment for the Humanities, and Maris Vinovskis of the University of Michigan.

Public interest in these stories was aided immeasurably by reporters, editors, and columnists with whom I worked over the period in which the chapters were originally published, among whom were Dean Wylie and Gary Speaker of the *Los Angeles Times,* Kenneth Cooper and Judy Mann of the *Washington Post,* Bob Brown and Eric Brady of *USA Today,* Claudia Pryor and Lynn Scherr of ABC's "20/20," and Joanne Fuchs of CNN.

Finally, the members of my family—Nancy, Jonathan, and Nicholas—have been extraordinarily supportive and tolerant of all the household and telephone-line disruptions the research and writing of this book have entailed, let alone the inevitable high anxiety of a resident writer. They are justly relieved that I have moved on to something else.

Kensington, Maryland   Clifford Adelman
September 1994

Lessons of a Generation is dedicated to the 22,652 people in the high school graduating class of 1972 whose extraordinary cooperation and loyalty to federal surveys and record gatherings, proddings, and temperature takings over a fourteen-year period have enlarged our national wisdom well beyond that of other nations. As you have shared your lives (albeit anonymously) with your fellow citizens, so may we share our reflections on the lessons of your lives, both with you and with your children. You have been our teachers; we have been your students. We hope we have listened well.

The Author

Clifford Adelman is senior research analyst in the Office of Research, U.S. Department of Education. He earned his B.A. degree (1964) in English at Brown University, and his M.A. degree (1965) and Ph.D. degree (1976) in the history of culture at the University of Chicago. Before joining the Department of Education in 1979, he taught at the City College of New York and Yale University and served as associate dean and assistant vice president for academic affairs at the William Paterson College of New Jersey. During this period, two books of his were also published, *Generations* (1972) and *No Loaves, No Parables: Liberal Politics and the American Language* (1975).

Adelman's work in the Department of Education has focused on projects concerning reform in higher education, testing and assessment, and the development and use of large-scale national data archives. He designed and managed the higher education work of the National Commission on Excellence in Education (*A Nation at Risk* [1983]), and was staff director and amanuensis for the higher education report that followed, *Involvement in Learning* (1984). He designed, edited, and wrote large parts of the series on assessment that followed *Involvement in Learning*, including *Assessment in American Higher Education* (1985), *Performance and Judgment* (1988), and *Signs and Traces: Model Indicators of College Student Learning in the Disciplines* (1989).

Lessons of a Generation

Chapter 1

Accounts and Stories:
Tracking a Generation

> We all come to know each other by asking for accounts, by
> giving accounts, by believing or disbelieving stories about
> each other's pasts and identities. . . . The narrative of one
> life is part of an interconnecting set of narratives; it is em-
> bedded in the story of those groups from which individuals
> derive their identity.
> —*Paul Connerton*, How Societies Remember, *p. 21.*

This book offers some accounts that have waited a long time to be
given.

These accounts derive from the richest archive ever assembled
on a generation of Americans. They are available to us now because
of the foresight and wisdom of decisions made nearly a quarter
century ago by individuals in the old Office of Education in the
former Department of Health, Education, and Welfare. I was still
in graduate school when these decisions were made. Two decades
later, my own life and understanding were enriched immensely as
a result, and I hope yours will be as well.

Note: Chapters Two, Three, Four, and Five were originally published as
monographs by the U.S. Department of Education between December 1990
and October 1992. During this period, there were continual minor corrections to the data base for the postsecondary education transcript sample of

It was a fashion at the time, a fashion that has now become a permanent idea, to believe that higher education has significant and long-term effects in the lives of individuals (Feldman and Newcomb, 1969; Hyman, Wright, and Reed, 1975). But no one knew for sure. No one knew precisely how different educational choices we make in our lives from adolescence to adulthood—choices of courses in high school, choices of whether and when to attend college, choices of curricula and other activities in college—play out in combination with other life choices. These include marriage, divorce, parenthood, military service, community activity, and, most important, choices to work in different occupations and industries. No one knew precisely how educational choices affected our economic, social, and cultural well-being. And what can be said of individual well-being could also be said of national well-being; what could be said of one narrative could be said of what Connerton (1989, p. 21) called an "interconnecting set of narratives"—that is, a story about all of us.

Uncertainty has a way of nagging. The wise men and women responsible for the archive I have used in writing this book asked a simple question: What if we were to take a single generation, a single cohort of Americans, all born in roughly the same year, pick them up in their senior year of high school, and follow them in life choices for a long period of time? Follow them in and out of school, college, work, family, community life, aspirations, plans, opinions, and so forth in sufficient detail (for example, courses taken, reasons for leaving a job) to generate a multidimensional portrait of their

---

the class of 1972. All data that appear in this book have been drawn from the final corrected version of the transcript data tapes, hence are slightly different, at times, from the data that appeared in the monographs. In addition, all four chapters have been revised and expanded. In the course of revision, I have reduced the technical content of the studies. Readers who drink data and wish to see even more tables, standard errors, and technical notes are referred to the original publications, all of which are available from the Office of Research, U.S. Department of Education: *Light and Shadows on College Athletes* (1990); *Women at Thirtysomething: Paradoxes of Attainment* (1991; 2nd ed., 1992); *The Way We Are: The Community College as American Thermometer* (1992); and *Tourists in Our Own Land: Cultural Literacies and the College Curriculum* (1992).

lives? If such data were gathered over ten, fifteen, or even twenty-five years, we would have not a snapshot but a motion picture—and in that motion picture, a drama that would help us explain the consequences of choice and circumstance. In fact, it would provide far more detail on choices than our nation had ever possessed.

In the language of those who conduct surveys, a snapshot data base is called *cross-sectional,* and the most widely known examples come from the U.S. census. Whatever their subject, cross-sectional data bases say, this is the way it is at a given moment in time. By comparing moments, we can see the way it was and the degree to which it has changed. But all we really see are a series of current status reports on large groups of people. We do not see how the status of individuals in one snapshot is any different from the status of individuals in the previous snapshot, because even in census reports, we are not looking at the same people. Snapshots also offer no clues as to why the overall picture has changed. The dynamics of change must be inferred, and inference on the basis of snapshots is risky. In the motion picture of a longitudinal study, reasoned the planners of the archive I examine here, inference is less risky because the clues and dynamics are inherent in an evolving story about a single group of individuals.

Thus was born the *National Longitudinal Study of the High School Class of 1972* (NLS-72). There is no other reference point quite like it. While there have been other longitudinal studies in the United States that have tracked educational and labor-market experiences of large national samples (see Resource D), there is no group as large from a single age cohort that anyone has followed in such detail from high school to "thirtysomething." For that reason, in part, what you will read here must be the baseline against which subsequent cohorts will be measured. And, indeed, there are subsequent cohorts. The National Center for Education Statistics, which designed the NLS-72 and its successors, has created two other studies involving cohorts roughly ten years apart: the *High School and Beyond* (HSB) study, covering the high school classes of 1980 and 1982, and the *National Educational Longitudinal Study* (NELS-88), which picked up its subjects in the eighth grade in 1988. Most of these eighth-graders graduated from high school in 1992.

It may be tempting to respond to what you will read in this

book that "it's different today." Honestly, you don't know that. None of us does. Until we actually see what happens to the high school classes of 1982 and 1992, until their stories play out to "thirtysomething," we do not know that anything is different. Unfortunately for our curiosity, no fourteen-, sixteen-, or eighteen-year-olds will take pills that turn them overnight into a group of thirty-five-year-olds with histories just because we are impatient for comparable contemporary data. In the world of longitudinal studies, we simply have to wait for people to age.

When I was green and running over college, I had the accidental privilege of studying writing with the late Pulitzer Prize-winning poet John Berryman. Berryman's first lesson was about first sentences and first paragraphs. He would take an opening sentence such as Tolstoy's "Happy families are all alike; each unhappy family is unhappy in its own way" and spend an hour prodding us to figure out why these were carefully and brilliantly chosen words to introduce the 900 pages of *Anna Karenina*. Full of challenge and ambiguity, that first sentence tells us something important about those 900 pages and how Tolstoy would like us to read them.

Similarly, if the introduction to any book is honest, it tells the reader how the author thinks the rest of the book should be read—and why. For this book, the introduction is a tough task because I hope to cover a lot of issues. To form the core of the book, I render four accounts drawn from the records left by members of the high school class of 1972 that cover their lives from roughly age fifteen to age thirty-two. These accounts concern four groups of people—women, athletes, individuals who attended community colleges, and all the college students in the sample (from the standpoint of their cultural literacy).

The first group, women, was selected on the basis of a specific demographic characteristic that inherently involves a complexity of choices. The second group, athletes, was selected to illustrate what happens to people with a special talent who choose—or are pressured to choose—to develop that talent. The third group, community college students, was selected to trace what happens to people as a result of a choice they made to associate with a specific type of institution. And the fourth group, the entire sample of college students from the perspective of their cultural literacy, was selected to explore what people who choose a common educational experience might actually learn. To be sure, some of these groups appear in more than one account. Each account, however, is self-contained and covers the choices, achievements, and disappointments of the group under discussion. Where appropriate, these accounts also examine the accuracy of public perceptions about the education and labor-market experiences of these four groups as they became adults. Indeed, following these accounts, I provide some reflections on the context of becoming an adult in the United States during the period 1972–1986 and the changing shape of higher education during that period.

When these four accounts were first published by the U.S. Department of Education in slightly different form between 1990 and 1992, each of them received considerable attention from either the media, Congress, government agencies, educational associations, or combinations of the above. In many ways, the responses to these reports were as revealing as the reports themselves and taught me a great deal about how our polity deals with unusual or uncomfortable information from powerful sources of data. In reworking these accounts, I will share some of that learning with you.

In these opening pages, I want to tell you

- Who these accounts are about and who they are not about
- What kinds of records the accounts are based on, why it is important that these records be accurate, and how one knows when they are not accurate (frankly, I want to scare the wits out of you with respect to information you may currently accept as sacred)
- How a historical approach to these records is different from a strictly statistical approach, and why quantitative history is a better framework than social statistics for interpreting national archives composed of longitudinal data (frankly, I also want to persuade you that history by the numbers is better than both history without numbers and social statistics with no soul)
- Why I picked these four stories, as opposed to other stories that might be told with the same records, and, allied to that, what these stories have in common

Therefore, this opening chapter is heavy on methodology. It is important stuff.

The Cohort: Half a Generation

It might have been the high school class of 1971 that was studied
if the federal paperwork had been completed sooner. It might have
been the class of 1973—or even the class of 1974—if the federal
budget's astrological signs had been aligned a year earlier. So let the
class of 1972 stand in for the generation that passed out of adolescence in the early 1970s.

The specific subjects of the NLS-72 archive were selected in
their senior year of high school. In this particular cohort (and its
peer cohorts of the same period), 25 percent never made it to the
senior year of high school. So the archive, however rich, starts with
three-fourths of the generation. Furthermore, because the studies in
this book focus principally on the nature and effects of education,
my primary subjects are those individuals who continued their education after high school in any way, in any type of institution, and
at any time up to 1986 when they were thirty-two years old. Roughly
two out of three people who were high school seniors in the spring
of 1972 acquired some postsecondary education at some time during
the next fourteen years. Some took only a course or two in a college
or a trade school. Some took dozens of courses but never earned a
degree. Some earned Ph.D degrees. Two-thirds of high school seniors continuing their education is a lot. But the bottom line of this
tally reads very simply: two-thirds of three-quarters of a generation
is still half a generation.

Some will argue that the other half is wholly forgotten. That
is not true (Adelman, 1993). The scholarly literature and popular
literature on education, as well as the literature of public policy
(particularly on youth employment), all devote considerable attention to school dropouts and to comparisons between high school
graduates who do and do not go to college. The analyses I am able
to undertake in this book are artifacts of the archive: they are determined by the data, and the NLS-72 sample does not include school
dropouts. It does include those whose formal education ended in the
high school graduation line, and they appear in discussions of high
school performance and labor-market experience. But the four accounts in this book ask questions that require subjects who have
engaged in voluntary intentional learning as adults and records of

precisely what was studied by these individuals. The sponsor of this archive, after all, was the U.S. Department of Education.

Samples, Surveys, and Records

About 3 million people graduated from high school in the spring of 1972, and over 1.8 million of them went to college, community college, and/or trade school by the time they were thirty. The 3 million high school graduates are represented in the NLS-72 study by 22,652 individuals. These people were selected in three stages. In the spring of 1972, a representative national sample of 1,061 high schools was drawn. Within each high school, eighteen seniors were selected at random. These people participated in a base-year (1972) survey that asked them hundreds of questions about family backgrounds, high school experiences, plans and aspirations, and opinions. After the spring of 1972, a supplementary sample of 257 high schools (and eighteen students within each school) was drawn to compensate for nonresponse in the first sample. High school records were obtained for virtually everyone in both groups. Scholastic Aptitude Test (SAT) and American College Test (ACT) scores were obtained for all students who took those tests (9,200), and roughly 19,000 students took a special learned-abilities test that was developed for the NLS-72 study.

Over the next fourteen years, subsamples of this base-year group were surveyed five times: in 1973, 1974, 1976, 1979, and 1986. The extraordinary loyalty of the participants should be evident from the fact that in 1986—fourteen years after graduating from high school—12,841 of them (87 percent of those asked) filled out a sixty-five-page questionnaire covering virtually every aspect of their lives between age twenty-five and age thirty-two, providing month-by-month accounts of employment, schooling, and family life, as well as other data (Tourangeau and others, 1987). Survey response rates such as these are what statisticians call "robust." Compared to response rates for most other longitudinal studies, "robust" is an understatement.

Of course there were extremes. On the one hand, my colleagues are fond of telling the story of one anonymous student who returned every survey form blank, folded into a paper airplane, in a box with a block of cement, with postage to be paid by the U.S. government. On the other hand, we are told, students from one high school used the arrival of the follow-up NLS-72 surveys as the occasion for class reunions. They would break out a case of wine and spend an evening rehearsing their lives for each other and for posterity. We are pleased to have provided the occasion for such accounts and connections.

In the 1979 survey, 14,750 respondents indicated that they had attended at least one college or trade school since high school graduation, and they subsequently granted the government permission to obtain their transcripts from these institutions. These transcripts were gathered in 1984, twelve years after the cohort graduated from high school. Over 19,000 valid transcripts were received for 12,600 students. This collection, referred to in this book as the *postsecondary education transcript sample* (NLS-PETS) is probably the most unusual portion of the archive; it is the one on which all the analyses in this book will pivot.

The fifth follow-up survey in 1986 is also critical to most of the analyses in this book because it provides a full history of 12,841 participants' labor-market experience and family formation in young adulthood. Of this group, 64 percent were also in the NLS-PETS. The felicitously large overlap between the two is a by-product of the sampling design for the fifth follow-up. It was not an element of that design.

The base-year survey was designed so that it is possible to extrapolate to the general population of three million high school seniors in the spring of 1972. Every student in the base-year sample was assigned a unique weight representing his or her position in the general population of high school seniors. The weight assigned was in inverse proportion to the probability that a given student would be selected in a purely random procedure. Thus, for example, a black student from a rural high school in Iowa would carry a relatively high weight; a white student from a suburban high school on Long Island would carry a relatively low weight. In the NLS-72 archive, the student carries that weight into subsequent surveys or "panels" (for example, the 1976 survey or the 1986 survey), in which the weight is modified by the demographic characteristics of participants in that panel.

The further removed a panel is in time from the base-year sample, the less inferential and more descriptive the analyses of that panel must be. That is, a claim made for the people in the group under analysis rests on stronger grounds than does the same claim extended to the general population of the class of 1972. But the person who wound up in, say, the 1986 follow-up survey retains a portion of his or her 1972 weight in the archive, and this portion justifies a modicum of inferential analysis from the 1986 group to the larger population of adults who had both graduated from high school and were thirty-two or thirty-three years old in 1986. The weights are extremely important, and all the data in this book are weighted according to the panel or combinations of panels from which they are derived. So when you look at a table and see that the number of people on whom the data for that table are based is, say, 5,127, what you are seeing is the number of people in the NLS-72 study, not the number of people they represent in the population. In this case, the 5,127 are the people in the NLS-PETS who earned bachelor's degrees. The weights for that panel are such that the 5,127 represent 732,511 people in the high school class of 1972. You do not always see this weighted number, but the percentages in the table are based on it.

Tell Me Lies, Tell Me Sweet Little Lies

College transcripts, high school records, and SAT or ACT test scores are what Webb, Campbell, Schwartz, and Sechrest (1966) call "unobtrusive measures." All these records are artifacts designed to record student behavior and are produced and provided by parties other than the students themselves. As such, they differ considerably from survey data. They provide evidence against which to judge how modest, honest, or forgetful people may be when making claims on surveys regarding their activities and achievements. Although institutional idiosyncrasies may render some transcripts difficult to read or compare with others, transcripts do not exaggerate, they do not lie, and they do not forget. Depending on the question, however, people responding to surveys do all three of the above.

For example, as I am writing this chapter in 1993, the National Center for Education Statistics is gathering the college transcripts for the next generation in the longitudinal studies series, the high school class of 1982. In the course of telephone interviews at age twenty-eight, nine respondents indicated that they had attended a certain very prestigious university. However, when the Department of Education's contractor for data gathering requested these transcripts, the university claimed that only one of the students had attended at any time in the previous decade. The university administrators checked alumni records. They checked records of their professional schools and graduate departments. They double-checked. "Well," a colleague of mine remarked, "I guess if you are going to lie about where you went to school, you might as well say that one."

If one does not corroborate assertions with unobtrusive evidence, these lies accumulate. In 1986, we asked survey respondents in the NLS-72 to indicate their highest level of educational attainment. Of all questions that could be asked of high school graduates at age thirty-two, this is the first question one would expect to be asked by the U.S. Department of Education. Some 8,205 respondents to the survey (out of 12,841) were also in the transcript sample, so I could ask the same question of postsecondary transcripts gathered two years earlier and compare what the transcripts showed with the survey responses. I did, and here is what I found:

- Of those who claimed to hold a doctoral or first professional degree (medicine or law, for example) at age thirty-two, 6.2 percent had not even earned a bachelor's degree by age thirty.
- Of those who claimed the bachelor's as their highest degree at age thirty-two, 11.5 percent not only held no degree at all but had earned less than sixty undergraduate credits by age thirty. Of this group, in turn, 87 percent were not even in school between the ages of thirty and thirty-two, so had no chance to earn a degree during that period.

The magnitude of these differences lies beyond standard errors of measurement. Based on this evidence, along with previous analyses demonstrating that high school students misperceive the type of curriculum in which their transcripts say they were enrolled (Rosenbaum 1980; Rumberger and Daymont, 1984), I, for one, am skeptical about using survey data to determine educational attainment. When Fetters, Stowe, and Owings (1984) matched transcripts against student survey responses to questions about grades, coursework, and courses in the High School and Beyond longitudinal studies, variances in the quality of response by race, gender, and academic ability were considerable. These findings are not comforting. Furthermore, these researchers demonstrated that students exaggerate the extent of their coursework, and that "there generally is a decay in the quality [of survey responses] as the recall period lengthens" (p. 31). To be sure, Fetters, Stowe, and Owings were referring to high school transcripts, but since postsecondary transcripts and careers are more complex, one suspects these discrepancies would be greater in higher education, and greater still in the NLS-72 archives, in which the recall period on surveys can be as much as fourteen years.

I often ask the people who call the U.S. Department of Education with questions about college curricula if they can list the courses they took in college. While they like the question, they usually struggle for ten minutes or so to come up with, at best, 75 to 80 percent of the titles. The older they are, the longer they struggle for diminishing returns. Some two decades after graduate school, I cannot reconstruct my transcript.

Cleaning Data and Constructing Analysis Files

The massive amounts of data in an archive such as the NLS-72 will be grist for the mills of historians, economists, sociologists, and public policy analysts for decades to come. As a historian, I believe that data should be as accurate and complete as possible. The "public release" NLS-72 data tapes contain binary information that is three times removed from its source. Students responded to questions on a survey form, a U.S. Department of Education contractor created coding schemes for categorizing those responses, and coders made judgments in placing the responses into those schemes. Likewise, registrars at thousands of postsecondary institutions used their own protocols to create transcripts, a contractor developed schemes to render the information on those transcripts comparable, and coders made judgments that took the literal information on the transcripts and transformed it by the rules of the code. By the time the information got on the data tapes, then, two potential distortions had occurred. This happens on all national surveys. It is scary.

Major distortions are comparatively easy to spot: one begins to perform analyses, and the results do not make sense. There is obviously something wrong or something missing. There are two ways to deal with this problem, depending on where it arises. The first is simply to accept the data as given and to eliminate all odd cases in any analysis. Had I followed this procedure in the matter of degrees earned, for example, the analyses would have been based on the records of about 10,100 students, not 12,600. That is a 20 percent reduction in the sample size.

The second way to deal with the problem (and the one I have preferred here) is to go back to the original source, to look at the literal response or entry, and to correct the coding. For example, I noted some strange data on students whose highest educational attainment was the associate's degree. According to the raw data tapes, a significant percentage of those students had earned more than 120 undergraduate credits—twice the number of credits usually required for the associate's degree. I then asked the data base to identify the institutions that had awarded the associate's degrees to these people. The answers included (in significant numbers) Smith; Oberlin; Vassar; the University of North Carolina, Chapel Hill; Indiana University; and so on. These institutions do not award the associate's degree. When I asked the data base to produce the literal names of the "associate's degrees" entered on the transcripts of those students, the answers included "A.B.," "AB," "Arts," and "AM," among others. Evidently, the coders had entered any degree beginning with the letter A as an associate's degree. A significant number of bachelor's degrees and master's degrees had been so coded, and women were disproportionately represented among those affected.

This was the tip of the iceberg. On further investigation, following the same trail back to the original degree designation and matching the degree against other information on the transcript, it appeared that approximately one out of every six degrees had been misclassified. That is not an insignificant proportion. Each miscoding had to be corrected, and these were only the most obvious of the corrections to the transcript file. There were thousands of other corrections, including those for missing dates (of terms or degrees) where those dates could be inferred from other transcript information, and those for missing credit information for courses in which grades had been recorded.

A College Course Map: Taxonomy and Transcript Data (Adelman, 1990a) describes the massive task of recoding the 485,000 course entries on the transcripts and the creation of a new course taxonomy that would reflect, as accurately as possible, what the students in the PETS data base had actually studied. If one out of every six degrees had been misclassified, you can imagine the ratio for misclassified courses. Without that new course-coding system, the analyses in this volume would have been impossible to undertake.

The quality of people's responses to survey questions is sometimes just as shaky as their claims to degrees. We tend to take people's word when they are asked what they do for a living and who employs them. But a college transcript file such as the PETS allows researchers to rein in some obviously inflated notions. For example, if someone's occupation is coded as "veterinarian," yet the transcript file showed that he or she does not possess the requisite degrees, that person is not a veterinarian. The coder may not have taken the time to classify the person appropriately (possibly as "clinical laboratory technologist" or "animal caretaker, excluding farm"), but that can be done in the course of programming. The same process can be used for other occupations—such as architect, engineer, lawyer, actuary, psychologist, and elementary school teacher—that require specific credentials or levels of education. You will note, particularly in Chapters Two and Four, that I have taken the 400-odd occupational codes used in the NLS-72 and aggregated them into forty-plus "jobs," many of which are defined with reference to other variables, including educational attainment and industry.

Why Fix the Account? History by the Numbers

Why bother with all of this? What is the point of making painstaking efforts to clean data bases such as the NLS-72? Numbers are icons in contemporary culture. We too readily assume that a number produced by an authoritative source represents a known and unassailable reality. We do not ask how the number was produced, and even if we do ask and know something is wrong, we accept statistical adjustments to the number in place of corrections of fact. We accept reality by algorithm. It is easier and quicker to follow a set problem-solving procedure, and accuracy loses out to timeliness in the context of our electronic lives. We want to know now and are willing to pay for today's data with considerable margins of error. When public or institutional policy is developed on the basis of those margins of error, however, we pay in more concrete ways for our mistakes.

There is a temperamental difference between quantitative historians and social statisticians in regard to numbers, one that reveals different views of the epistemology of evidence. Most historians work with pre-electronic cultures and periods and with samples that are not scientifically drawn. The construction of data from parish records, maps, artifacts, pamphlets, diaries, drawings, or clothing is slow and involves the constant search for corroborating evidence. All such records, historian Marc Bloch (1953) wrote, must be cross-examined. The historian is concerned with the relationship between the resulting number or mark and the reality. If the reality has not been identified or perceived correctly, the mark is wrong. The social statistician, however, does not focus on the relationship between mark and reality but on the mark itself, since the reality expresses itself directly in the mark and not through artifacts such as records, drawings, or clothing. In the electronic world of designed samples within which the social statistician works, the origin of the mark is taken for granted.

In the future, social historians will use the NLS-72 archive, but in our time the principal users are social statisticians. As long as they tend to accept the mark, I want to make sure it is the right mark. The case of the bachelor's degrees miscoded as associate's degrees (which affects women more than men because women's colleges were more likely to use "A.B." as the designation for bachelor's degrees) is the kind of case that breaks the boundaries of chance, the statistician's benchmark. Had the coding error gone uncorrected, it would appear that women's educational attainment was lower than it was in fact. No one wants these errors to multiply into myth a century from now. So we fix them. The alternative is to throw out cases that do not seem to make sense and thus to reduce the population under analysis.

History or Statistics? The Accounts in This Book

This book is hardly the first collection of analyses based on the NLS-72, though it may be one of the first to use the whole archive. Of the hundreds of articles and books that have used NLS-72 data since they began to appear in 1974 (see Taylor, Stafford, and Place, 1981; Maline, 1993), it appears that a quarter describe and analyze discrete portions of the data set (such as high school records), another quarter compare discrete portions of the NLS-72 data to data from other sources (about student educational aspirations, for example), and the remaining half test hypotheses on relationships among several variables drawn from different portions of the archive (for instance, the impact of college grades on early career earnings). These studies play by tight statistical rules and are dominated by standard, account-oriented, social statistics: X is correlated with Y better than Z; C explains Q percent of the variance in B. They often worry about sampling; they always worry about the effects of using different statistical models. Some wind up telling us more about research methods than about the subject at hand.

The accounts I offer are less governed by tight statistical rules and models because I see the NLS-72 archive as a set of guides to understanding both the experience and spirit of a generation. These guides provide an empirical history of selected aspects of human life, but that history is not an end in itself. It calls out for connections to trends in the larger society that the data base, however rich, does not offer. These connections are difficult to perceive at present because we are still living them. The course of history, however reflected in tidy numbers, is inherently sloppy.

Nevertheless, from the days of Herodotus, historians have made quantitative statements. If one said that public officials had a growing interest in health matters in the late nineteenth century, that statement is, in effect, quantitative, and one had better have the evidence for "growing." If you said that the movement of populations from rural to urban centers in colonial America in the mid-eighteenth century was significant, you have made a quantitative statement and had better possess the evidence for "significant." If I say that the interest of the Grimm brothers in the evolution of languages was typical of European intellectuals at the turn of the nineteenth century, I have really made a quantitative assertion and had better have some evidence of "typical." The language of history—whether social, economic, or intellectual history—is often a language of quantity (you see, I have just done it again—consider "often").

From the historian's point of view, let alone from other perspectives, ours is eminently a statistical century. We have counted everything. Our record keeping overwhelms us. No institution in our society has been exempt. Numbers and aggregations abound at the smallest units of social analysis—village, firm, school. It is downright difficult to avoid such data. The important question is how should one use them.

Do We Want to Be Certain or Reasonable?

A historical approach to data such those in the NLS-72 archive cannot claim causal relationships between phenomena; all it can say is that one set of phenomena is associated with another. A quantitative exploration of such associations may lead to correlations, but not to explanations of cause and effect. At best, the historical approach can use numbers to suggest the strength of the associations. There is too much in the story of this generation that is not quantifiable to allow anyone to push the analysis further than that. For example, the NLS-72 surveys all asked questions about why people did or did not pursue a course of conduct, such as going to college or quitting a job. The response options, however, do not reveal the intensity of a respondent's feelings or the weight of the explanation in the respondent's mind.

As a second—and related—principle, a historical approach must often settle for what is reasonable, as opposed to what is certain, but it must try to render its analyses as persuasive as possible by eliminating ambiguities in numbers and by clearly defining the population. For instance, in defining the universe of people necessary to analyze earnings at age thirty-two, we want to be sure that the people in that universe were consistent labor-market participants, not occasional participants or new entrants to the work force. The economic literature shows that years of work experience are directly related to earnings, and we want to control for that powerful and commonsense relationship before asking other questions. For similar purposes of control, the social statistician would use a regression analysis and seek certainty; I would rather limit the universe and seek reasonableness.

These principles of association and reasonableness derive, in part, from the fact that individuals do not always make choices for "rational" economic or educational reasons. There is an emotional content to the life of a generation that data cannot capture. A wise friend of mine once asked me whether the members of the class of 1972 were happy at thirtysomething. Did the surveys ever ask them how satisfied or pleased they were at their progress, their whole lives, their communities, or their society, which, of course, is our society? Not really. The surveys asked whether they were satisfied with school and job and for a number of dimensions of those satisfactions, but nothing more. There are no direct statements from participants on the meaning of the data they produced or on their times and experiences. There are no texts in the traditionally understood sense of that term. And when there are no texts, it is hard to get at the lives that are lived behind the mask of data.

During the years in which the class of 1972 came into adulthood, Angus Campbell and his colleagues did ask a different sample of the population about satisfaction with various "domains" of life such as marriage, friendships, housing, health, leisure, and work (Campbell, Converse, and Rodgers, 1976; Campbell, 1981). While I will spend more time with these findings in the last chapter of this book, we can get a taste of the overall pattern of satisfaction by looking at responses to the question, "Is life in the U.S. getting better, staying the same, or getting worse?" (Table 1.1). With the exception of the age group approaching retirement, the generation of which the class of 1972 was on the cusp was the only one with a marked increase in pessimism. Some aspects of the accounts in this book may help explain why.

Think of any generation as a biological organism. It may not be the best analogy, but it gets close to the historical method I have in mind. We make empirical observations of this organism's evolution and know that many forces are acting both on and within it. However, we cannot ascribe a given stage in the organism's development to any one or even any small group of those forces, not

**Table 1.1. General Population Surveys of Satisfaction
with Life in the United States, 1971 and 1978.**

Age group	*Ratio of responses: worse/better*[a]		
	1971	*1978*[b]	*Change*
18–24	1.3	2.1	+0.8
25–34	2.7	1.9	–0.8
35–44	2.1	2.1	None
45–54	2.3	2.2	–0.1
55–64	1.9	2.3	+0.4

[a]The higher the number, the more people who thought life was getting worse.

[b]The 1978 figures are those for the 1971 age group seven years later. Thus, the people who were aged eighteen to twenty-four in 1971 (roughly the class of 1972) were twenty-five to thirty-four when they were resurveyed in 1978.

Source: Adapted from U.S. Bureau of the Census, 1980, Table K, p. LX.

with statistical certainty, not with the power of laws of theoretical science. Historians are not that exact and cannot pretend to be, any more than biologists can be statistically certain of cause. Historians work "outward and upward from the sources" in a kind of "qualitative empiricism" (Forster, 1978, p. 74).

So, while this book will present the reader with many numbers, it is important to understand the kind of numbers involved and their limitations. The numbers reflect choices made by individuals in situations that had multidimensional boundaries. The choices were controlled selections—that is, individuals did what was possible for them to do under the circumstances. While it is not my intention to write a metaphysics of choice behavior, it is extraordinarily important to understand that when decisions are made to pursue one path as opposed to others, when those selections occur in a stream of time, when circumstances change and choices can be reversed, and when this whole drama is being played out in the three million private lives of the class of 1972, it is incumbent on us to represent what happened in all its diversity. With all due respect to colleagues and friends, this is not a job for a statistician.

How I Learned to Stop Loving the Mean

Once upon a time, my employer, the U.S. Department of Education, held an annual rite at which the average SAT and ACT scores of U.S. high school students were presented, by state, on a large piece of paper. This piece of paper was called The Wall Chart, and it contained more information than average test scores. Whatever else was up against that wall, though, it was the test scores that made the newspapers. Not merely the mean score, by state, but also the change from last year's mean score to this year's mean, expressed in points. Missouri up 3 points; Alaska down 2 points. The Wall Chart was read as stock tables are read, but with far less faithfulness to the realities it represented.

After all, not everybody takes the SAT or ACT, not even all college-bound high school students. Furthermore, a change of 3 points in mean score on the SAT, whether in Missouri or nationally, may be no change at all. It depends on the distribution of scores. This is not the occasion for an essay on reporting test scores. But it is an occasion to point to the differences between the kind of information that results from means and the kind of information that is reflected in distributions.

Mean scores represent central tendencies. Central tendencies are convenient. They are neat marks that can be used as shorthand indicators. The newspapers love them. Although all responsible reporting of means includes the standard deviations from the mean, you will never meet a standard deviation in the daily news. Even though a standard deviation is fairly simple to explain, it's too hard to explain in the newspapers. (However, one could always try a crude statement such as, "If you know the mean and the standard deviation of anything, you know the range of results for the vast majority of people whose behavior is being measured. Anything more or less than the outer boundaries of that range is unusual.") We live in a culture that likes pithy propagandistic statements such as "men always test better than women," even though these statements do not represent the richness and variety of human performance very well (as Chapter Two will illustrate).

What I have learned in preparing these accounts is that, provided one has a large group, the way the group's behavior is distributed with respect to a given characteristic (for example, numbers of credits earned in foreign language courses) tells us a lot more than the central tendency. A distribution enables us to isolate populations at the extreme ends of performance and to ask questions about these populations. A distribution enables us to identify the "deviant cases" and to find out what makes them so. Distributions enrich the accounts. So one of the reasons that you will be presented with many numbers is that I would rather give you rich accounts than poor ones.

Statistical Significance Versus Historical Significance

In presenting statistics, I include standard errors of measurement for those cases in which they are both relevant and important. In any sample, let alone one subject to longitudinal pokings and proddings, there are bound to be errors. Some errors are due to missing data—for instance, when a respondent did not answer a question on a survey or when a transcript we requested was never received. (When a trade school for training barge pilots on the Mississippi sank with all its records, for example, the transcript files for some students in the NLS-72 were obviously incomplete.) Other errors are due to survey bias and random mistakes. Bias is avoidable; random error is not.

In general, the smaller the sample of people one is talking about, the greater the effects of errors. But it doesn't always work out that way, and that is what the notion of statistical significance is all about. Statistical significance, though, is very different from historical significance. We all make judgment calls about data that may not be statistically significant but that may be historically significant. Conversely, there are many statistically significant observations that do not reflect the slightest ripple of the character of their times. What is subject to aggregate quantification may not be as important in history as the deviant case—the unique situation (the Finland Station), the remarkable individual (Leonardo da Vinci). The graduation rates for varsity football and basketball players did not become historically significant until 1990, when Congress passed the Student Right-to-Know Act (P.L. 101-542). That act has since become a powerful symbolic indicator of the kinds of information about higher education that are regarded as important in current public policy. We can now judge the social values implicit in the new policy and connect them with larger trends in our culture.

My point is that the mere presentation of numbers, even along with their appropriate indicators of statistical significance, is insufficient. Historians in particular cannot simply collect data as ends in themselves (Hunt, 1986). Numbers do not absolve anyone from staking out speculative lines of inquiry that go beyond the boundaries and capacities of a data base. We cannot strike the pose of the self-portrait Albrecht Dürer sent to his physician without adding the caption (as Dürer did), "There, where my finger is pointing: that's where it hurts."

The Role of the Universe

One of the most persistent frustrations of both the general public and policy makers with the work of number crunching and poll taking is that no two statistical descriptions of the same empirical phenomenon seem to agree. How does this happen, and what do the studies in this book do about it?

It Depends on How You Ask the Question

The best way to demonstrate what typically happens is by example. Let us use one of the most deceptively simple and frequently asked pair of questions in higher education: What percentage of the people who go to college earn a bachelor's degree? How long does it take them to do it? The key to what results when these two questions are asked is the definition of the universe, or the denominator in the equation. Who is included among those who "go to college"? Anyone who simply registers for a course, whether he or she earns any credits or not? Anyone who registers with the intention of earning a bachelor's degree? Anyone who attends only four-year colleges? Anyone who enters any kind of college at any time in his or her life?

Table 1.2 presents six different universes (denominators) that can be used to answer the first question, and (not surprisingly) six different answers to that question. With the exception of the universe that contains all 22,652 NLS-72 participants, the data for both the universes and the answers comes from the PETS. What do we know about this sample? First, it is based on student records (collections of transcripts) that cover twelve years of the participants' history. Second, most of the people from the class of 1972 who are in this sample are those who entered any kind of postsecondary institution by October 1979 (when they were twenty-five or twenty-six years old) and for whom the National Center for Education Statistics was subsequently (in 1984) able to obtain at least one transcript. Third, the weighting of the data in the PETS accounts for nonresponse (for example, for people for whom transcripts were requested but not received). So while there are virtues to these data, no matter what universe we choose, there are also some limitations.

In this book, I try to make sure that the reader always knows (either from the context or from a note to a table) what universe I am talking about and why. All analysts want you to see what they want you to see. Analysts can jiggle a universe in an infinite variety of ways to produce preferred hypotheses. Thus, a reader should always ask *why* a universe is being defined the way it is, and the burden of explanation is on the analyst. There are important occasions in these studies in which the data in Table 1.2 help explain, for example, why women graduate from college faster than men (Chapter Two) and why black varsity athletes eventually graduate from college at a higher rate than all other black students—indeed, at a higher rate than a large proportion of white students (Chapter Three).

As for how long it took NLS-72 bachelor's degree recipients to earn their degrees, the definition of that universe is more complex than one might think. Using the PETS group, I started with all the people who earned the bachelor's degree but dropped those whose records contained either notations of missing transcripts or transcripts with missing dates. I wanted to be sure, in calculating the time it takes to earn a bachelor's degree, that I had both a date for first entry into any kind of postsecondary institution and the date on which the bachelor's degree was conferred. I also dropped students with transcripts that contained anomalous term-date information that could not be resolved. The unit of analysis here is time;

Table 1.2. Highest Degree Earned by NLS-72 Students, by Subgroup
and Race/Ethnicity, 1972–1984.

		Degree	
			Bachelor's
		Associate's	degree
Universe	None	degree	or higher
Universe 1[a]			
All	72.3 (.16)[b]	4.9 (.06)	22.8 (.15)
White	70.2 (.18)	5.2 (.07)	24.6 (.17)
Black	84.2 (.32)	2.9 (.10)	12.9 (.31)
Hispanic	86.9 (.46)	4.2 (.26)	8.9 (.44)
Universe 2[c]			
All	51.0 (.25)	8.8 (.11)	40.2 (.23)
White	48.5 (.25)	9.1 (.12)	42.4 (.26)
Black	67.4 (.58)	6.1 (.21)	26.5 (.57)
Hispanic	70.9 (.82)	9.5 (.53)	19.6 (.83)
Universe 3[d]			
All	43.5 (.24)	10.2 (.12)	46.4 (.24)
White	41.2 (.25)	10.4 (.13)	48.5 (.27)
Black	59.8 (.63)	7.5 (.26)	32.7 (.62)
Hispanic	64.5 (.94)	11.6 (.65)	23.9 (.97)
Universe 4[e]			
All	41.5 (.24)	10.3 (.13)	49.3 (.24)
White	39.2 (.25)	10.4 (.17)	50.4 (.27)
Black	57.6 (.68)	7.8 (.28)	34.5 (.66)
Hispanic	62.1 (1.0)	12.4 (.69)	25.6 (1.0)
Universe 5[f]			
All	35.8 (.27)	1.9 (.06)	62.3 (.26)
White	33.7 (.28)	1.9 (.06)	64.4 (.27)
Black	52.7 (1.0)	2.1 (.12)	45.1 (1.0)
Hispanic	55.9 (1.7)	3.5 (.16)	40.6 (1.8)
Universe 6[g]			
All	27.8 (.25)	2.0 (.06)	70.3 (.24)
White	25.9 (.25)	1.9 (.06)	72.2 (.25)
Black	44.6 (1.0)	2.5 (.16)	52.9 (1.1)
Hispanic	49.6 (2.1)	2.4 (1.0)	48.0 (2.1)

Note: Rows may not add to 100.0% due to rounding.

[a]All students in the base-year sample. $N = 22, 652$.

[b]Standard errors in parentheses.

[c]All students for whom postsecondary transcripts showing any
earned credits were received. $N = 12,336$.

[d]All students who earned more than ten postsecondary credits at any
time between 1972 and 1984. $N = 10,734$.

**Table 1.2. Highest Degree Earned by NLS-72 Students, by Subgroup
and Race/Ethnicity, 1972-1984, Cont'd.**

---

e All students who attended either two- and/or four-year colleges
and who earned more than ten postsecondary credits. N = 10,364.
f All students who attended only four-year colleges and who earned
more than ten postsecondary credits. N = 5,772.
g All students who entered college within six months of graduating
from high school, who attended only four-year colleges, and who earned
more than ten postsecondary credits. N = 4,797.

therefore, any mark of the data that does not allow for an accurate
calculation of time disqualifies that record from the universe.

Table 1.3 provides the upshot of asking the question with
these restrictions. It shows that the mean elapsed time to degree was
4.54 *calendar* years, a figure that represents almost five full *academic*
years. That figure, in itself, ought to demonstrate that the death of
the "normal" four-year bachelor's degree is not a recent phenomenon.

Furthermore, the standard deviation for mean time to degree
of all bachelor's degrees received was 1.46 calendar years. By putting
the mean and standard deviation together, we can say that roughly
84 percent of the NLS-72 students who received bachelor's degrees
between 1972 and 1984 did so within six (4.54 + 1.46) *calendar* years
of the day they first entered college—no matter when they first entered. This figure provides a powerful range of reasonableness for
time to degree.

When the question is asked a different way (year of degree
and not time to degree), the data indicate that 88 percent of all those
in the NLS-72 who received bachelor's degrees by 1984 had done so
by the end of calendar year 1978, 6.5 years after graduating from
high school. It also turns out that 88 percent of those who received
bachelor's degrees entered college directly from high school.
Whether one uses Table 1.2 or these figures, it is obvious that entering college directly from high school dramatically increases the
chances of completing a bachelor's degree. And it turns out that this
is true regardless of race, gender, or socioeconomic status.

The Answer Depends on Your Source

One of the most persistent matters of concern in higher education
is retention. Boards of trustees, state legislatures, and Congress fre-

Table 1.3. Years to Earn a Bachelor's Degree, by Gender,
Race/Ethnicity, College Major, and Institutional Type, 1972–1984.

Student and institutional category	Mean[a] (years)	Standard deviation (years)	Standard error	Percent of universe
All bachelor's degree recipients	4.54	1.46	.02	
Gender				
Men	4.68	1.51	.03	53.9%
Women	4.38	1.37	.03	46.1
Race/ethnicity				
White	4.52	1.44	.02	89.8
Black	4.66	1.64	.09	7.9
Hispanic	5.24	1.61	.17	2.3
Student major[b]				
Business	4.63	1.57	.06	16.4
Education	4.41	1.40	.05	17.8
Engineering/ computer science	4.78	1.72	.12	5.2
Physical sciences/ math	4.51	1.44	.11	4.0
Humanities	4.55	1.46	.10	5.9
Fine/performing arts	4.54	1.26	.09	4.7
Biological sciences	4.37	1.10	.07	5.7
Health sciences/ services	4.65	1.41	.09	6.8
Applied sciences	4.76	1.58	.13	3.8
Applied social sciences	4.57	1.43	.08	8.0
Vocational-technical	5.00	1.78	.25	1.3
Vocational services	4.66	1.19	.16	1.4
Other	4.90	1.88	.22	1.8
Institutional type[c]				
Doctoral	4.57	1.39	.04	40.3
Comprehensive	4.56	1.51	.04	47.7
Liberal arts	4.31	1.37	.07	8.6
Other	4.69	1.60	.14	3.4

Note: The universe includes all NLS-PETS students who earned a bachelor's degree, had no transcripts missing, and had no missing dates for either entry to postsecondary education or bachelor's degree. Low-side anomalies due to odd transcript entries have been removed. N =3,995.

**Table 1.3. Years to Earn a Bachelor's Degree, by Gender,
Race/Ethnicity, College Major, and Institutional Type, 1972–1984, Cont'd.**

[a]Time to degree was calculated by subtracting the date of first entry to any postsecondary institution from the date on which the bachelor's degree was awarded.

[b]In shaping the NLS-72 data base for the studies in this book, I used several configurations of undergraduate majors. The most common configuration I used, with twelve categories, is displayed in Resource A. Table 1.3 happens to use a different configuration with fourteen categories because I wanted to highlight applied and vocational fields.

[c]See Resource A for definitions of these categories.

quently ask questions about students who were enrolled at Old Siwash last year but not this year. The questions are asked in particular about members of minority groups. The institution is punished in the public eye for not ensuring that students return. Furthermore, students who do not return are presumed to be dropouts, deviant cases. This is a deficit model: the institution has deficits, the student has deficits. There are only sinners, no saints.

This is a grim, and false, picture. A national transcript sample like the PETS blows it up. These twelve years of empirical student records from a single cohort challenge almost all the terms, definitions, and assumptions of the debates on retention and dropout. They allow us to describe postsecondary careers with a confidence we have not previously enjoyed. The reasons should be obvious: geography and time.

A national collection of records from the same group of students, no matter where they went for their postsecondary education or when, crosses both state lines and the border between public and private institutions. There is no other system of tracking students that can do that. Some states can track within state borders, in public institutions only, and do it very well. But the result is an incomplete picture. In addition, only complete long-term student records can demonstrate that many students who disappear from one institution without a credential turn up, after a period of time, in another. Retention rates at Old Siwash are not as important to the present analysis as retention rates in the entire U.S. system of higher education; in fact, retention rates at Old Siwash are irrelevant.

The data presented in Table 1.4 provide some hints of the

Table 1.4. Number of Postsecondary Institutions Attended, 1972–1984.

Highest degree earned	1	2	3+
None	75.6%	20.0%	4.4%
Certificate/license	70.4	23.3	6.3
Associate's	62.4	27.1	10.5
Bachelor's	56.1	34.4	9.5
All students	68.1	25.2	6.7

Note: N = 10,183.

extent to which the NLS-PETS generation moved from one institution to another at all levels up to the bachelor's degree. In this table, I have excluded from the NLS-PETS universe any student who earned a bachelor's degree *plus* any postbaccalaureate credits or degrees, since changing institutions between undergraduate and graduate programs is not at issue here. More recent data indicate even greater interinstitutional mobility. Of all 1986 bachelor's degree recipients, only 51.5 percent attended only one institution (National Center for Education Statistics, 1987, p. 11). Of course, one might say that the second or third or fourth institutions attended involved incidental contact (for example, a summer school course). No doubt this is true in some cases. But for the people in the NLS-72 group who attended more than one institution, the time lapse between first and last enrollment in higher education indicates that something else may be at work, a stopping out and a dropping back. Some 43 percent of the bachelor's degree recipients in this group who attended three or more institutions, for example, took more than 6.5 calendar years to earn their degrees, and it is highly unlikely that that time period involved continuous enrollment punctuated by summer school courses at institutions other than Old Siwash. Such data do not answer all the questions about retention and mobility, but they certainly indicate that—in fits and starts—people persist.

Four Stories

If you had graduated from high school in the spring of 1972 and were about to go to your twenty-fifth reunion, what would you want to know about your class (besides whatever happened to Marvin Jones)? Probably, you would be most interested in the basic demographics: who got married and who got divorced (and how many times), and who had how many kids, wound up in different jobs, earned college and graduate degrees, owned businesses, became rich or poor, and so forth. All of this information is in the NLS-72 archive. For example, by age thirty-two, 68 percent had been married, 66 percent had natural children, 29 percent of those married had been divorced or separated, and 39 percent of the latter group had remarried. One large portion of demographic information is missing, however. While we know who died, there are no data on the physical health of the generation (other than the comparatively rare cases of people who said they left a job or quit school because of health problems).

You might also want to know how people's opinions and aspirations had changed: whether they still valued money more than anything else, whether they still felt it was important to correct injustices in society, or whether their desire to obtain Ph.D.'s had mellowed. This information, too, can be derived from the 4,000-plus questions that were asked of respondents over the fourteen years of the five follow-up surveys.

But significant pieces of the spiritual history of the generation are missing. For example, if you went to your twenty-fifth reunion, you might want to find out if people's sense of humor had changed, what their most significant failures had been, how their relationships with spouses, children, and/or lovers had changed, what they typically think about while commuting to work, and whether—if they could do it all over again—they would do it the same way. These are narrative questions precluded by the form of national surveys.

Three other missing pieces of spiritual history are more obvious: sex, religion, and politics. The longitudinal studies of the National Center for Education Statistics are government surveys, and government agencies are justly sensitive about asking people questions on their sexual, religious, and political activities and views, even when respondents are guaranteed anonymity. The NLS-72 surveys never asked any questions about sexual activities, practices, or attitudes, thus leaving a large part of psychological life for young adults wholly private. The NLS-72 archive records respondents' religious affiliation only as seniors in high school. We have no idea if—or how—those affiliations changed. Based on survey responses, we know whether people are registered to vote, when they voted in elections, and whether they ever participated in political organizations. But we have no idea if they were Democrats, Republicans, or something else; no idea if they judged themselves to be conservative, liberal, or something else; or if any of these simple political barometers changed over time.

A national interpretation of this archive is somewhat different from the poll conducted for a twenty-fifth high school reunion. From a national perspective, the NLS-72 archive was designed to teach all of us what aspects of our lives may be different as a result of schooling, what kind of learning makes a difference, what the institutions and organizations responsible for education can do to make a better difference, and what we, as individuals, can do to ensure that our society and economy benefit fully from the investments we have made in learning. One can argue that key elements of private life such as sex, religion, and politics are developed in concert with schooling, and that the social and economic history of a generation is incomplete if it does not account for them. True. But we work with the artifacts at hand.

Of the hundreds of inquiries that can be undertaken using the NLS-72 from a national perspective, this book takes up only four. I selected these four studies because, in different ways, each has been a concern of public policy, newspaper stories and editorials, or virulent polemics, and because, in all cases, the arguments used have relied on incomplete, spurious, or outright imaginary data. Why have the topics of these studies been concerns of public policy and argument? Because each reflects a configuration of values that our society has yet to define fully or agree to, because all of the topics, broadly speaking, are "economic" stories, and because they all illustrate the nature and effects of life choices. That is, they are about investments of time and effort that have different "yields" to both individuals and society. We are still struggling for understanding and consensus on what these investments and their yields should be. What the stories of the class of 1972 show us are the dimensions of this struggle.

Chapter Two follows the NLS-72 women for fifteen critical years, using the entire range of the archive but emphasizing labor-market experience and changing attitudes toward school, work, and various life values. One could perform the same kind of analysis using any large demographic grouping—for example, race. And one could perform the analysis using more sophisticated statistical techniques. But from the moment I started to explore the data of the NLS-72 archive, there was no question that the most fascinating and stunning story to emerge was that of the women of this generation and what they had and had not attained.

It is standard practice when examining social statistics to ask the computer for cross-tabulations by race/ethnicity, gender, and socioeconomic status (SES) for every variable or group of variables. I did this. Columns of numbers marched by like so many troops in a military parade. But as they passed, a contingent literally leapt from the printouts. The women's story is unmistakable and powerful. There is no other story like it in the archive, and it is about a very large group of people.

Chapter Three is about a very small group of people— smaller than you think, and that is part of the point. The research for this chapter was motivated by the introduction of what became the Student Right-to-Know Act. There was a popular perception that college varsity athletes, particularly football and basketball players, never graduated and were thoroughly exploited by their institutions in the process. This perception was a product of anec-dotal evidence. No one believed any data existed that could either confirm or deny the mythology. But it is obvious that the NLS-72 archive can do it, as can any long-term longitudinal study that includes high school records and college transcripts.

One could perform a similar kind of analysis with any group in a generation whose lives are largely defined in terms of a special talent or activity, and around whom a social mythology arises. In-deed, Chapter Three also compares the careers of college varsity athletes with those of students in the performing arts. Chapter Three is ultimately about the way we treat "stars" in our society. It is also about the corruption of education by the entertainment industry.

Chapter Four offers a portrait of people in the class of 1972 who come to inhabit the great economic middle ground of our nation through the choices and circumstances that led them to use community colleges along the way. The community college turns out to be a unique entity among U.S. educational institutions in terms of the way it functions in people's lives. To highlight this unique status, Chapter Four pays considerable attention to long-term patterns of attendance in postsecondary institutions and to indicators of economic mobility for students who were originally (at age eighteen) from the lowest socioeconomic bracket. While I have to guess about this, I have little doubt that members of the class of 1972 are still attending community colleges twenty years later. There is no other institution that can accommodate them as well over such a long period.

Chapter Five was occasioned by a spate of editorials, op-ed pieces, and heated campus exchanges in the late 1980s over the comparative exposure of U.S. undergraduates to information about Western civilization and non-Western/nonmajority cultures. These exchanges are continuing under the rubric of "cultural diversity." In all the heat, no one ever cited national data concerning what people actually study in college because no one had those data. The reconstruction and cleaning of the PETS archive made such data accessible, at least for the generation of the NLS-72. The analysis presented here was undertaken to provide an empirical base against which to judge the various anecdotes, single-campus studies, and disputes about this topic. Ultimately, the account is about the values we declare when we choose to invest time and effort in studying particular subjects. It is also an "economic" account in that it treats acquired areas of knowledge as potential commodities.

So, four studies: demographic group, group with a special talent, institutional effects, and curricular choices. Each one tells us something different about the 1.8 million people in the class of 1972 who continued their education after high school (and, by extension, the 5.6 million people in the other high school graduating classes of the early 1970s). Do the accounts add up to anything? Do they enable us to describe a "spirit" of this generation? Do they enable us to determine how these millions of adults can influence our culture, economy, and polity? What can these 1.8 million adults learn from their own records that they can use to help us all rethink what we do in school and work life? The last chapter tries to answer those questions. It gets outside the data base and puts the class of 1972 into the swirling currents of the history through which it moved in the 1970s and early 1980s.

In light of those questions, though, it may be helpful to illustrate, however briefly, the way I will use the NLS-72 data to present guidelines for determining economic influence, and then to indicate why our assessment of this influence must be preliminary.

The Knowledge Content of Work

There is one economic theme that I stress in this book and one on which I am prepared to make some leaps of faith. I propose, very simply, that what you study is what you learn and that what you learn comprises a large part of what you bring to the workplace. There is a direct line from formal education and training to the way one will exercise—and even change—one's work. To draw that line, one can start with education and look toward work, or start with job status and look backward at education and training.

If we start with the evidence of education, we can use both the high school records and the college transcripts of the NLS-72 to argue that people who have devoted considerable time and effort to studying specific subject matter are likely to bring the knowledge and skills they acquire to their jobs, no matter what those jobs might be. This is not a simple matter of majoring in a field in college and later working in that field. It may involve majoring in one field, such as international relations, and working in another, such as management in an industry producing durable goods. The more cases of this kind one can find among those in management positions in a particular industry, the more plausible the hypothesis that managers in that industry are internationally oriented and knowledgeable. But the more likely outcome of starting by identifying everyone who studied international affairs and asking where they would end up in economic life at age thirty-two would be a scatterplot: some are teachers, some are musicians, some are social workers, some are computer technicians.

We can also start with occupational status at a given point in time and look backward. Let us take all those members of the class of 1972 who were managers or salespersons in 1986 and who had attended any kind of college. Do their records show that they studied a sufficient amount of internationally oriented material to acquire a global outlook and/or be literate in a language other than English? Whether they earned a degree or whether they majored in an internationally oriented field would be a secondary variable in this interpretation. The primary variables are course-taking patterns. Table 1.5 illustrates this particular case. Based on the records of the class of 1972, the table is a de facto map of what the current generation of thirtysomething managers brought to their jobs in the way of international knowledge and orientation in the late 1970s and 1980s. The pattern here is clear. The map may help explain

Table 1.5. The Internationally Oriented Education of NLS-72
Students Who Were Managers or Salespersons in 1986.

| Area of study | Postsecondary credits | | | | |
	None	1–4	5–8	9–12	13+
Any foreign language and international studies					
Bachelor's degree	48.9%	16.3%	16.0%	6.8%	12.0%
No bachelor's degree	85.0	8.0	3.0	2.0	2.0
Elementary/intermediate Spanish, French, or German					
Bachelor's degree	66.2	10.6	14.2	3.7	5.3
No bachelor's degree	90.2	3.8	3.5	1.3	1.2
Advanced/literature in Spanish, French, or German					
Bachelor's degree	94.3	3.0	1.3	0.3	1.1
No bachelor's degree	99.2	0.5	0.2	0.1	0.0
Non-Western culture, history, and society					
Bachelor's degree	83.8	11.0	3.3	1.2	0.7
No bachelor's degree	96.9	3.0	0.1	0.0	0.0

Note: The universe includes all participants in the 1986 follow-up survey who indicated an occupation as manager or administrator in financial services, manufacturing, communications, or human services industries, or as sales manager/sales personnel in either wholesaling or manufacturing/construction. $N = 1,298$.

why U.S. industry was slow to compete aggressively on the world economic stage during that period. This situation may change, and the class of 1972 may yet contribute to the change. But it is difficult to offer specific predictions, and for the same two reasons that all my propositions about the spirit of this generation are preliminary.

Two Unfinished Stories

There are two reasons we would be making great leaps of faith in 1993 to answer questions about the "spirit" of the generation.

The first is that the story of the NLS-72 is itself incomplete. Originally, a sixth follow-up at age forty was planned. For some reason, it was dropped. The story currently ends at thirtysomething, and that is too early. We have a once-in-a-lifetime opportunity to follow a generation into its forties and to test many hypotheses about the effects of education, career choice, and family formation on people from different backgrounds. We know, for example, that the period of life between the ages of thirty-two and forty is likely to be more critical for women's education and career development than for men's. But we will never know anything about that, let alone any other topic, for sure unless we reinstate the sixth follow-up survey. It will not be cheap ($3 to S4 million), but for a national archive as unique and rich as this one, it will be worth the investment.

The second reason questions about the spirit of the class of 1972 cannot be fully answered is that there is presently no way to compare that class to other classes. For example, using the NLS-72 alone, one could trace the growth and decline of altruism in the generation through attitudinal questions, choices of courses in college, and labor-market history. Were the members of the class of 1972 more or less likely to devote themselves to human service? Is a devotion to human service in academic study, careers, and voluntary work a sufficient indicator of altruism? If researchers constructed such an indicator, how would we know that it was unusual or noteworthy unless we had time-series data?

In this respect, the other longitudinal studies of the National Center for Education Statistics will eventually provide needed comparisons. The most complete and comparable of these studies is the ten-year follow-up (at age twenty-eight) for the high school class of 1982, an undertaking that also includes an eleven-year post-secondary transcript sample. The data from this effort should be ready for analysis in the near future. When they are, it is my hope that we will start turning the accounts of these archives into stories.

Chapter 2

Women at Thirtysomething: Paradoxes of Attainment

I am sure that readers of this book remember the tone of the newspaper columns at the end of that *annus mirabilis* of 1989. The shadow of the year 2001 was over everything. Columnists ranging from Samuelson in *Newsweek* to Abelson in *Barron's* worried then—and worry now—that the U.S. work force will be wholly eclipsed by work forces in other advanced postindustrial nations, that we are unprepared for the upheavals and opportunities of a global economy, and that, ultimately, our standard of living will fall. Their recitations defined the "going mood," and the going mood hasn't gone away.

But the going mood overlooks a going reality that few have marked: if we play it right, if we allow our oft-stated beliefs in rewards for educational achievement to govern, if economic justice can determine economic strategy, the women of the United States will make the difference. We will not be eclipsed, and our standard of living will not fall. If we play it right, and just.

The United States will enter the next century with a remarkable edge over its global competitors. U.S. women, of all races, are the best educated and trained in the world and will constitute 64 percent of the new entrants to our work force by the turn of the century. U.S. women now make up more than half of enrollees and degree recipients at all levels of higher education except the doctoral (and even there, the gap between men and women should disappear within a decade) and first professional sectors.[1] The changes in women's educational attainment since 1971–72, the year our respondents were seniors in high school, and 1990–91, the most recent year for which data are available, as Table 2.1 shows, have been rather dramatic.

Table 2.1. Percent of Degrees Awarded to Women.

Degree	1971–72	1990–91[a]
Associate's	43.1%	58.9%
Bachelor's	43.6	54.5
Master's	40.6	56.4
First professional	6.2	39.2
Doctoral	15.8	42.5

[a]U.S. citizens only.

Source: Snyder, 1993, pp. 272 (Table 252), 275 (Table 255), 278 (Table 258), 281 (Table 261), and 284 (Table 265).

In contrast, in the late 1980s, women constituted only 45 percent of the total enrollment in higher education in Italy and Great Britain, 42 percent in West Germany and the Netherlands, and 34 percent in Japan.[2] In terms of general access and attainment in higher education, the issue of women's educational equity in the United States is largely passé. That battle has been won, fair and square. Labor-market equity, sadly, is another issue.

"Americans are missing something," Kerstin Keen of Volvo said to me during a break at a conference of the Organization for Economic Cooperation and Development in Washington in June 1989. "You're not utilizing women as well as you have prepared them." Keen, who presented a report on education and training[3] on behalf of the European Round Table, a consortium of twenty-four major corporations involved in cross-national human resource development, added that "in most of Europe, the problem is precisely the opposite."

The most telling evidence of this unhappy paradox comes from the archive of the NLS-72. While there are dozens of stories in these records, the most stunning is that of the women.

The reason I begin with this story is that it inevitably winds up being the story of just about everyone in the class of 1972. Its many facets reflect the journey of that class through school and college, family formation, and work life.

Thesis and Approach

The story in this chapter is at once inspiring and dispiriting. The women in the class of 1972 made a number of investments in their personal educational capital that, in many respects, were of higher quality than those made by men. According to the rules, these blue chip investments should have paid off in women's careers. As of age thirty-two, however, women's yield on these investments was disappointingly low, indicating a residual bias against women in the labor market that undermines our national economic well-being. This thesis builds on many others that have explored the social utility of equity (see Harvey and Noble, 1985).

As this thesis plays itself out through the story of the NLS-72 women, I hope the reader will recognize that that story is fundamentally different from the mass of status attainment studies that have consumed sociologists for decades as well as from the considerable body of economic literature dealing with "return on investment" in education (see, for example, Murphy and Welch, 1989). This story is different from the status attainment studies because I believe that occupational status is not as important a factor as productivity within an occupation. First-rate computer programmers who can shorten the time and sharpen the focus of analyses of health care problems, for example, are more important to our economy and society than mediocre lawyers. This story is also different from the return-on-investment studies because it pays attention to the precise nature and quality of the human capital investment, not to generalized measures or models.

While I do not explore all of them, the paths to and through this thesis are made possible by a number of characteristics of the NLS-72 data base: its longitudinal nature; its inclusion of the unobtrusive evidence of postsecondary transcripts; its degree of detail on the occupations and industries in which people worked; its degree of detail on family formation and civic participation; and its inclusion of information on the emphases of work, job satisfaction, changing educational and occupational aspirations, and attitudes toward money, careers, family, and so on.

This account is descriptive, not reductive. The methodological tradition that uses various regression analyses to explain the last drops of human behavior does not govern the presentation. If all I offered you at the end of this excursion was an observation such as "the socioeconomic status of unmarried women is more affected by years of schooling than is the status of married women," or "parental socioeconomic status and type of college attended explain 29 percent of the variance in educational attainment between men and women," I will have shortchanged you.

The categories of analysis in this story are far more discrete than you will find in the typical sociological or economic study of women's attainment. Whereas those studies usually employ a half-dozen aggregate occupational categories (for example, "professional/technical"), I have constructed forty-three "jobs" from the variables in the NLS-72 archive. Whereas those studies normally use five aggregates for college majors (for example, "science/engineering"), I use fourteen. These more specific categories are the labor-market and educational analogues to what historian Fernand Braudel called "daily life." They get us closer to the particular, provide a richness of description that helps us better understand precisely where and how women succeed, and suggest where the unhappy paradoxes in U.S. economic life may lie.

Women's Academic Experience and Achievement

Let us look at the NLS-72 women first with an emphasis on the evidence of their superior academic performance. In economic terms, academic performance is one of the principal elements of the *quality* of human capital investment. The first variable to consider is overall high school class rank. No matter how one slices the high school class of 1972, women's mean class rank exceeded that of men by a minimum of ten points. Table 2.2 shows the basic demographic slices for all NLS-72 students who continued their education in any way after high school. No matter what the category of analysis, a much higher percentage of women than men were in the

Table 2.2. Mean High School Class Rank of Those
Who Received Any Postsecondary Education
Between 1972 and 1984.

Race/ethnicity and socioeconomic status	Men (by percentile)	Women (by percentile)
All	54.6	66.0
Race/ethnicity		
White	55.6	67.3
Black	44.1	55.5
Hispanic	48.4	58.5
Socioeconomic status		
Lowest quartile	50.0	61.7
Middle quartiles	52.8	65.3
Highest quartile	58.7	69.3

Note: N = 11,252.

highest quintile of their high school graduating classes. Of all students who went on to college, for example, 40 percent of the women—but only 24 percent of the men—ranked in the top quintile of their respective classes. In dealing with the class of 1972, college admissions officers were very generous to men.

The same conclusions arise if the analysis focuses on curricular backgrounds. Among students who took more than four semesters in each of the key elective components of a precollegiate curriculum (math, science, and foreign languages) women outranked men in the top quintile by a minimum of 20 percent. To be sure, fewer women than men took the minimal college preparatory curriculum in math and science, so one can always argue that the top group of women is self-selected. Even so, these women beat men on conventionally male turf, as have those in more recent cohorts (Hafner, 1989).

When one turns to third-party measures of educational performance, some surprising findings about the putative gender gap in test scores emerge. If we match women and men in the class of 1972 who took equal amounts of a modest precollegiate curriculum in math and/or science in high school, the difference in their SAT and ACT scores was negligible, at least among whites (Table 2.3).

I use standard deviation units (SDUs) in Table 2.3 because

Table 2.3. Influence of High School Curriculum on SAT Scores
of Women and Men in the High School Class of 1972.

High school curriculum	Male-female differential in SDUs[a]			
	All	White	Black	Hispanic
All students	-.21	-.19	-.26	-.41
>4 semesters foreign language	-.19	-.22	+.04	+.27
>4 semesters math	-.11	-.05	-.30	-.54
>4 semesters science	-.12	-.07	-.30	-1.03
>4 semesters math and science	-.10	-.02	-.58	-1.07

Note: The universe includes all students for whom both SAT/ACT scores and high school records were available. ACT scores were converted to the SAT scale. A minus sign indicates the women's score is less. N = 9,197.

[a]Standard deviation units. An SDU greater than ±1.0 is an enormous difference. An SDU less than ±.10 is virtually no difference at all.

they are a far more responsible and accurate way to measure difference in test performance than mean scores. Why? Because the standard deviation takes account of the incredible variation in the backgrounds of the large populations that take national examinations such as the SAT or ACT, and it is neither fair nor accurate to judge the performance of a group of people without accounting for this degree of variance. Given the more accurate presentation of the SDU, I wish we could do away with mean scores on such indicators as the SAT, but neither the daily papers nor the nightly newscasts could handle the change.

The data in Table 2.3 also confront the conventional wisdom that men always test better than women. This is a complex issue with a huge literature (see Diamond and Tittle, 1985). The case is not so easy. Using SDUs as our measure, we learn that, overall, the women of the NLS-72 who took a college preparatory curriculum including a solid background in math and/or science did just as well on the SAT as men with the same curricular backgrounds (for similar observations see de Wolf, 1981; Pallas and Alexander, 1983). But we also learn that simple comparisons of test scores between men and women are not in themselves very revealing. The race and SES of male and female test takers are more revealing. Among those who took the SAT or ACT, a higher percentage of women than men came from the lowest SES quartile, and this difference resulted principally from the overrepresentation of women among black SAT test takers. Indeed, as one moves from the lowest to the highest SES quartile, the percentage of women scoring in the higher bands on the SAT increases more than does the percentage of men (see Resource C, Table C.3). Even the more sophisticated comparisons between women's and men's performances on the SAT (for example, Rosser, 1989) are not persuasive because they do not account for these effects.

To be sure, common achievement tests in specific subjects would tell us more about the adequacy of high school preparation than do tests of general learned abilities such as the SAT (Jencks, Crouse, and Mueser, 1983). Unfortunately, the NLS-72 archive does not include such tests. But the correlations between the SAT, for example, and College Board Achievement tests are high enough (Gardner, 1982) to justify use of the former in the present analysis.

Moving on to College: Aspirations and Choice

Educational aspirations tend to be ideal goals, while educational plans are more realistic and far more indicative of an individual's academic self-confidence. As high school seniors, the NLS-72 women had lower educational aspirations than the men, and their plans were lesser still. When asked the "highest level" of education they *planned* to attain as opposed to the highest level they "would like to attain," 16 percent of the women (versus 11 percent of the men) who aspired to the bachelor's degree reduced their expectations. But none of this seemed to make a difference in the long run. As Table 2.4 makes amply clear, women's eventual educational attainments exceeded both their aspirations and plans, something that cannot be said for men. The data reflected in Table 2.4 are reminders to watch what people do, not what they say.

Part of the difference between the aspirations and plans of young men and women (and it is difficult to determine just what part) may be due to the attitudes of their parents (Brook, Whiteman, Peisach, and Deutsch, 1974; Sewell, Hauser, and Wolf, 1980). The attitudes of parents were reported by NLS-72 students themselves— which is significant in that a child's perception of parental attitudes surely affects his or her actual behavior more than any direct expres-

Table 2.4. Aspirations for, Plans for, and Achievement of
Bachelor's Degrees, 1972–1984.

Highest degree earned to 1984	If aspired to bachelor's degree (N = 9,049)		If planned bachelor's degree (N = 7,768)	
	Men	Women	Men	Women
None	41.4%	37.3%	37.1%	32.2%
Certificate/license	1.4	2.7	0.9	1.7
Associate's	6.3	7.6	5.7	6.1
Bachelor's	40.2	43.4	44.1	49.3
Master's	6.6	7.9	7.5	9.2
Doctoral/first professional	4.1	.1	4.6	1.2
All bachelor's degrees and higher	50.9%	52.4%	56.2%	59.7%

Note: The universe includes all NLS-PETS students who answered
questions in the base-year survey on educational aspirations and plans. N
= 11,877.

sion on the part of parents. While I am sure the situation reflected
in Table 2.4 has improved as a result of women's educational attainment, the increasing visibility of female leaders in public life, and
two decades of changing representations of women's lives in the
media, Table 2.5 shows that, in the eyes of their children, the parents of the class of 1972 had lower educational aspirations for their
daughters than their sons.

   In their helpful review of the complex literature on this
topic, Kaufman and Richardson (1982) point out that the dynamics
of relationships between children and parents, particularly in the
case of working mothers and their daughters, are crucial in determining who aspires to what. These dynamics are beyond the reach
of surveys such as the NLS-72, but the data provide other frameworks for understanding the apparent gender-role stereotyping reflected in Table 2.5.

   For example, those students in the NLS-72 who had *not* entered postsecondary education by 1984 illuminated these gender-role
disparities when, in the fall of 1973, they provided reasons for not
going on at that time. Only 3 percent cited discouragement by parents or teachers, but women were more likely to refer to family
factors (to be sure, including marriage). Overall, the men were more

Table 2.5. Parents' Educational Aspirations for the
Class of 1972.

| | For sons | | For daughters | |
Educational aspirations	Father	Mother	Father	Mother
Graduate degree	16.2%	17.0%	9.5%	9.7%
Bachelor's degree	42.4	43.2	40.4	38.9
Some postsecondary education	31.5	30.9	36.5	39.1
No postsecondary education	9.9	8.9	13.6	12.3

Note: The universe consists of all students who responded to questions in the base-year survey on their father's and/or mother's educational aspirations for them as children. N reporting father's aspirations =16,142. N reporting mother's aspirations = 17,213.

likely to cite personal preferences, self-doubt, and personal excuses than circumstance that referred in any way to others.

In these observations about aspirations and educational choice, we have the beginning of a secondary theme in this analysis: the women in this account are oriented more toward others than toward themselves. This theme will emerge again when I consider differences in women's and men's subsequent education and workplace experiences.

Women and Men in College and Elsewhere

The women in the class of 1972 entered postsecondary education directly from high school at the same rate as did men, but, regardless of socioeconomic status, were more likely (29.3 percent) than men (26.6 percent) to have won scholarships during the first two years following high school graduation. The combination of these two factors—no delay in going to college and scholarship support in the early years of postsecondary education—helps explain why those women who earned bachelor's degrees did so faster than the men: 66.8 percent of the women who earned bachelor's degrees between 1972 and 1984 did it in 4.5 years. The comparable figure for men was 54.7 percent. Although scholarship support is less critical to degree attainment in community colleges, the same pattern holds for those who received associate's degrees: 41.5 percent of the women who earned associate's degrees at any time between 1972 and 1984

did so within 2.5 years of high school graduation. The comparable
figure for men was 34.6 percent. These are significant differences.
They begin to tell us a story.

To sum that story up to this point: among the participants
in the NLS-72, women's academic performance in high school was
far superior to that of men. In terms of national measures of general
learned abilities, the impact of women's course of study in high
school, particularly in math and science, was equivalent to that for
men. At the same time, women's educational aspirations were lower
than those of men, an attitude influenced, no doubt, by their parents' lower educational aspirations for daughters than sons. Nonetheless, women continued their education at the same rate as did
men, were rewarded more with scholarships for postsecondary education than men, and completed degrees (associate's and bachelor's) at a faster pace than did men.

Women and Men of the Curriculum

It should not surprise you to discover that there is a men's curriculum and a women's curriculum in college and that the differences
are even more pronounced than they were in high school. What we
observe in the gross credit production statistics for those in the high
school class of 1972 who earned bachelor's degrees at any time
through 1984 are unfortunate clichés. Even when we look at individual courses (and there are 1,037 course categories in our taxonomy), we see a very convincing empirical confirmation of what
some economists would call segmentation.

Of the total time (measured in credits) spent in college by
men and women in the class of 1972 who earned bachelor's degrees,
what percent was accounted for by different courses? End Table 2A
illustrates a trichotomous pattern. There is a group of common
courses in which women and men spent roughly equivalent
amounts of time (for example, General Biology), a second group of
courses in which women spent considerably more time than men
(for example, Developmental Psychology), and a third group in
which men spent considerably more time than women (for example,
Business Law). The women's curriculum was dominated by human
services and humanities courses, the men's by business and core

science and engineering courses. Of course, given the fields in which these men and women majored in college (see Resource C, Table C.4), these distributions—measured in temporal units—are wholly expected.

Men, Women, and Statistics

The study of mathematics has long been regarded as an occupational "gate-keeper" (Sells, 1973). It has been well demonstrated that because women have historically studied less mathematics than men (a pattern resulting from gender-role socialization), they are diverted from curricula that lead to the higher-paying jobs in technical and professional fields (Fox and Hess-Biber, 1984). What has not been examined in such studies, though, are the mathematics backgrounds of men and women in the same occupations. In anticipating that discussion, I want to lay out some data that are inaccessible without a transcript sample such as the NLS-PETS.

We have already seen that those women who studied as much math as men in high school performed just as well on measures of general learned abilities such as the SAT. A similar observation can be made of the college cohort within the NLS-72, with one significant qualification: men and women studied different types of mathematics in college (for a confirmatory study at one institution, see Whiteley and Fenske, 1990). We can best observe these differences with reference to the field of statistics.

The NLS-PETS course-coding scheme allotted seven distinct classifications for the study of statistics in higher education, reflecting the fact that statistics is often presented in college as an applied field. The percentages of men and women who studied statistics in these various disciplinary contexts are shown in Table 2.6. These are not mutually exclusive groupings. People who took a statistics course in math may also have taken a biostatistics course or econometrics. The fields in which women were as likely as men to learn statistics (the biological and social sciences) are not surprising, and those in which women were far less likely than men to learn statistics (economics and business) are also not surprising. They are by-products of student majors and the normal requirements of those majors. Economic statistics is a requirement for economics majors,

Table 2.6. How Women and Men Studied Statistics in College,
1972–1984.

| | Men | | Women | |
| | Bachelor's degree recipients | All | Bachelor's degree recipients | All |
Statistics courses taken				
Math statistics	26.6%	16.4%	19.1%	10.9%
Economic statistics	3.5	2.0	1.0	0.5
Business statistics	10.0	3.6	6.2	2.3
Biostatistics	1.2	0.6	1.1	0.5
Psychological statistics	3.2	1.8	3.3	1.9
Social statistics	1.3	0.8	1.7	0.8
Educational statistics	0.1	0.1	0.8	0.4

Note: N for all = 10,734 (includes only those NLS-PETS students who earned more than ten postsecondary credits between 1972 and 1984); N for bachelor's degree recipients = 5,127.

of whom 77 percent in the NLS-PETS were men. Educational statistics is not normally a requirement for education majors, of whom 73 percent were women.

With the exception of remedial math (taken after high school in equal percentages by men and women), more men than women studied math in college no matter what kind of math is at issue. But in the case of statistics, the ratio of women to men was higher than that for any other kind of math. Among bachelor's degree holders, 72 women for every 100 men studied statistics in one form or another, whereas, for example, only 43 women for every 100 men studied calculus. The point is that for those women who studied college-level mathematics after high school, statistics was a more important path than it was for men.

Within-Field Differences

For all the familiar expectations concerning what men and women study in college, there are some fascinating patterns that defy superficial explanation. Most of these involve within-field differences, and two cases are of particular interest. The first case concerns the study of foreign languages (see Table 2.7). Women in the NLS-PETS were more likely to study a group of languages I call *ana-*

Table 2.7. Percent Completing at Least One College Course in
Specific Foreign Languages, 1972–1984.

	All		Bachelor's degree recipients	
Language studied	Men	Women	Men	Women
Synthetic group				
German: introductory and intermediate	5.9%	5.0%	9.4%	8.7%
German: advanced/literature	0.9	1.0	1.6	2.0
Russian: introductory and intermediate	0.7	0.6	0.9	1.0
Russian: advanced/literature	0.2	0.3	0.3	0.5
Latin	0.8	0.7	1.3	1.3
Analytic group				
French: introductory and intermediate	5.7	11.4	9.3	18.9
French: advanced/literature	0.8	2.2	1.6	4.5
Spanish: introductory and intermediate	10.2	14.3	15.4	20.8
Spanish: advanced/literature	1.0	2.3	1.7	4.0
Chinese: introductory and intermediate	0.2	0.3	0.3	0.7

Note: N for all = 10,734 (includes only those NLS-PETS students
who earned more than ten postsecondary credits between 1972 and 1984):
N for bachelor's degree recipients = 5,127.

lytic—that is, languages whose typical subject-verb-object sentence
structure is easily recognizable to native speakers of English. Men
held the edge, but a lesser one, in studying another group of languages I call *synthetic*. To a native speaker of English, the sentence
order of these languages often involves a delayed element of meaning. It is also true that languages in this synthetic group are more
highly inflected than those in the analytic group. That is—to put
it crudely—synthetic languages have many phonetic elements that
determine the status of words and meaning, such as suffixes that
indicate case, gender, mood, and tense.

Do these data imply that women prefer to follow familiar
logical sequences (English syntax resembles those of French or Chinese far more than it does German or Latin) and that men prefer
meaning games with delayed completion of the sense of sentences?

Because more women than men in the NLS-PETS studied foreign languages at any level, the weight of the hypotheses embedded in these questions is not great. But the course-taking patterns are noticeable nonetheless. It may be that a higher proportion of men took German or Russian because they were majoring in scientific or engineering fields, though I doubt it. But it is also obvious that women who took German and Russian were more likely to study them at advanced levels. This was a consistent feature of foreign language study in the NLS-PETS group: women persisted to advanced course levels, hence were more likely to be proficient. Men did not. And proficiency is the measure of quality in foreign language study.

The second case of within-field differences falls in the English curriculum, where the most telling cultural comparison is between men's domination of science fiction courses and women's domination of folklore/mythology courses. This dichotomy is reinforced by a similar pattern involving technical writing (men) and creative writing (women). These courses are electives, and student choices express proclivities. Do they imply that men are, in fact, more analytical than women? Not really, since the ratio of women to men in all linguistics courses was 3:1, and linguistics is a highly analytical field. What student choice here suggests, instead, is that men are consistently drawn to technological phenomena or technological representations of phenomena. Indeed, for example, women dominated all fine arts courses except those in film studies, including photography, cinematography, and video (the most technologically oriented of the fine arts). One interpretation of these patterns is that they are legacies of previous gender stereotyping in both formal schooling and informal learning. However, my immediate point in presenting these examples is that the curricular paths pursued by these men and women in college were distinct, but in more subtle ways than traditional comparisons of gross categories have revealed.

College Performance and Degree Attainment

The curricular experience of college is but part of this story. More important are the near-term outcomes of that experience. I have already noted that women who earned the bachelor's degree did so faster than men, even though in the class of 1972, a lower percentage of women than men earned the degree. Part of the explanation for the comparative speed at which women earned bachelor's degrees may lie in a combination of the type of institution from which they received the degree and their major.

A very low percentage of women majored in fields such as engineering or architecture, in which extended programs of more than four years are the norm. These programs are far more likely to be offered at doctoral degree–granting institutions and specialized schools of technology than at any other schools. Comprehensive colleges are the home of the vast majority of programs in business and education, neither of which, in the 1970s, required an extended period of enrollment. Liberal arts colleges rarely offer extended programs in professional or occupational fields, and in general, students attending liberal arts colleges tend to complete bachelor's degrees faster than students who receive their degrees from other types of institutions. Some 60 percent of the women (versus 51.8 percent of the men) received their bachelor's degrees from institutions whose major academic programs were geared to the traditional four-year time frame.

The NLS-PETS data base is not the first longitudinal study to demonstrate that women earn consistently higher grade-point averages in college than men (see, for example, Feldman, 1974; Astin, 1977), but the data in our transcripts allow us to see that this pattern holds no matter what field they studied (Table 2.8). The differences in performance are greatest between women and men who majored in science, business, and engineering (traditionally male fields). To be sure, there was a greater degree of self-selection going on among women who majored in those fields, but the NLS-72 data suggest that, with the exception of business, the same can be said for men (that is, whether they were male or female, business majors were students of weaker academic backgrounds).

If we use the *course*, rather than the major, as the arena of academic performance, the same pattern holds. A noteworthy example involves statistics and calculus. Even though the ratio of women to men completing courses is much higher for statistics than for calculus courses, and even though it has been well demonstrated

Table 2.8. Mean Undergraduate Grade-Point Averages for
Women and Men Who Received Bachelor's Degrees,
by Major, 1972-1984.

Major	Women's GPAs	Men's GPAs
All	3.07 (.44)	2.92 (.46)
Engineering/computer science	3.17 (.34)	2.96 (.49)
Science and math	3.18 (.45)	2.98 (.49)
Business	2.96 (.47)	2.79 (.44)
Education	3.05 (.41)	2.89 (.39)
Humanities	3.16 (.45)	3.10 (.50)
Arts	3.13 (.42)	3.08 (.41)
Social science	3.08 (.46)	2.95 (.48)

Note: N = 5,127. Standard deviations are in parentheses.

that men are more confident than women in their abilities to learn math (Fennema, 1984), women did better in both courses, as Table 2.9 demonstrates.

The NLS-72 data suggest that the experience of this kind of achievement in college had a striking impact on the further educational plans of women in the class of 1972. When they were surveyed in 1976, the proportion of those who aspired to graduate degrees vaulted over that of men, and it remained higher through the 1979 follow-up survey (Adelman, 1991).

Those women who actually followed through on the first step to achieving their aspirations and entered graduate school by 1984 appear to be more qualified than the men. Using grade-point average as a proxy for such qualifications, 43.6 percent of the NLS-72 women who entered graduate/professional school had earned undergraduate grades of A– or better. The comparable figure for men was 34.5 percent. However, a smaller proportion of women than men earned at least ten credits after receiving the bachelor's degree, and a much lower percentage completed any kind of graduate or first professional degree by age thirty or thirty-one (the outer limit documented on the college transcripts). But given both the undergraduate achievement of these women and their shifting aspirations, I suspect that if we returned to them at age forty, we

Table 2.9. Grades in Key Mathematics Courses, 1972–1984.

Grades	All[a]		Bachelor's degree recipients	
	Men	Women	Men	Women
Statistics				
A/A-	26.2%	33.5%	28.8%	35.2%
B/B-	35.0	36.2	35.8	35.8
C/C-	30.1	24.2	27.9	23.9
D/F	8.7	6.2	7.5	5.1
Calculus				
A/A-	21.1%	31.8%	23.6%	36.3%
B/B-	35.8	31.0	37.5	32.0
C/C-	35.9	28.9	33.0	26.5
D/F	8.2	8.3	5.9	5.1

[a]Includes only those NLS-PETS students who earned more than ten postsecondary credits between 1972 and 1984. $N = 10,734$.

would find greater parity in graduate degrees, though this would differ by field (see Berg and Ferber 1983).[4]

Women and Men in School at Thirtysomething

The NLS-PETS provides unobtrusive evidence of the education of the class of 1972 through age thirty. But the fifth follow-up tacks two years onto this history through survey data. Confining the universe of analysis to those people who were both in the PETS *and* continued their education beyond 1984 produces a more reliable portrait of women and men in school in their early thirties because we know their prior educational histories for sure. Of these people, 21 percent reported being formally enrolled in school at some time between the summer of 1984 and the summer of 1986. Who were these people? What and where were they studying? End Table 2B presents the basic data. I see the highlights as follows:

- A higher percentage of the women (22.9 percent) than men (19.9 percent) continued their education between ages thirty and thirty-two.

- Although a higher percentage of women (49.3 percent) than men (45.3 percent) in this group had never earned any degree previously, a lower percentage of women (48.6 percent) than men (52.1 percent) were seeking a degree at the bachelor's level or above.
- The curricular preferences of women and men observed in the PETS data changed in four notable fields. In accounting and computer science and technology, women moved into the majority. In fine and performing arts and education courses for subject certification, men moved into the majority.
- At every level of credential through the master's degree, an equal or higher percentage of women than men said they completed the requirements for the credential during this period; but this pattern did not hold at the doctoral and first professional degree levels.

The most striking of these findings is women's move into the fields of accounting and computer science. It is not wholly glib to attribute this trend to labor-market demand. The women of the class of 1972, as we will see, came to value earnings in career selection more than did men, and as the years passed, more of them sought the knowledge that would allow entry into higher-paying occupations. Given the fact of women's weaker mathematics backgrounds, the efforts women made in these fields are notable. To be sure, the computer field includes data processing, but only 9 percent of the NLS-PETS students who studied computer-related topics between 1984 and 1986 took data processing. The vast majority studied general computer science and computer programming.

Summing Up: Women and Educational Capital

In all these data on background and academic attainment, women's aspirations were less inflated than men's, their plans more realistic, their focus on goals more intense. They were not full of their own self-confidence, whether in their ability to learn math or the likelihood that they would earn a Ph.D. Unlike the men of the class of 1972, the women did not strut. Instead, they did what they say they would do. In fact, they did more than they said they would do.

Perhaps, as Mary Belenky and her colleagues wrote in *Women's Ways of Knowing* (1986), these women acted because they discovered "personal authority." To varying extents, they transcended the expectations of parents and communities and developed their own destiny in ways that men did not. Further education is the fulcrum of this development, and advanced education and training—along with realistic plans and determination—are the basic currency of the world economy of the twenty-first century.

Women not only sought further education but developed more positive attitudes toward it than did men. All the post–high school NLS-72 surveys asked respondents to indicate their degree of satisfaction with various aspects of their postsecondary education. Confining the population to PETS students and the results to two points in time (age twenty-five for all those who had attended a postsecondary institution up to that point and age thirty-two for all those who had attended any postsecondary institution between ages twenty-five and thirty-two), I found that a higher percentage of women than men were "very satisfied" with every major aspect of their postsecondary education. The difference was consistently greatest with reference to "skill development" and "intellectual growth"—that is, with reference to self. The women of the NLS-72—more than the men—believed that they benefitted from higher education.

The Anvil of the Labor Market

These women's beliefs, however, did not hold up in the labor market, where all the evidence of women's superior educational performance and commitment was discounted. Between ages twenty-five and thirty-two, a substantially higher percentage of women than men from the class of 1972 experienced genuine unemployment (that is, they were in the labor force, not working, but looking for work), and this phenomenon held stubbornly true even in the face of educational attainment. As Table 2.10 demonstrates, the lowest rates of unemployment among women to age thirty-two were for those who had no children and had earned a credential less than the bachelor's by age thirty. Of these women, about 25 percent were nurses and health technicians and another 18 percent were in business and

Table 2.10. Women's Experience of Unemployment from Age
Twenty-Six to Thirty-Two.

Degree status and children	Total unemployment in months, 1979–1986					
	None	<6	6–12	13–24	25–36	37–84
Men	66.3%	11.9%	7.9%	5.5%	4.8%	3.5%
Women without children	54.6	16.4	10.4	8.7	4.6	5.4
Women with children	41.3	12.3	11.2	12.3	8.5	14.5
Women with no degree						
Without children	47.9	16.6	12.4	10.3	6.1	6.7
With children	38.5	11.3	11.6	11.2	8.5	19.1
Women with degree less than bachelor's						
Without children	61.4	13.9	9.0	8.7	3.0	4.0
With children	42.6	11.7	8.8	13.4	10.2	13.5
Women with bachelor's degree						
Without children	57.3	16.8	9.4	7.7	4.0	4.9
With children	44.6	14.1	12.0	13.5	7.5	8.3

Note: The universe includes all NLS-PETS students who participated in the 1986 follow-up survey, who indicated an occupation for 1985,
and who provided information on unemployment. $N = 7,384$.

financial service support occupations such as secretary and bank
teller, both historically low-paying fields. And even though their
rates of unemployment were comparatively low, they were still
higher than those for men. This general, sad relationship is not
unique to the generation of the NLS-72 (Harvey and Noble, 1985).

Women who received bachelor's degrees not only experienced higher rates of unemployment than those with lesser credentials, but were also found disproportionately in such lower-paying
and traditionally female occupations as nursing/health technology
(11 percent), school teaching (22 percent), and office/financial service support (9 percent). This distribution of women in the labor
market holds regardless of the admissions standards of the colleges
they attended. Indeed, using the same data set, Conaty, Alsalam,
James, and To (1989) demonstrated that college selectivity is neg-
atively correlated with women's earnings at age thirty-two.

The "screening hypothesis" proposes that educational attainment sorts people with lesser credentials out of high-paying

occupations (Taubman and Wales, 1975). Given women's experience, this hypothesis seems to cut both ways in terms of economic benefits to individuals. Education screens in as well as out, and the occupations into which it screens, from schoolteacher to physician, have widely different wage rates. For this reason, I have some difficulty with the theory of dual labor markets (Piore, 1975), which lumps all professional/technical workers and all managers/administrators together. Had I followed this classification scheme in the analysis of occupational outcomes and earnings, railroad conductors would have been in the same class with CEOs,[5] and real differences between men's and women's occupations and earnings would have been masked.

In 1972, Lily Tomlin's switchboard operator, Ernestine, observed that AT&T was "not subject to city, state, or federal legislation." But the company agreed early in that year with the General Services Administration to promote 50,000 women from telephone operators to line workers, telephone installers, and regional office managers. By midyear, AT&T was running magazine ads featuring female line installers belted to telephone poles and was assuring the country that it employed "several hundred male telephone operators" and that there were "no all-male or all-female jobs at the phone company." But by the time the high school class of 1972 was fully ensconced in the labor market, whatever the then-unitary telephone company had done had left little impact on earnings differentials between women and men.

The Shame of Earnings Differentials

The subject of differences in earnings between men and women is hardly new in either the scholarly or op-ed page literature. But the NLS-72 archive offers a unique prism for analysis and suggests paths through the topic that, to the best of my knowledge, have not been adequately explored.

The NLS-72 data allow comparisons only among groups of people in the same cohort with similar labor-market histories. Thus, all the comparisons I use here are based on people who (1) indicated an occupation for 1985, (2) provided data on earnings for 1985, (3) indicated they had held at least one full-time job at any time between September 1979 and February 1986, and (4) provided basic histories (every month employed, hours worked, and so forth) for up to four jobs held between September 1979 and February 1986. My purpose in setting those conditions was to ensure that earnings and experience comparisons were based on people who were consistent labor-market participants. Of the 12,841 people in the 1986 follow-up survey, 8,696 met all these conditions. Of that group, two-thirds were also in the PETS transcript sample. I focus principally on the PETS sample group (N = 5,864) because the transcripts allow us to analyze its experience with unobtrusive measures of educational history and attainment.

The archive teaches us that the key factors in interpreting earnings differentials between men and women who continued their education beyond high school include children, years of job experience, experience of unemployment, occupation, industry, type of employer, highest earned degree, college major (for bachelor's degree holders), and amount of mathematics studied in college. Race/ethnicity appears to be an issue only in combination with highest degree earned. As previously demonstrated with respect to bachelor's degree holders only (Conaty, Alsalam, James, and To, 1989), family background and the characteristics of colleges attended have much less influence on earnings compared to college academic experiences and labor-market history.

A few other longitudinal panel studies have focused on earnings, though not always as the key dependent variable (Sewell and Hauser, 1975; Alexander, Eckland, and Griffin, 1975; Jencks and others, 1979). A noted example is the work of Suter and Miller (1973), whose female subjects were drawn from the National Longitudinal Surveys of Labor Market Experience, sponsored by the U.S. Department of Labor. The panels in this data base do not come from a single cohort, and they include people who never graduated from high school. In this case, for example, the panel covered women between the ages of thirty and forty-four in 1967 and followed their career behavior for five years. However different this longitudinal panel is from ours, Suter and Miller found some similar relationships to those reported below concerning years of job experience, educational attainment (using the proxy of years of schooling), and occupation (in very broad categories) on the one hand and earnings on the other. Using regression analyses, Suter and Miller determined that 38 percent of the earnings differentials between men and women could not be accounted for after adjusting for these factors.

Why Earnings?

The "earnings function" is an important feature of my analysis because it is traditionally interpreted in the economic literature as a proxy for productivity (technically, "marginal productivity"). The human capital theory (Becker, 1975) holds that knowledge commands a premium in the labor market and that people sacrifice current earnings by investing in acquiring knowledge. That acquisition presumably renders them more productive, a factor that should be reflected in greater earnings—the return on their investment. These knowledge and skill investments should be even more reflected in earnings, according to the theory, if the goods or services produced are in high demand, restricted supply, or both.

Some sociologists (for example, Collins, 1979) dispute the productivity variable in this theory on the grounds that the very nature of organizations in which people work renders accurate assessment of merit, knowledge, and skill almost impossible. Those who are most productive, this counterpoint asserts, are rarely in command, hence rarely earn as much as those who exploit the political and social systems of organizations to reach positions of power. Although I will return to this intriguing observation, the reader should note that most of the comparisons in my analysis are within occupations, not within organizations, on the grounds that people's educational and training investments are directed toward occupations—not organizations or firms. In the United States, at least, a young person does not usually say, "When I grow up, I'm going to work for IBM," but instead, "I'm going to be a computer engineer." Furthermore, when the units of analysis (people) are first sorted by background characteristics, education, and occupation, the case is stronger for interpreting earnings in terms of productivity.

Dean (1984, p. 5) has correctly pointed out that there are "productivity effects" resulting from education—including technological improvements and management efficiency—that "may or may not be fully reflected in the earnings" of those involved. Indeed, the whole notion of productivity effects, to which I will return, takes us beyond the human capital or growth accounting use of earnings as a proxy for productivity. But for the moment, let us follow through the traditional analysis.

What I hope to demonstrate is that even when one accounts for the obvious correlates of low wages, at age thirty-two the men of the NLS-72 were paid more than the women, a fact that may have little to do with productivity. This result held even for those who worked part time in 1985 (7 percent of the total employed). In other words, there is an anomaly in the labor market that is probably the result of bias. It is hard to imagine why employers would pay more for the similar labor of one group of people over another when the second group has demonstrated equal or superior qualifications. There are exceptions to this earnings pattern, and they will be noted.

Economists have explored all kinds of approaches to the nature and locus of what Becker originally (1957) called the *discrimination coefficient*—the unexplained difference between men's wages and women's wages when all other factors are held constant. Is it the belief of employers that women evidence higher job turnover rates? Is it because employers do not obtain sufficient information about employees' potential productivity when they are hired but instead judge them with statistical models of group behavior that may be thoroughly outdated (England, 1984)? Is it ingrained in the nature of certain industries and types of firms (Lyle and Ross, 1973)? Is it the result of gender typing of jobs and gender segmentation within occupations (Treiman and Hartmann, 1981)? What perverse system of occupational classification, rates—and hence pays—a dog pound keeper higher than a nursery school teacher on the grounds that the latter (typically a woman) acquires the requisite knowledge and skills merely by virtue of being a female (Steinberg, 1984)?

The NLS-72 archive contributes only indirectly to these provocative and instructive inquiries; however, it provides strong evidence for a recasting of the central observation: that within knowledge-based occupations, women are not just equally as qualified as men—they are on average better qualified. And to the extent to which more and more better qualified women enter the work force, their wages should rise relative to those of men (Smith and Ward, 1984).

Women With and Without Children

The most important distinction made in this analysis is between women who had children at any time up to age thirty-two and those who did not. With the exception of divorced, widowed, or separated women, marital status did not make a significant difference for women in terms of either years of job experience, number of jobs held, or earnings at age thirty-two. On the other hand, marital status did seem to make a difference for men, principally because more men who remained single to age thirty-two were in school after the age of twenty-six than were men who were married by age thirty-two. Married men thus had more years of job experience (a mean of 8.23 versus 7.44 for single men), hence higher earnings (a mean of $27,003 versus $20,837 for single men). This difference in mean income is too great to be attributed to school time alone).

To compare the earnings of working women with those of working men, I have set the basic parameters of the two groups as analogously as possible. Childbirth and caring for young children are unique features of women's lives that, through age forty, often remove them from the labor force for a period of time (Leibowitz, 1975). Women with children thus usually have fewer years of job experience than both men and women without children, and the number of years of job experience is directly related to earnings (Polachek, 1984).

While, as Sewell, Hauser, and Wolf (1980, p. 562) observe, "there is no self-evident temporal or causal interpretation of the association between marital/child status and *occupation*," there is no doubt that "child status" has a strong impact on earnings differentials. Hanoch (1980) observed that not only are the number and age of children inversely related to a mother's annual hours of work, but also that the higher the level of education, the greater the differential in working time between women with children and those without children. These basic relationships over a nine-year period (1976–1985) are shown in Table 2.11. Remember, the data in the

Table 2.11. Job Experience and Earnings of Men, Women Without Children, and Women with Children.

	Mean years work experience, 1976–1985	Mean earnings, 1985
Men	8.0	$25,022
Women, no children	7.8	18,970
Women with children	7.5	15,016

table are for the group of NLS-72 people I previously defined as consistent labor-market participants! Thus, the reader might ask why the earnings of women with children are so much lower than those of women without children (let alone men) compared to the differences in mean years of work experience. The principal difference lies in occupational distribution. A higher percentage of women without children were in such higher-paying occupations as engineer, architect, lawyer, or accountant, and a higher percentage of women with children worked in such lower-paying fields as nurse, health technician, or teacher. Also, while only 7 percent of the entire group under the microscope here were part-time workers in 1985, 14 percent of the women with children worked part time.

Occupation, Job Experience, and Earnings

End Table 2C presents the earnings differentials for the NLS-72 women without children and men in thirty-three occupations. In seven of the thirty-three, women without children earned more than men at age thirty-two. In three of these occupations, women had more years of job experience: computer programmer, electrical engineering technician, and buyer or purchasing agent. In the other four, women constituted the majority of employees: research worker, not elsewhere classified; high school teacher; editor/reporter; and computer equipment operator. In three of these cases, however, the earnings advantage for women was slight.

To be sure, "occupation" may not be a useful category of analysis because what people call themselves isn't always what they actually do. "Work role" or "position" (Collins, 1979) is probably more accurate. Principally for that reason, I do not place as much emphasis on "occupational status" as do other researchers using longitudinal panel data (Sewell, Hauser, and Wolf, 1980; Smart and Pascarella, 1986). Nor does occupational status pay the rent. Nonetheless, despite the messages from the *Glamour* magazines of this world, women seem to have achieved pay equity in occupations requiring substance more than fluff (though, as End Table 2C shows, substance is no guarantee of pay equity).

It also seems that women achieved pay equity in some occupations as a correlate of the amount of mathematics they studied in college. If we take those who earned more than eight credits in college-level mathematics of any kind (college algebra, analytic geometry, calculus, statistics, and so on) and match the 1985 earnings of women without children and men, the occupations in which mathematics course taking seemed to make a difference for women are indicated in Table 2.12.

We can conclude that women's study of mathematics made a significant contribution to their earnings in business-related occupations, even in the case of managers in manufacturing industries, where the pay gap between men and women has historically been small.[6] In addition, among the forty-three occupations that underlie these analyses is a residual category, "Other," that covers dozens of occupations and is populated by a fairly large group. Within this group, women without children who took more than

Table 2.12. Differences in Earnings, Within Occupations of Women Without Children and Men, 1985.

Occupation	All	Earned more than eight credits in college math
Accountant	− 9.1%	−2.6%
Engineer	− 5.0	−1.9
Manager (financial institution)	−29.1	+4.5
Manager (wholesale/retail)	−49.3	−5.2
Manager (manufacturing)	− 3.0	+7.0

Note: A Minus sign indicates that women's earnings are less.

eight college-level credits in math earned, on average, 16.5 percent *more* than men with the same mathematics background. That indicates a more generalized effect of mathematics course taking for women. For the class of 1972, more math meant more money—for women, in particular.

When the analysis is confined to those who earned the bachelor's degree and looks at men and women with similar undergraduate backgrounds, the basic theme does not change, but the variations become more skittish. End Table 2D lays out mean years of employment and mean 1985 earnings by twelve aggregate categories of undergraduate major for men, women without children, and women with children. All men and all women without children had exactly the same mean years of job experience (5.63) for the period at issue, but men's average earnings were 30 percent higher than those for women without children.

This differential held for majors in the social sciences, applied social sciences (a category including communications, home economics, social work, and library science), and biological sciences. In other cases (education, physical sciences, and engineering, for example), the difference in years of work experience does not seem to justify the magnitude of the earnings differential. Yet in all three cases in which women without children earned more than men (business, humanities, and fine/performing arts), women had more years of job experience.

To underscore these differences, let us match them against undergraduate performance data while simultaneously asking if the differences can be explained by one of the key variables in women's career/labor-market experience: time out for the birth of a child and the care of an infant (I used a mean of four months as the demarcation line for this variable). As Nakamura and Nakamura (1989) have demonstrated, this time out also has delayed effects, reducing the overall labor-market participation of women with children the year after childbirth (Nakamura and Nakamura call this phenomenon the *inertia model*). In Table 2.13 I have used earnings to rank undergraduate majors by the extent of men's advantage, from least to most. In general, the lower the percentage of women in a major who later take time off for childbirth, the lower the earnings differential.

Table 2.13. Academic Performance, Time Out for
Childbirth, and Earnings Differentials in 1985,
by Major, for Bachelor's Degree Recipients.

Undergraduate major	Men's earnings advantage	Women's mean GPA advantage	Women who took leave for childbirth
Fine/performing arts	1.0%	.08	8.8%
Humanities	3.5	.07	19.0
Business	10.2	.12	7.6
Engineering	11.8	.16	0.0
Education	20.5	.17	17.3
Applied sciences	24.4	.04	15.0
Applied social sciences	28.2	.17	8.9
Biological sciences	31.1	.07	16.3
Physical sciences	35.4	.19	17.8
Health sciences and services	36.6	.17	19.4
Social sciences	40.8	.14	13.1

The case is not neat, as the humanities and applied social sciences show, but some of the anomalies can be explained fairly easily (for example, schoolteachers' schedules allow for maternity leave in a less disruptive manner than is the case in other occupations). In general, the higher the percentage of a group that takes four or more months off, the lower the mean years of job experience for that group, hence the lower the earnings expectation. There is no doubt that maternity leave played a role in the earnings differential (but the comparative percentage of men and women in each major who had earned graduate degrees, for example, plays no role), though how great an influence requires more sophisticated statistical analyses than the methodology of this account allows.

On the other hand, there was no pattern of relationship between differences in academic performance (grade-point average as the indicator) and differences in earnings, a finding that contradicts Pascarella and Smart's (1990) conclusions with respect to the Cooperative Institutional Research Program (CIRP) students at age twenty-seven, as well as a majority of previous studies on grade-income relationships (Cohen, 1984). If grade-point average is a proxy for effort and persistence, and effort and persistence are characteristics valued by employers, then women's pay, after adjustments for occupation and career interruption for childbirth, should more closely approximate that of men.

Earnings and Race/Ethnicity

Analyzed in terms of race/ethnicity, women's earnings evidence what I call a labor-market "race premium" that is largely a function of degree attainment. As End Table 2E indicates, whether or not they had children by age thirty-two, black and Hispanic women who earned bachelor's degrees had higher earnings than the white women. The data in End Table 2E also supply some fuel for the argument that at levels of education below the bachelor's degree, earnings differentials may be influenced as much (if not more) by years of job experience as by educational attainment. The only category of white women who earned more at age thirty-two than black or Hispanic women consisted of those who had no children and whose highest degree was the associate's. The mean years of job experience for that group were the highest of any of the eighteen groups of women represented in End Table 2E.

Between the bachelor's and graduate degree levels, there was an also stunning race premium in the labor market for black men that was not present for any other race-by-gender group. Black men who earned a graduate degree of any kind had earnings 31.6 percent higher than those whose education stopped at the bachelor's level (the comparable premium for white men was 2.1 percent). But the earnings of black women in those two groups evidenced no change whatsoever. This is not wholly a labor supply and demand issue: while black women accounted for 61 percent of black bachelor's degree recipients from the class of 1972, black men accounted for 64 percent of black graduate (including professional) school enrollees. Having persisted and succeeded despite tremendous odds, black women of the class of 1972 seemed to hit a plateau of education and earnings that black men did not (for similar data from a slightly earlier period, see Freeman, 1976).

Career Paths and the Emphases of Work

In the analysis of the NLS-72 archive, it also pays to look at some differences in the dramas of career development of men and women (Table 2.14). Overall, there was a greater degree of deflation of

Table 2.14. What Did They Plan to Do at Age Thirty When
They Were Nineteen? What Were Their Actual
Occupations at Age Thirty-Two?

	Men		Women	
Occupationᵃ	Planned	Did	Planned	Did
Clerical worker	0.9%	5.5%	13.5%	21.2%
Craftsperson	8.5	12.5	0.5	2.0
Operative	2.0	5.2	0.6	1.4
Laborer	1.4	2.6	< 0.1	1.5
Homemakerᵇ	0.0	3.5	13.7	15.5
Homemaker-student	0.0	0.3	0.0	1.0
Manager/proprietor	16.9	20.1	4.9	10.1
Professional 1ᶜ	24.7	17.5	31.0	17.5
Professional 2ᶜ	21.5	8.1	11.3	4.6
"Buy/sell"	1.8	6.8	0.8	3.4
Schoolteacher	6.6	3.2	16.7	9.8
Other	15.7	14.7	7.0	12.0

Note: The universe includes all students in the NLS-PETS who answered the question on expected "kind of work . . . when you are 30" in the 1973 follow-up survey and participated in the 1986 follow-up. $N = 7,249$.

ᵃThe occupational categories of the 1973 question do not match those of 1986 perfectly. For example, the 1973 "Sales" category covered (among other occupations) insurance agents. For 1986, I expanded the sales category to "Buy/sell," and insurance agents are not included. Instead, they are grouped with accountants and stockbrokers to match the 1973 category, "Professional 1."

ᵇIncludes all who did not indicate a job of any kind outside the home between 1979 and 1986. It thus includes full-time homemakers, full-time homemakers who were also students (indicated here as a subcategory), and others.

ᶜIn 1973, "Professional 1" included accountants, artists, nurses, engineers, librarians, writers, social workers, actors, and athletes. "Professional 2" included clergy, physicians, lawyers, scientists, and college professors. In the 1986 configurations, a more elaborate coding scheme was used, and scientists were classified as Professional 1 and librarians as Professional 2.

men's career expectations than of women's—perhaps more evidence of women's realism. If one rates the first four occupational categories in the table (clerical worker, craftsperson, operative, laborer) as of lower status than the others, the shift from expectations at age nineteen to occupational reality at age thirty-two was greater for men than women. Conversely, the ratio of people in business occupations to those who planned business occupations was greater for women than for men.

Career development is overlooked by the vast literature on status attainment because that literature is not concerned with productivity or productivity effects—however measured. The more critical question is what we can learn from such comparative deflations as we see in Table 2.14 (educational aspirations to actual degree attainment, and occupational aspirations to actual occupation) about the attitudes, behaviors, and knowledge men and women are bringing to the economy and the workplace. That is where the rubber hits the road for the nation. Who do we want setting the tone and conditions of our economy? Individuals who are knowledgeable, always learning, realistic, determined, motivated, and willing to share knowledge, one assumes. These are "productivity effects" that go beyond the proxy of earnings. They are more difficult to quantify than earnings (Haveman and Wolfe, 1984) and are best deduced from attitudes and behaviors in both the workplace and private life.

In this light, recent work on women's psychological development may hold economic significance. Whether female or male, those who reach the stage of what Belenky, Clinchy, Goldberger, and Tarule (1986) call *constructed knowledge,* who integrate self-knowledge and external *procedural knowledge,* who have a high tolerance for ambiguity, who are challenged by complexity, and who learn and work in ways that connect the human environment to the knowledge environment can affect the workplace in powerful ways. What do these abstract phrases mean in action? They mean taking a given task/role and expanding it by knowledge and personal disposition. For example, if one of a person's routine tasks is preparing references for use by others, task expansion might consist of annotating the references, enlisting the assistance of co-workers in hunting down references of special interest, finding new forms of communicating the product to audiences that would otherwise never benefit, and utilizing these new audiences as sources of additional material. In this way, the routine becomes a kaleidoscope with new patterns, discoveries, and interest. Women are more likely to follow this path than are men.

Women in the Workplace

Despite the discouraging pattern of earnings differentials, a much higher percentage of women than men who attended college reported at age thirty-two that their learning and training were very relevant to their work. This phenomenon held regardless of highest degree earned. For example, 40 percent of the women whose highest degree was the master's (but only 29 percent of the men) found their education very relevant to work; 27 percent of the women whose highest degree was the associate's (but only 21 percent of the men) found a similar relevance.

Given equal educational achievement, these data suggest that productivity effects for women may be greater than those for men. That is, the chances are that people who use their education in their work are controlling and changing the nature of their work more than people who do not use their education in their work. The NLS-72 archive provides some indirect support for this assertion in data concerning what people work with on the job—ideas, people, paper, things. At age thirty-two, more men than women of the NLS-72 said they worked a great deal with ideas on the job, while more women than men said they worked a great deal with people. But as the level of education rises, the spread between men and women narrows on both counts. And when the population is restricted to those who earned the bachelor's degree and who found their education very relevant to their work, the proportion of women who claimed to work "a great deal" with ideas exceeds that of men. We expect higher education to yield a greater orientation toward ideas, and the NLS-72 working women fulfilled this expectation more than men did.

Some perceptive employers agree with this analysis. "Women come into the workplace like immigrants," says Harold Tragash, vice president for human resources at Rorer Pharmaceuticals. They are "determined to succeed on the basis of *what* they know, not who they know." Tragash sees women more likely than men to "influence co-workers from a technical knowledge base" (personal communication, November 1989). Yes, the "stock of knowledge" represented by human capital is a source of technological change (Mincer, 1989), but not unless it is shared. Only people who share that capital can change the knowledge content of work. Changing the knowledge content of work is critical to innovation in manufacturing, services, and public administration. Innovations stemming from this supply side of knowledge that today's women in particular bring to the job can make the difference in our economy in the twenty-first century. Again, these are productivity effects.

Unfortunately, as Kanter (1977) observed, women with this determination and knowledge are not placed in decision-making roles, are shunted out of the communication network, and are "stuck" or "encapsulated" in ways that hinder not only their own mobility but also their effectiveness. Men, however, seem to thrive on the model of ascription I describe in Chapter Three when telling the story of college varsity athletes: their success, advancement, and ultimate economic status have been based far more on a social network than on the stuff of learning in higher education. We can infer that their jobs probably involve more of what Collins (1979) calls *political labor* as opposed to *productive labor*. We can also infer from earnings data that the U.S. workplace, in general, rewards hustling more than knowledge. Indeed, as the data in Table 2.15 demonstrate, the NLS-72 men on the whole were less likely than women to be satisfied with aspects of their work bearing on productivity, but were more satisfied with their own opportunities for advancement. Although these differences are not large, they reinforce a pattern of evidence that suggests women are more enthusiastic and potentially productive workplace participants at the same time that they are underrewarded.

Even though the NLS-72 archive contains no direct information on women's experience of sexual harassment, it would be myopic not to acknowledge that sexual harassment is likely to play a role in this analysis of workplace behavior. Sexual harassment, it has often been stated, is not really about sex: it is about power, about the ways in which some men function as political creatures in the workplace. It is not new; it does not postdate the Anita Hill–Clarence Thomas confrontation. In fact, sexual harassment suits were all over the media in 1980 when most of the class of 1972 was hitting their stride in the workplace and when women were tipping the balance in higher education (among other landmarks of that year, the first women graduated from the U.S. service academies).

Table 2.15. Aspects of Job Satisfaction Among Men and Women, 1986.

	Percent "very satisfied"	
Job elements	Men	Women
Working conditions	20.5%	22.6%
Relationships on job	29.5	33.8
Development of new skills	19.5	22.3
Use of education on job	21.1	24.0
Opportunity for promotion in firm	16.5	13.4
Opportunity for career advancement	20.0	17.0

Note: The universe consists of all participants in the 1986 follow-up survey who indicated both a current occupation and as many as four jobs held between 1979 and 1986. $N = 10,155$.

The exercise of power that gross sexual harassment reveals is not only discriminatory and psychologically damaging, but also inhibits women's sharing of knowledge and skills, hence undercuts productivity. It is as much an economic threat as a social disease.

Women's Values and Choices

Research has demonstrated that women make occupational choices for more complex, and more personal, reasons than do men, and those reasons do not always include maximizing economic self-interest (Treiman and Hartmann, 1981; H. S. Astin, 1984). While the socialization issues surrounding this finding are well documented, the currently fashionable argument (see, for example, Mickelson, 1989) is that women will continue to perform well in school and college and contribute their knowledge to the workplace irrespective of what should be traditional economic rewards—that is, they do not care as much as do men because women's idea of "value" is different.

The data in the NLS-72 archive provide both support for this assumption and evidence against it. There is no doubt that, over time, earnings became more significant in career and job choice for the NLS-72 women than for the men. Between 1973 and 1986, the percentage of women rating income/salary as more important than *all* other considerations in selecting a career more than doubled to

20 percent, while the comparable figure for men remained flat at 17 percent.

Over the same period and compared to other life values, however, money became more important to men than to women. Table 2.16, playfully entitled, "Bucks, Ego, and Life Values," reflects a not-so-playful web of choices. Here is how the table works. The value attached to "bucks," or in the words of the NLS-72 survey question, "making a lot of money," is expressed in a ratio to the mean of responses to other values, such as "having strong friendships." The ratios for all respondents were set on a scale that was divided by mean and standard deviation to yield four ranges. The

Table 2.16. Bucks, Ego, and Life Values: Attitudes of Women and Men Toward Money and Self, 1973-1986.

	Ranks lowest in life 1	2	3	Ranks highest in life 4
Money				
Men				
1973 (age 19)	17.7%	24.6%	43.0%	14.7%
1979 (age 25)	15.4	30.5	36.7	17.5
1986 (age 32)	11.4	29.6	39.1	19.9
Women:				
1973 (age 19)	27.7	21.6	42.8	7.9
1979 (age 25)	19.2	34.0	36.9	10.0
1986 (age 32)	14.8	34.7	39.9	10.7
Self				
Men				
1973 (age 19)	12.4	44.7	24.7	18.3
1979 (age 25)	7.6	35.3	42.7	14.4
1986 (age 32)	6.5	35.8	43.3	14.5
Women				
1973 (age 19)	15.8	46.9	24.2	13.2
1979 (age 25)	8.2	42.1	40.6	9.1
1986 (age 32)	8.1	43.8	39.8	8.4

Note: The universe includes all NLS-72 students who participated in the 1973, 1979, and 1986 surveys and who answered, on all three occasions, a series of questions concerning the relative values they placed on various life goals. *N* = 12,236.

"right tail" (value = 4) describes people for whom money is the most important value in life. Between age twenty-five (1979) and age thirty-two (1986), the percentage of women rating money as a life value higher than other life values barely moved. This seems to be a function of family formation. That is, one of the major values that competes with money in the ratio that produces these data is "being able to give my children better opportunities." The percentage of women who indicated that their "children's future" was a "very important" value rose considerably during the period between ages twenty-five and thirty-two.

There was also a parallel between the increasing importance of money and what one might call an "ego" variable—that is, a tendency to value activities and achievements referring principally to oneself (success, having lots of money, leisure time) rather than others (children, community, broader social concerns). Table 2.16 demonstrates that the self-centeredness of both men and women drops considerably between the ages of nineteen and twenty-five and then levels off, but that, on balance, men remain more self-centered than women. This gap held through an age of explosion in dual-career couples, and through trends accompanying that explosion: increased use of day care, improvements in men's cooking skills, and pages of magazine fillers and television news features on these trends.

Though contradicted, in part, by Astin and Kent (1983), the general trend of men's comparative self-centeredness is supported by the NLS-72 respondents' descriptions of their degree of activity in various voluntary organizations at age thirty-two. Men are more likely to be active in what I call "personal development" organizations such as sports clubs or hobby groups (34 percent of men versus 26 percent of women), and women more likely to be active in community service groups or organized volunteer work in, for example, hospitals (15 percent of women versus 9 percent of men). Regardless of how the NLS-72 women's other life values changed, they still gave more of themselves than men.

What the NLS-72 Women Teach Us

However intriguing the argument that women will continue to attain and contribute to the workplace irrespective of rewards may be, it nonetheless condones labor-market exploitation and economic stagnation. Basically, it implies that women are going to do what they always do, so economic rewards are superfluous; hence, why bother? From the perspective of national economic development, let alone elementary justice, that argument spells disaster.

Why? First, because it does not encourage anyone's educational achievement. It certainly does not tell men that genuine knowledge counts. Indeed, we have seen a notable slide in men's school performance in recent years (Adelman, 1993), in part because some of them seem to believe that to learn is "feminine" (Stockard and Wood, 1984). Second, because the argument does not encourage the sharing of knowledge for the good of any enterprise. If we take women's knowledge contributions for granted or ignore them at the same time that we treat men's knowledge as proprietary and rewardable, we have a half economy. Third, because the rest of the world does not behave that way. Other postindustrial nations may not educate as high a percentage of women beyond high school as we do, but their economies do not leave women as underutilized. And the rest of the world is starting to pass us by.

It was a coincidence that 1972 saw both the beginning of the NLS-72 and passage of the Women's Educational Equity Act, which gave a boost to the subsequent course of women's participation and attainment in postsecondary education. The framers of that legislation were concerned principally with the justice of equal treatment, as they should have been. But our national rhetoric has since come to proclaim that education is also an economic investment on behalf of the whole society. The history of the high school class of 1972 strongly suggests that women can prove the case. The coming century is theirs to do so, but if the market ensures women's attainments through just rewards, the benefits surely will belong to all of us. That's playing it right—and just.

Aftermath: Glass Ceilings or Glass Walls

In January 1992, ABC's "20/20" did a segment that revolved around this story. The crew shot for three hours in my office (and used five minutes, of course, but one expects that). I tried to keep the focus of discussion on three or four major points: women are learning better than men, do not puff up about it, share their knowledge, and are hence more likely to be productive workers. I did not harp excessively on the pay equity issue because the real story is much bigger than pay equity. But that's not what the media wanted to hear. They wanted me to say that women suffer in the labor market solely because men are sexist, not because (as I believe) men cannot see how women's commitment to education and ways of working are models of economic promise. In an awkward moment that made the final cuts, they forced me to the simplified, propagandistic position.

During the shooting of the "20/20" segment, I used the sound bite, "We're talking about glass walls more than glass ceilings," and I had hoped the producers would find three or four typical working women in their thirties to demonstrate just how the whole unfortunate employment and earnings game plays out. Instead, they chose two women at the pinnacles of elite professions (medicine and law), with six-figure salaries. The glass walls were never mentioned, and the only glass ceiling that made it to your living room was the one to the penthouse.

As long as we read women's education and labor-market stories as penthouse stories, we are never going to address the problem. I say "we," because the messages of this story are as much for men as they are for women—if not more so. I am sure men understand that if national well-being requires that we work harder and more consistently at learning and that we give more of our learning on the job, then if men do not participate in these activities, we will still have a half economy. Men and women have come to participate together in most occupations that do not rely heavily on physical strength. In those occupations, men must join women in styles of learning and work that will benefit all of us—and that may be the most difficult challenge. As Senator Paul Simon of Illinois said during a Congressional hearing that utilized the study reported in this chapter, we cannot legislate "changing people's attitudes and behaviors in the workplace so that knowledge is respected a lot more than it is, and sharing of knowledge is respected more than it is" (Committee on Labor and Human Resources, U.S. Senate, 1991, p. 11). But we can put public pressure on employers to live up to what they tell us all the time about what they want in terms of knowledge, learning ability, and sharing. Watch what they do, not what they say.

Notes

1. Women's share of first professional degrees varies widely by field, as the following chart, using 1990–91 data, illustrates:

Field	Percent female[a]	Field as percent of first professional degrees[a]
Pharmacy	61.7%	1.7%
Veterinary medicine	57.4	2.9
Optometry	44.1	1.6
Law	43.1	53.4
Medicine	36.0	21.2
Dentistry	32.2	5.0
Theology	23.8	7.7
Other fields	26.9	6.5
All	39.2%	100.0%

[a]Among U.S. citizens only.

Source: Snyder, 1993, p. 285 (Table 265). It should be noted that some of these first professional fields do not require the prior receipt of a bachelor's degree and that, in those cases, the first professional degree is the equivalent of a bachelor's.

2. These are 1984 data for total enrollment in higher education. At what is known in international data as "degree level 6"— that is, baccalaureate enrollments—the figures are: Italy, 46 percent; United Kingdom, 45 percent; West Germany, 38 percent; Netherlands, 33 percent; and Japan, 24 percent (Department of Education and Science (United Kingdom), 1987, p. 8 (Table 4)).

3. See European Round Table (1989).

4. The indirect evidence comes from the Survey of Earned Doctorates conducted annually by the National Academy of Sciences. In 1991, the mean age at which women earned Ph.D.'s was 36, compared with 33 for men. The range was 29.1, for female doctorates in chemistry (a field in which women constituted 23 percent of the doctorates) to 42.7 for female doctorates in education (a field in which women constituted 58 percent of the doctorates). See Ries and Thurgood (1993, pp. 76–79).

5. The occupational and industry codes used in virtually all sur-

veys and studies sponsored by the National Center for Education Statistics are the same as those developed and used by the Bureau of the Census. Each code consists of three digits. For economy, most studies use only the first digit. The series of occupational codes beginning with the number "2," for example, has two sections—"Managers and Administrators, Except Farm" and "Sales Workers." This series covers such disparate occupations as bank officers, funeral directors, postmasters, railroad conductors, bar managers, elementary school principals, "managers and administrators, not elsewhere classified"—the only category in the scheme that accommodates a CEO, advertising agents, "hucksters and peddlers," newsboys, and stockbrokers. The results of using only the first digit are thus bizarre, yet no one ever questions them. We have decades of data built on the garbage dumps of such lack of discrimination.

6. Previous studies (for example, Lyle and Ross, 1973) have found that the most equitable distribution of men and women across occupations within a firm occurs among firms in heavy industry with significant international markets. To be sure, occupational distribution is not the same variable as earnings. But equitable distribution indicates that a corporation takes a positive and active stance toward women's employment opportunities, which, by extension, should be reflected in pay.

End Table 2A. Women's Courses and Men's Courses: A Sample Among Those Who Received Bachelor's Degrees, 1972–1984.

	Percent of total credits earned	
Courses	Women	Men
Common courses (spread[a] <30%)		
English composition (regular)	2.97%	2.96%
General biology	2.11	1.84
General psychology	2.10	1.72
Introductory sociology	1.50	1.11
Physical education activities	1.33	1.50
World/Western civilization	1.18	1.15
Literature: general	1.19	0.92
U.S. government	1.02	1.18
Introductory communications	0.90	0.89
U.S. history (surveys)	0.74	0.82
Bible studies	0.58	0.64
"Women's courses" (spread[a]>30%)		
Music performance	1.61	1.06
Spanish: elementary/intermediate	1.30	0.88
Nursing (general)	1.27	0.01
Developmental psychology	1.13	0.46
French: elementary/intermediate	1.12	0.56
Art history	1.04	0.52
English literature	0.96	0.56
American literature	0.93	0.64
Educational psychology	0.90	0.33
Elementary education	0.85	0.11
Social work (general)	0.57	0.15
Anatomy and physiology	0.54	0.19
"Men's courses" (spread[a] >30%)		
Calculus	1.02	2.80
General chemistry	1.49	2.24
General physics	0.78	2.09
Introductory economics	1.13	2.04
Introductory accounting	0.74	1.27
Advanced accounting/cost accounting/auditing	0.67	1.48
Organic chemistry	0.59	1.09
Business law	0.40	0.88
Introduction to management	0.37	0.87
Electrical engineering	<0.01	0.85
Geology (general)	0.50	0.80
College algebra	0.46	0.72

[a]Spread is defined as the difference in the percentage of credits earned by the two groups—for example, that for general biology—is (2.11- 1.84)/ 2.11 = 13%.

End Table 2B. Women and Men in School After Age Thirty,
by Degree Objective, Institutional Type, and Educational
Satisfaction, 1984–1986.

	Men		Women		All
Enrolled, 1984–1986	19.9%		22.9%		21.4%
Enrolled full time at any time, 1984–1986	6.2		5.5		5.9
Degree objective					
None	13.6	(N.A.)[a]	21.1	(N.A.)	17.6
Certificate/license	20.3	(56.3)	16.0	(68.4)	18.0
Associate's	14.0	(16.7)	14.0	(17.9)	14.1
Bachelor's	20.0	(28.1)	22.6	(28.0)	21.4
Master's	19.3	(31.8)	16.5	(32.5)	17.8
Doctoral	8.8	(34.4)	4.2	(14.9)	6.3
First professional	4.0	(59.0)	5.3	(46.0)	4.7
Institutional type					
Vocational	11.4		7.2		9.2
Community college	26.5		29.2		27.9
Four-year college/ university	48.4		56.3		52.6
Independent graduate/ professional school	11.5		4.6		7.9
Other	2.3		2.6		2.4
Enrollees very satisfied with					
Teachers	34.5		42.0		38.5
Quality of instruction	27.6		36.4		32.3
Curriculum	22.5		30.8		26.9
Skill development	23.9		32.8		28.6
Intellectual growth	36.0		43.9		40.2

Note: The universe includes all NLS-PETS students who also participated in the 1986 follow-up survey and who indicated that they had enrolled in a postsecondary school between the fall of 1984 and the spring of 1986. $N = 1,557$. Due to rounding, not all columns total 100.0%.

[a]The percentage of each subgroup saying they completed the requirements for the credential to which they aspired is indicated in parentheses.

End Table 2C. Average 1985 Earnings in Selected Occupations
of Women Without Children and Men, 1985.

Occupations	Earnings of men	Earnings of women without children	Differ- ential	Women in occupation	Bachelor's degree recipients
All	$25,022	$18,970	31.9%	43.4%	53.1%
Science/technical/health					
Computer programmer	23,536	26,134	(11.0)[a]	32.3	53.4
Computer systems analyst	34,091	32,797	3.9	24.2	63.6
Electrical engineering technician	21,305	26,681	(25.2)	14.5	14.5
Engineers (all)	38,804	36,942	5.0	6.7	100.0[b]
Engineering/science technician, not elsewhere classified	28,139	17,969	56.6	23.8	8.3
Scientist	28,975	21,053	37.6	28.8	100.0[b]
Pharmacist	32,312	27,987	15.4	35.3	100.0[b]
Physician	39,054	31,458	24.1	25.0	100.0[b]
Health technician	22,237	20,998	5.9	75.0	50.0
Economist	34,770	33,594	3.5	31.8	100.0[b]
Research worker, not elsewhere classified	18,708	19,086	(2.0)	56.4	70.3
Human services					
Social worker	18,391	16,942	8.6	68.6	82.9
Elementary school teacher	21,403	19,661	8.9	87.0	100.0[b]
High school teacher	17,538	18,130	(3.4)	50.7	100.0[b]
Other teachers, not elsewhere classified	19,254	16,009	20.3	67.7	88.9
School administrator	26,268	18,622	41.1	56.5	100.0[b]
Therapist	24,168	20,858	15.9	75.0	81.3
Manager: human/health services	23,782	19,205	23.8	63.9	70.5
Business/finance/management					
Personnel/labor relations	34,895	31,552	10.6	56.8	65.9
Accountant	31,082	28,484	9.1	37.3	73.6
Bookkeeper	14,740	14,258	3.4	95.2	25.4

End Table 2C. Average 1985 Earnings in Selected Occupations
of Women Without Children and Men, 1985, Cont'd.

Occupations	Earnings of men	Earnings of women without children	Differ-ential	Women in occupation	Bachelor's degree recipients
Buyer/purchasing agent	25,385	31,783	(25.2)	39.0	58.5
Manager: financial services	34,386	26,633	29.1	40.3	64.7
Manager: wholesale/ retail	28,365	19,002	49.3	25.3	47.6
Manager: manufacturing	32,879	31,930	3.0	22.8	56.6
Manager: communica- tions industries	30,074	23,508	27.9	48.3	60.0
Real estate agent	31,017	30,516	1.6	28.9	57.9
Estimator/investi- gator	23,123	17,476	32.3	66.0	52.8
Production controller	22,333	18,380	21.5	53.1	21.9
Other					
Editor/reporter	20,873	25,438	(21.9)	54.3	66.7
Lawyer	33,671	28,667	17.5	37.5	100.0[b]
Police	28,376	21,444	32.3	15.4	36.9
Computer equipment operator	17,534	18,581	(6.0)	67.9	19.6

[a]Items in parentheses indicate occupations in which women earned more than men.

[b]Occupation defined to include only those with requisite degrees.

End Table 2D. Years of Job Experience and Earnings at Age Thirty-Two, for Men and Women with Bachelor's Degrees, by Major.

Majors	Men		Women without children		Women with children	
	Mean years employment, 1979-1985	1985 earnings	Mean years employment, 1979-1985	1985 earnings	Mean years employment, 1979-1985	1985 earnings
All	5.63	$27,834	5.63	$21,361	5.42	$16,933
Business	5.87	31,098	5.91	33,230	5.52	19,483
Education	5.84	21,651	5.80	18,544	5.55	17,524
Applied social science	5.40	25,635	5.48	21,423	5.70	17,377
Engineering/computer science	5.87	40,047	5.78	35,320	—	—
Physical science/math	5.84	32,209	5.51	22,777	5.13	17,915
Biological sciences	5.19	29,508	5.30	22,022	4.93	19,464
Health sciences	6.04	29,971	5.79	25,380	5.48	16,656
Applied sciences	5.59	22,317	5.54	21,761	4.96	12,373
Humanities	5.00	20,113	5.48	20,959	5.21	17,865
Fine/performing arts	4.85	15,993	5.60	18,337	5.43	14,820
Social sciences	5.44	26,890	5.43	18,191	5.25	16,023

Note: The universe includes all NLS-PETS students who earned bachelor's degrees, participated in the 1986 follow-up survey, and indicated that they were employed and had earnings in 1985 and had held a full-time job at any time between July 1979 and December 1985. N = 3,068.

End Table 2E. Race/Ethnicity, Mean Years of Job Experience, and Earnings for Women, by Highest Degree Earned, 1985.

Highest degree earned	White	Black	Hispanic
None			
Without children			
Mean years experience	7.69	7.46	7.70
1985 earnings	$15,469	$15,363	$19,055
With children			
Mean years experience	6.48	6.69	6.55
1985 earnings	$13,968	$14,277	$15,687
Associate's			
Without children			
Mean years experience	8.19	5.80	6.95
1985 earnings	$18,474	$10,915	$16,890
With children			
Mean years experience	7.21	5.14	6.62
1985 earnings	$13,022	$14,647	$11,407
Bachelor's			
Without children			
Mean years experience	7.44	6.95	6.42
1985 earnings	$21,091	$24,394	$21,586
With children			
Mean years experience	7.07	7.19	6.91
1985 earnings	$16,617	$18,538	$19,960

Note: The universe includes all women students in the NLS-PETS who also participated in the 1986 follow-up survey and who indicated that they had held a full-time job at any time between October 1979 and December 1985. N = 3,420. Mean years of job experience covers the period October 1976–December 1985.

Chapter 3

Light and Shadows
on College Athletes

The fall season of 1989 came upon us early. Dogged by a decade of scandals and suspensions, squabbles over admissions standards, and sloganeering over racism, college athletics moved from the sports pages to the legislative chambers. While college presidents fought with the National Collegiate Athletic Association (NCAA) over voluntary disclosure of the status of athletes as students, bills on required disclosure of graduation rates slouched their way toward law in both House and Senate.[1]

It is a sign of our cultural values that the question of whether varsity college athletes (particularly football and basketball players) actually graduate is of greater concern in national policy than whether college students study any college-level math after high school (only half do), whether business administration majors study any international affairs or foreign languages (not much), or whether our engineering majors have demonstrated proficiency in English sufficient for quality communication with clients (they have not). The members of these groups outnumber varsity athletes in the offending sports by fifty to one and have a far greater impact on the quality of life in our nation.

It is also sadly obvious that no research grant ever brought national visibility to a university as a Final Four or Bowl appearance does, though how much such appearances have to do with the fundamental reasons people establish colleges and universities, or the reasons that state and federal taxpayers continue to support them to the tune of $100 billion annually, is a mystery. College varsity sports, as Thelin and Wiseman (1989, p. 9) remark in the only extant major review of a weak literature, "is a world turned upside down with its own peculiar logic, code, and organizational behavior." Indeed, it is a world turned upside down when national mythology supersedes national educational development.

If college varsity athletes received a disproportionate share of federal financial aid and if those who received that aid failed to graduate, there might be some justification for concern in public higher education policy. But they do not receive a disproportionate share of federal aid to begin with, principally because locally provided athletic scholarships are worth a great deal more than Pell grants (General Accounting Office, 1987).

Nonetheless, we argue over graduation rates of athletes. And the arguments that fill the newspaper columns and the legislative chambers too often refer either to anecdotal information or single-institution studies or NCAA conference studies or outright popular mythology (for example, see Axthelm, 1980; American College Testing Service, 1981; National Collegiate Athletic Association, 1989; Purdy, Eitzen, and Hufnagel, 1982; Weistart, 1987). In most cases, the data are gathered and reported by or for interested parties.

We must be careful not to impose values retrospectively on this issue. It is said that increased interest in sports, whether passive or active, occurs when emotional life is empty and when community life weakens. We need heroes and heroines, and we need company. Maybe that was true in the late 1980s, but all the objective indicators of the 1970s say that sports was not as prominent a phenomenon in U.S. life as it is today. For example, personal consumption of sports supplies and spectator sports tickets was actually lower in 1978 than in 1970 (Peterson, 1981), and this type of data tends to be more accurate and indicative of interest than self-reported uses of time (Robinson, 1978). When we consume less in a particular sphere of human activity, we are less likely to be emotionally involved and less likely to be upset with the foibles of the most visible representatives of that activity, present or past.

To illustrate the poles of contemporary references to the college graduation rates of athletes, consider the following two statements from highly regarded sources. The first is by Donald Kennedy, former president of Stanford University; the second is by Richard Lapchick, director of Northeastern University's Center for the Study of Sport and Society:

> For football players to earn degrees in many of the most athletically successful programs is appallingly rare. Graduation rates for football (and basketball) players are often less than half those for the student body as a whole [Kennedy, 1990, p. A25].

> Student-athletes, in general, have very high graduation rates, usually higher than non-athletes. Based on data from the NCAA, the student-athletes from all sports combined who were enrolled as freshmen in 1980–1981 posted a median graduation rate of 66.6% compared with 59% for all students at those particular schools [Lapchick, 1990, p. 6].

Where the former president of Stanford got his figures, no one asked, and he did not tell. And when the NCAA announces its graduation figures, one has to take a deep breath—particularly given the highly ambiguous way in which the data are reported and confined to the 291 NCAA Division I colleges and universities.[2] Lapchick unwittingly confirms this judgment when he refers to graduation rates "at those particular schools." He might have said more.

The NLS-72 data base was not designed with a study of college athletes in mind. It is a naturalistic data base, and, as such, has both virtues and limitations when compared to targeted, intrusive studies. The principal virtue of a naturalistic data base when dealing with a particular subgroup of students who attended college can be expressed simply: "That is the way it was." Those are the fish that were in the sea. The study did not sort the fish first, letting some in and some out. Instead, we let the sloppy course of history determine our subjects. The disadvantage of this approach is lack of statistical power. That is, in a natural sample of all students who were in the same high school class and went to any kind of college at any time over a twelve-year period, varsity athletes will be a small percentage of the whole, no matter what sport is at issue. As the 1984 survey of undergraduates by the Carnegie Foundation for the Advancement of Teaching demonstrated, a *maximum* of 7 percent of students at four-year colleges participated in "intercollegiate athletics" (Boyer, 1987, p. 181). Seven years later, the Knight Foundation Commission's report on intercollegiate athletics claimed that 254,000 students at the 828 NCAA institutions participated in intercollegiate sports (Knight Foundation Commission on Intercollegiate Athletics, 1991, p. 3), approximately 6 percent of the undergraduate population at those NCAA institutions. If the major high-visibility, television contract college sports (men's football and basketball) are at issue, varsity athletes make up an even smaller percentage of the whole. Thus, whatever quantitative statements one may make about these people, one runs the risk of large standard errors of measurement.

Identifying Varsity Athletes in the Archive

The first task in this analysis was to drag a number of nets through the sea of NLS-72 data to identify and describe distinct groups of athletes. The history of this task is instructive, principally because it confronted a formidable obstacle right away: none of the five NLS-72 surveys ever asked the questions, "Were you a varsity athlete in college?" and "If so, in what sport(s)?"

In the absence of a direct question, the task involved flagging all instances of the 21,500 course titles in the postsecondary transcript sample (PETS) that were coded under the category "Physical Education Activities" and that used any of the following terms (verbatim or in abbreviated form): *varsity, intercollegiate,* or *team practice.* These courses were given new course category codes as varsity athletics. There were two such codes: one covering football and basketball (the "major" sports), and one covering everything else (the "minor" sports). At least this recoding effort told me who had received an entry on his or her transcript (credit-bearing or not) for participation in varsity athletics. Not all colleges enter such information on transcripts, but at least one could be absolutely sure that the students who carried one or both of these two new course codes were, in fact, varsity athletes.

Following this methodology strictly meant that some students who were clearly varsity athletes were not identified as such. There was one group of students who had earned between five and sixteen credits in basketball, football, track, or tennis, and I seriously doubt that those were mere physical education credits. There was another group whose transcripts included six or more course entries under the "Physical Education: Activities" code with generalized, ambiguous titles such as "Advanced Sports," "Independent Study," "Team Activities," and "Competitive Athletics"—and these students were *not* physical education majors. But in none of these cases were the terms *varsity, intercollegiate,* and *team practice* used. Hence, the students were not flagged as varsity athletes.

I included women's basketball under major varsity sports because, of all women's sports, basketball receives the most media attention. Critics will argue that, because there is no professional league for women's basketball, colleges do not serve as the minor leagues as they do for the National Football League and the National Basketball Association, hence women should not be included among the varsity athletes whose careers should interest us. The criticism is a sad commentary, even though the premise is honest. Some 17 percent of the varsity athletes in major sports in my sample were women. Again, critics, citing NCAA data, will judge that percentage to be high, but NCAA data do not cover varsity athletes in *all* four-year colleges. No women's college, for example, was a member of the NCAA in the 1970s. But all the women's colleges attended by students in the NLS-PETS were included in this analysis.

Six Comparison Groups

A cascading logic was used to sort students into six groups (that is, students in group 1 could not be part of any other group even if they met the conditions for membership, students in group 2 could not be part of groups 3 to 6, and so on). The first condition for each of these groups was that their students' pattern of college attendance be confined principally to four-year colleges. Of the 12,599 students in the NLS-72 transcript sample, 8,101 fell in those patterns, and they comprise the basic universe for the study in this chapter. The weighted N for this basic universe is 1,149,952. I stress the weighted Ns in this analysis because some of the subgroups are small, and the reader will otherwise have no clues to how realistic the numbers are. Of the basic universe, just under 3 percent were varsity athletes in any sport in college.

The six groups identified were the following:

1. *Varsity athletes (major sports).* Each student in this category had at least one transcript entry (credit-bearing or not) under the new code, "Physical Education: Major Varsity Sports." Some of these students participated in both major and other varsity sports but, according to the logic by which the groups were set up, were included only in the category of major varsity sports. Thus, a person who played both varsity basketball and varsity baseball was counted only as a basketball player. The weighted N for this group was 17,204, or 1.4 percent of the universe.

2. *Varsity athletes (minor sports).* Students in this category had at least one transcript entry under the new code, "Physical Education: Other Varsity Sports." Baseball and track were the most frequently indicated sports in this group, followed by tennis, golf, swimming, and soccer. The weighted N for this group was 13,203, or 1.1 percent of the universe.

3. *Performing arts students.* This is a key control group discussed at some length later in this chapter. Students in this category had indicated in the base-year survey that they had been very active in one or more performing arts in high school. On their college transcripts, they earned more than six credits in performing arts courses involving actual performance (for example, class piano but not music theory courses; acting but not stagecraft). The size of this group was half again as large as the total of varsity athletes in all sports: 3.9 percent.

4. *Intramural sports participants.* Students in this category claimed to be very active in athletics on all three occasions in which they were asked in the surveys (1972, 1974, and 1976). Yet

their transcripts showed three or fewer sports credits, even in basic physical education activities courses. One assumes that these people were active in either intramural or personal athletic endeavors. If other varsity athletes exist in the sample, some are probably included in this category. The number of students in this category was greater than that of groups 1, 2, and 3 combined and constituted 8.6 percent of the universe. This population estimate is probably low. The Carnegie Foundation survey of undergraduates showed 14 percent engaged in intramural sports for more than two hours per week, termed an "active" participation rate (see Boyer, 1987, p. 181).

5. *Nonathletes.* Students in this category never claimed to be active in athletics. In addition, their college transcripts show zero sports credits. This is a large group: 30 percent of the universe.

6. *Everybody else.* Some people in this group were active in athletics on one or two occasions on which they were surveyed but not on all three occasions. Some earned sports credits. But none of them met any of the membership criteria for the other five groups except the college attendance pattern. This residual group is the largest of the six: 55 percent of the universe.

From this point on, and depending on the variable under discussion, the reader should *not* interpret *any* table as representing the entire NLS-PETS. To repeat: *all* data in *this* chapter refer only to the students who met the basic college attendance pattern criterion. Therefore, some of the data in this chapter will differ from data in other chapters.

Performing Arts and Varsity Athletics

Why single out performing arts students in this analysis? There are both cultural and practical rationales for doing so. Professional performing artists, principally musicians and actors, share professional athletes' cultural glitz. They represent an aristocracy of dreams to which we all, in a secret part of our souls, aspire. The period during which the class of 1972 came of age witnessed an explosion of media outlets worldwide and a corresponding corporate endeavor to fill every electronic moment with something, ergo, an expanding labor market for our dreams. Even if your rock group was called Neon Cucumber and made only one album, there was a moneyed network to try you out, to put you on tour, and to splay your faces and costumes all over two numbers of *Rolling Stone*. Even if you played supporting roles in a half-dozen high school productions, sooner or later you too could become at least a minor member of somebody's brat pack. Tucked into the Saturday night-at-nine slot and lasting a half season, you did 137 autographs after the opening show and still get residuals from reruns in Parador. Your moments on the electronic waves survive.

As industries, then, both performing arts and athletics possess high visibility, high glamour, and mythological power. When Kareem Abdul-Jabbar told *Newsweek*'s Pete Axthelm in 1983 that "some people think that a sports hero can be above life," he understated the psychology of this power (Axthelm, 1983, p. 129). Our media have canonized the secular dreams of thousands of young people to become stars of the playing field, stage, or screen. And college can serve as an incubator of those dreams. Even though the odds against success are overwhelming, the dreams do not die easily. This cannot be said for any other extracurricular activities in schools. By comparing the careers of the NLS-72 athletes to those of the performing arts students, though, it will become apparent that our colleges favor one of these special talents over the other.

Performing arts students also serve a more practical need in this chapter because they are an important component of the National Study of Intercollegiate Athletes carried out by the American Institutes for Research (AIR) for the Presidents' Commission of the NCAA in 1988–89. A large and complex study, the AIR undertaking looked into a variety of aspects of the lives, backgrounds, psychological development, college experiences, finances, perceptions, and so forth of college athletes in forty-two NCAA Division I schools. It also included a transcript sample of 2,077 students at twenty of those schools.[3] The AIR study delved deeper on a much narrower playing field than this study does, and in that respect, it is valuable. In other respects, its value is limited: none of the students in the study had graduated from college, survey responses and even test scores were imputed for the 20 percent of the sample who failed to respond, the sampling was designed to produce quotas in various categories, the ratio of varsity athletes to other students in the study was 3:1, and the only athletes it examined were those at the 42 NCAA Division I schools (out of 291 Division I schools, which are themselves but a fraction of the 1,800 four-year colleges in the United States).

A critical feature in the conceptual framework of the AIR study is a control group of students with which college athletes are compared. Loosely defined, this control group consisted of "other students who devote a great deal of time to a particular extracurricular activity [other than athletics]" (American Institutes for Research, 1988b, p. 17). The 42 institutions themselves identified extracurricular activities based on the following criteria: they require fifteen or more hours per week, they involve competition, they involve "physical and emotional pressures associated with successful performance," they offer "career-related possibilities," the special talents necessary for these activities can be identified in individuals at a "relatively young age," and the activities offer such extraordinary personal (social and psychological) benefits to participants that severance ("terminating participation") may have severe consequences ("real costs") (p. 17).

What extracurricular activities, according to the AIR study, are characterized by these criteria? Here they are, with the percentage of the AIR extracurricular student sample that comes from each (American Institutes for Research, 1988a, p. 83):

Performing arts	37%
Student services, government	14
Work-study	12
Fraternity/sorority	10
Club sports/intramurals	8
Clubs	8
Newspaper/magazine/radio station	8
Other	3

The list is somewhat disingenuous. Only one of these categories of extracurricular activities really meets the six criteria. It is the same category, moreover, that would qualify on other, and more valid, criteria related to athletics, namely, performing arts.

What are those other more valid criteria? There are four. First, performing arts activities and the groups that execute them, such as orchestras, drama troupes, bands, and dance companies, are necessary to institutional culture in any college, and in some institutions, they contribute to the distinct identity of that culture. The performing arts are much like varsity athletics in this regard; they can provide the institution with identity, as well as lend a distinct coloring to student life that, for example, college newspapers, radio stations, and fraternities and sororities do not. Because the display of student talent in both athletics and performing arts is organized around discrete, nonroutine events, athletics and performing arts are also distinct from the daily and often routine activities associated with clubs, newspapers, radio stations, student services, and social organizations.

Second, in the case of both performing arts and varsity athletics, the extracurricular is co-curricular. There are degrees in performing arts, and, as I hope to demonstrate, there are de facto degrees in varsity athletics. There are no degrees in other categories in the AIR control group: clubs, student services, work-study, intramural sports, or Greek life. Along these same lines, the other extracurricular activities on the AIR list can function without faculty. Not so the performing arts. They require expert coaching, directing, instruction, and critique, just as do varsity athletics. And, in general, colleges maintain expert staff to perform those functions. Third, both performing arts and athletics, unlike the other extracurricular activities in the AIR universe, are continuous curricula. That is, both are tied to organized instruction in educational institutions from the elementary grades through college. Prospective schoolteachers and college faculty are trained in and can be certified or credentialed in both areas.

Fourth, collegiate-level performing arts are informed by normative values, and colleges are normative institutions. But college newspapers and work-study programs, for example, are not normative organizations. Amateur athletics *should* be normative, but what puts college athletics on the front pages of the newspapers today derives from the fact that they are not (Cullen, Latessa, and Byrne, 1990; Sperber, 1987, 1990).

Indeed, the differences between performing arts and varsity

athletics stem from the fact that the latter is not a normative enterprise. There are no $1 billion television contracts associated with college-based performing arts groups. There are no audiences of thirty million on New Year's day. Piano or ballet competitions in Moscow aside, there are no international Olympics of amateur dance, drama, or music. Yes, the media outlet explosion of the 1970s and early 1980s encouraged this generation to dream of fame, but the road was heartless; you had to *believe* in art.

Other differences should be obvious. There is but one sports academy in the United States that grants baccalaureate degrees but dozens of academies of music, theater, and film that do so. The professionalism in the curricula of those academies has been assumed by many colleges and universities under the rubric of "the conservatory degree." We do not give conservatory degrees in athletics (at least we do not admit that we give them), but we are very forthright about such degrees as the B.F.A. or the B.Mus. We do not pretend that these degrees do anything more than prepare individuals for professional roles in the performing arts. On the other hand, bachelor's degrees in music or drama are fundamentally different from conservatory degrees. They do not require as much specialized work, and they allow far more room for course taking across many fields of knowledge.

While performing arts students serve roles in college life analogous to those of athletes and while their extracurricular work meets the same six criteria articulated by AIR (time commitment, competition, pressure, career-related, early talent identification, severance consequences), those in the class of 1972 were a very different group of people. In addition, the labor-market experience of the NLS-72 cohort demonstrates that the career-related aspects of the performing arts were far more significant to their participants than were the career-related aspects of athletics.

Demography of the Sample

Table 3.1 provides basic demographic information on the six groups described above. It is not surprising to find that the percentage of blacks among varsity football and basketball players was more than double the figure for all blacks in the sample (18.0 per-

Table 3.1. Demographics of Varsity Athletes and Others.

	Varsity athletes (major sports)	Varsity athletes (minor sports)	Perform-ing arts students	Intra-mural sports participants	Non-athletes	Everybody else
Race/ethnicity						
White	79.0%	89.4%	91.9%	93.3%	90.2%	88.7%
Black	18.0	6.5	6.4	4.5	7.1	8.7
Hispanic/ Native American	3.0	4.1	1.7	2.3	2.7	2.6
Socioeconomic status						
Lowest quartile	17.7	5.9	7.6	11.4	13.3	13.4
Middle quartiles	49.6	37.1	40.6	41.0	43.2	44.2
Highest quartile	32.6	57.0	51.8	47.6	43.6	42.4
Gender						
Male	82.7	78.8	38.3	85.2	45.0	51.0
Female	17.3	21.2	61.7	14.8	55.0	49.0

Note: Columns may not total 100.0% due to rounding.

cent versus 8.1 percent). In light of the type of story that typically makes the sports pages, that percentage seems low. It isn't. NCAA data from the mid 1980s show a range of 17 to 24 percent of varsity football and basketball players who were black (Lederman, 1992). The lowest percentage of blacks in the NLS-72 was found among intramural sports participants. Blacks who were active in sports, and who were likely to come from lower-SES backgrounds to begin with, were more likely to participate in intercollegiate sports, where the scholarships lie.

Indeed, varsity football and basketball players (of all races) were also least likely to come from high-SES households and were most likely to receive scholarships. Students from high-SES back-grounds participated disproportionately in minor varsity sports (which are dominated by baseball and track, but which also include skiing, tennis, and golf—that is, the leisure sports of the upper middle class) and in the performing arts (the talents for which often require development through private lessons, and hence are generally inaccessible to the poor).

The demographic differences between nonathletes and "everybody else" were negligible in all categories with the exception of gender. The gender composition of all six groups, though, helps greatly in explaining their comparative academic performance.

High School Backgrounds

The conventional wisdom that varsity athletes, particularly those in major sports such as football and basketball, have comparatively weak academic backgrounds was borne out in the class of 1972. As the data in Table 3.2 indicate, college varsity athletes took far fewer foreign language courses in high school than anyone else and studied less math and science than anyone except the performing arts students. Intramural sports participants, in comparison, had the strongest backgrounds in math and science. At the same time, our future varsity football and basketball players took more semesters of trade and business courses in high school than did any of the other groups—that is, there was a larger vocational component in their high school curricula.

Whatever else they studied in high school evidently did not receive all that much attention. Their mean high school class rank (63rd percentile) was the lowest of all six groups (performing arts students had the highest mean class rank, at the 74th percentile). In addition, only 30 percent of the college varsity football and basketball players came from the top quintile of their high school classes, versus 42 percent of the other five groups. This combination of limited study in college preparatory subjects and lower academic performance may explain, in part, the significantly lower SAT/ ACT score profile of college varsity athletes in major sports (Table 3.3). Under the NCAA's Propositions 48 and 42, students whose *combined* SAT scores are below 700 are precluded from playing varsity sports in their freshman year. One out of four varsity athletes in the NLS-PETS would have been excluded under that rule had it been in effect in the 1970s. In fact, roughly two out of three varsity

Table 3.2. High School Curricula of College Varsity
Athletes and Others, 1972.

	Less than three semesters foreign languages	Less than five semesters math	Less than five semesters science
Varsity athletes (major sports)	68.3%	54.3%	70.5%
Varsity athletes (minor sports)	39.9	56.3	55.9
Performing arts students	42.8	62.1	80.6
Intramural sports participants	47.9	39.2	55.2
Nonathletes	46.6	54.5	65.1
Everybody else	52.6	53.6	64.8
All groups	50.1	52.9	64.7
	More than two semesters trades	More than two semesters business	More than four semesters fine/ performing arts
Varsity athletes (major sports)	15.3%	19.5%	3.1%
Varsity athletes (minor sports)	10.5	10.2	12.9
Performing arts students	3.3	12.3	63.1
Intramural sports participants	9.9	13.1	10.5
Nonathletes	7.5	16.5	16.9
Everybody else	6.9	19.1	15.6
All groups	7.4	17.4	17.2

athletes scored below the mean for the other five groups combined
on the SAT (and ACT converted to SAT scales).

What about the other comparison groups? Varsity athletes in
minor sports had the highest SAT scores, reflecting both their better
academic performance in high school and more classes in foreign

Table 3.3. SAT Scores of College Varsity Athletes and Others, 1972.

| | SAT ranges | | | | | |
	400–700	701–975	976–1148	1149+	Mean	Standard deviation
Varsity athletes (major sports)	24.2%	42.6%	16.1%	17.1%	913	217
Varsity athletes (minor sports)	9.3	29.5	25.5	35.8	1032	216
Performing arts students	6.3	42.3	32.3	19.1	1007	187
Intramural sports participants	5.5	38.0	33.7	22.8	1026	188
Nonathletes	10.1	38.3	28.0	23.7	1006	215
Everybody else	11.6	45.6	28.4	14.4	958	95

Note: The universe includes all students in the sample for the athletes' study whose records include either SAT or ACT scores (ACT scores were converted to the SAT scale). N = 6,161. Weighted N = 883,035. Because of rounding, not all rows total 100.0%.

languages and science. Performing arts students were distinguished by the paucity of their high school work in math and science and the significant amount of time they spent in formal fine and performing arts courses. But neither fact seemed to affect their high school class rank or SAT and ACT scores as much as it affected those of varsity football and basketball players. One reason for the higher ranks and scores was that women comprised over 60 percent of the performing arts students in the NLS-PETS, and as we have seen, the women's high school class rank was consistently higher than the men's, no matter what set of curricular controls are applied. A second reason, and one that also applies to varsity athletes in minor sports, was that a far higher percentage of performing arts students than varsity athletes in major sports (51.7 percent versus 32.6 percent) came from the top quarter of the SES range. SES is one of the strongest correlates of both high school performance and SAT and ACT scores (see Resource C, Table C.3).

College Performance: Some Positive Results for Athletes

One of the major findings of this study is that varsity athletes, including football and basketball players, completed the bachelor's degree at only a slightly lower rate than anyone else and that black varsity athletes completed the bachelor's at a higher rate (52.2 percent) than did all blacks in the sample (44.9 percent) and black nonathletes in particular (28.4 percent). The importance of this finding should not be understated, since the NLS-72 is the only extant source that accounts for *eventual* (twelve-year) degree completion. The NLS-72 is also unique in that its account is based on actual college transcripts and not testimony of football coaches or college presidents, let alone manipulation under the NCAA "adjusted graduation rate" formula. Finally, because it is a national data base, the completion rate reflects *all* institutions attended by the student over the twelve-year period, and not merely the institution at which he or she started out or the institution at which he or she played varsity sports.

Table 3.4 summarizes the data on highest degree earned and includes standard errors because the arguments about the comparative graduation rates issue need all the help they can get. The key column displays the sum of those students whose highest degree was, at a *minimum*, the bachelor's degree. Most of the differences in degree attainment rates among the six groups are statistically significant. The one exception involving varsity athletes in major sports lies in the comparison of that group to the residual group ("everybody else"). But in that case, the difference in graduation rates was slight to begin with.

As for blacks, who are of particular concern in connection with varsity football and basketball because of the perception that they are exploited (Edwards, 1985; Eitzen and Purdy, 1986; Leonard, 1986; Rudman, 1986), the numbers in some categories are too small and the standard errors too high, but the percentages of blacks earning bachelor's degrees suggest that participation in major varsity sports was not a drag on the degree completion rate in this generation, at least among the students identified as varsity athletes. It is also worth noting that a far higher percentage of black than white varsity football and basketball players who completed the bachelor's

Table 3.4. Highest Degrees Earned by Varsity Athletes
and Others, 1972–1984.

	None	Certificate	Associate's	Bachelor's and higher degrees combined
Varsity athletes (major sports)				
All	28.1%	0.7%	1.8%	69.3%
	(1.7)	(.03)	(.05)	(1.7)
Blacks	47.8	——	——	52.2
	(4.5)	——	——	(4.6)
Varsity athletes (minor sports)				
All	25.8	——	2.7	71.5
	(1.7)	——	(.10)	(1.7)
Blacks	31.0	——	——	69.0
	N.A.ᵃ	——	——	N.A.ᵇ
Performing arts students				
All	18.2	0.2	3.1	78.5
	(.92)	(.08)	(.11)	(.93)
Blacks	36.2	——	2.4	61.4
	(2.6)	——	(.14)	(2.6)
Intramural sports participants				
All	26.1	1.1	2.6	70.3
	(.81)	(.08)	(.20)	(.83)
Blacks	44.6	6.7	——	48.7
	(3.6)	(.29)	——	(3.7)
Nonathletes				
All	43.3	1.2	3.5	52.0
	(.45)	(.08)	(.15)	(.43)
Blacks	68.4	0.9	2.4	28.4
	(1.1)	(.02)	(.45)	(1.2)
Everybody else				
All	24.4	1.1	4.9	69.5
	(.25)	(.07)	(.15)	(.28)
Blacks	39.9	1.2	5.3	53.6
	(1.1)	(.45)	(.50)	(1.1)
All groups	30.1	1.2	4.1	64.7
	(.22)	(.05)	(.10)	(.22)
Blacks	50.2	1.0	3.9	44.9
	(.84)	(.27)	(.33)	(.89)

Note: Standard errors are in parentheses.
ᵃ *Ns* are too small for standard error.

degree also completed a graduate degree (28.7 percent versus 11.8 percent).

Varsity athletes in major sports start college at a disadvantage: they have less adequate high school preparation, lower high school performance, and lower SAT/ACT scores than other students. Yet, over the twelve-year period covered by the NLS-PETS, they do no worse than others in terms of college completion. Why? There are three major reasons: financial support, time of college entrance, and special services.

Financial Support

First, varsity athletes in major sports receive scholarships in excess proportion to their numbers during the traditional college attendance-pattern years. Some 55.9 percent of the NLS-72 varsity football and basketball players received college scholarships during the first two years following high school versus 49.6 percent of performing arts students and 31.4 percent of nonathletes. In contrast, the AIR study of 1987–88 (American Institutes for Research, 1988a) reported that 60.1 percent of football and basketball players at NCAA Division I schools were on *full* scholarships and that nearly three out of four had received athletic scholarships. It may well be that we passed out more athletic scholarships in the 1980s than we did in the 1970s, but these differences are more likely due to the broader representation of institutions in the NLS-72 sample. Whatever the case, a student receiving a scholarship is less likely to drop out of college for financial reasons and less likely to interrupt or attenuate study by taking on a job. Indeed, 69 percent of all those who attended four-year colleges *and* received scholarships in the first two years following high school graduation completed bachelor's degrees, compared with 52 percent of those who received no scholarship support at any time.

The AIR study provides an additional note on the financial care and feeding of varsity football and basketball players. Some 52 percent of those athletes reported that it was easy to get a summer job, while only 28 percent of varsity athletes in other sports and 32 percent of the AIR "extracurricular" group made the same observation (American Institutes for Research, 1988a, p. 11). Other researchers report that these summer jobs are often provided by "boosters"—alumni or friends of the college who specialize in supporting athletic programs and who sometimes do not hesitate to pad payrolls or otherwise deal under the table, even for athletes in non-revenue-producing sports (Sperber, 1990; Adler and Adler, 1991). It is hard to run away from special treatment.

It appears that the performing arts students were just as likely as varsity football and basketball players to receive scholarships at some time during their college careers, but the difference between these two groups is not statistically significant. At the same time, the difference between these two groups and all other subgroups in this analysis is substantial and significant. This is not a new story. Colleges recruit with scholarships those who can maintain institutional culture and student nonacademic life, and these scholarships are often given regardless of need—remember that performing arts students tend to come from higher-SES backgrounds than students in the other groups.

Time of College Entrance

A second factor contributing to the graduation rate of varsity football and basketball players is that they are more likely to enter college immediately on graduation from high school than most other comparison groups, and the differences are statistically significant. Immediate entrance to postsecondary education was a very strong correlate of degree completion for the class of 1972 (Table 3.5). Why do varsity athletes in major sports enter college with no delay? They have been recruited, and the coach wants them on campus in August, or sometimes as early as June, to start practice (Adler and Adler, 1991). If they are on campus in August for practice, they are registering for courses in September.

Varsity athletes in minor sports and performing arts students are even less likely to delay entering college. The reasons in this case are more traditional: their high school class ranks are higher, their SAT/ACT scores are higher (Table 3.3), and their SES profiles are higher (Table 3.1). That combination is more likely to lead to direct entrance and bachelor's degree attainment than any other set of circumstances.

Table 3.5. Time of College Entrance in Relation to Graduation
Rates for Varsity Athletes and Others, 1972–1984.

| | Time from high school graduation to college entrance | | | | |
	No delay	6–15 months delay	16–27 months delay	28–51 months delay	52+ months delay
Varsity athletes (major sports)	89.9%	6.5%	1.2%	2.4%	——
Varsity athletes (minor sports)	91.4	6.6	1.5	——	0.5
Performing arts students	90.4	4.8	1.1	2.1	1.6
Intramural sports participants	85.0	6.3	3.1	2.8	2.9
Nonathletes	72.1	8.8	6.5	5.4	7.1
Everybody else	86.1	6.9	2.5	2.9	1.4
All groups	82.0	7.3	3.7	3.6	3.2
Students from all groups who completed bachelor's degrees by 1984	66.3	51.3	42.6	45.2	19.2

Note: The universe includes all students in the study sample whose transcripts were not missing term-date information. N = 8,087. Because of rounding, not all rows total 100%.

Safety Net

While the NLS-72 archive does not include this information, the evidence of the AIR studies leaves no doubt that varsity football and basketball players have at their disposal a much broader safety net of supportive services than do other undergraduate students. It is much easier for them to receive help from tutors, academic counselors, teaching assistants, and professors than is the case for other groups of students (American Institutes for Research, 1988a, p. 44). And among black varsity football and basketball players, whether at predominantly white or predominantly black colleges, students perceive access to this supportive service network as very easy (American Institutes for Research, 1989a, pp. 34–35; Edwards 1985).

    The AIR studies provide national confirmation of the safety net that case studies and investigative journalism have documented in the past. The grouping of certain athletes in special classes with professors who are "friends of the program" (Adler and Adler, 1991) or, less euphemistically, "jock sniffers" (Sperber, 1990) is common. Likewise, the provision of special coaches who take care of athletes' registration for classes, track their academic performance, and negotiate with professors (Weistart, 1987), and the special arrangements made for summer school correspondence courses, are among the practices supporting varsity athletes that no other group of students experiences.

While one might question the motivation for this safety net, it certainly contributes to a higher graduation rate than would otherwise be the case given the academic backgrounds of varsity football and basketball players. As the following section demonstrates, the safety net steers these athletes along comparatively easy paths to degrees. If they do not graduate, yet another safety net awaits them. There are now seventy-eight universities participating in the National Consortium for Academics and Sports, a program that seeks out, counsels, and brings athletes back to school as adults to complete college. In the academic year 1990–91, some 921 athletes in this program completed bachelor's degrees ("School Helping Athletes . . . ," Oct. 20, 1991). These people were not twenty-three or twenty-four years old. And not all of them completed their degrees in the schools for which they played varsity ball. No wonder the NLS-72 twelve-year graduation rates for varsity athletes are high. No other group of former undergraduate dropouts is treated to this kind of support.

The College Record of Varsity Athletes: A Shadow Falls

The degree completion rate of college varsity athletes in major sports is only part of the athletes' story. When we begin to examine other factors in the college careers of varsity athletes, the apparent paradox of that completion rate—namely, that they finish in spite of significantly less adequate secondary school preparation than their high school peers—is unmasked and shown to be not especially paradoxical.

The second major set of findings of this analysis may be stated as follows: college varsity athletes, particularly football and basketball players, may complete bachelor's degrees at a respectable rate, but it takes them longer to do so than others, their grades are lower, and their curricula are—to put it gently—less demanding along the way.

We can take the time-to-degree data first. Overlapping the period in which the class of 1972 went to college, a basketball superstar of the 1980s, Larry Bird, also went to school. He entered Indiana University immediately from high school (having been recruited and therefore being on campus at the beginning of the academic year, as the formula would have it). Overwhelmed by the size of the place, he dropped out within a few weeks. He probably never generated a transcript. After a pause, he went to a junior college, but lasted only a few months. After about a year of working in the parks department in French Lick, Indiana, he was recruited to Indiana State University. The rest is history, but it was a long history.

Future NBA players, let alone superstars, are hardly typical. But in the data in Table 3.6, it is immediately and strikingly obvious that a far lower percentage of varsity athletes (no matter what sport is at issue) completed the bachelor's degree in 4.5 calendar years following high school graduation than other students. It is also obvious, however, that varsity athletes caught up to most other groups by 5.5 calendar years.

Given these differences in time to degree, it is not surprising to find that varsity football and basketball players are the group most likely to earn more than 132 undergraduate credits. Credits are

Table 3.6. Time to Bachelor's Degree When Received
Within Twelve Years of High School Graduation, 1972–1984.

	Within 4.5 years	Within 5.5 years	Within 6.5 years
Varsity athletes (major sports)	43.4%	78.1%	88.1%
Varsity athletes (minor sports)	44.1	79.6	85.8
Performing arts students	65.7	85.2	91.7
Intramural sports participants	63.1	84.2	90.8
Nonathletes	60.3	77.3	85.4
Everybody else	58.2	78.4	87.9
All groups	59.1	79.0	87.8

proxy measures for time, and students receive credits for passing courses. If a student's cumulative grade-point average or grade-point average within his or her major does not meet minimum standards, the student either stops out of college or continues taking courses at a reduced load until the standards are met. Varsity football and basketball players tend to have lower grade-point averages than do other students (see Table 3.9); hence, the chances are greater that these athletes will earn more credits along the way to the bachelor's degree. Even slightly lighter credit loads (for example, thirteen credits per semester as opposed to the fifteen-credit norm) can produce the same result. When athletes taking lighter loads still fail courses and thus risk losing eligibility, it is not uncommon for coaches to arrange for summer courses that will more than make up the difference in credits (Sperber, 1990).

Too, while the coach may have found ways ("red-shirting" being the most common) to stretch out athletes' eligibility to five years,[4] the more critical factor in terms of what happens to varsity athletes after they leave college is *what* they studied along the way. This is the story that the reader will never encounter in an NCAA report or in recommendations from such august bodies as the Knight Foundation Commission.

What Did They Study?

Whitner and Myers's (1986, pp. 665, 662) portrait of a college athlete provides typical anecdotal guidance to athletes' college curricula: "Because Mike was an entering freshman and an athlete, the difficulty of his course load was somewhat below that of most entering freshmen," with Mike himself expecting that college would be "just like high school. If you were good in your sport—they would pass you." More elaborate curricular games—including de facto correspondence courses and "directed studies," classifying athletes as learning disabled so they can be sheltered in courses with no reading, assignment of retroactive grades, and so forth—have been documented at many institutions (Sperber, 1990; Brede and Camp, 1987). The transcripts of the varsity athletes in the NLS-72 sample are filled with easy-to-spot examples of what Sperber calls the "hideaway curriculum": course titles such as "Recreation Internship," "Park Leadership," "Orientation to Anatomy," or "Team Sports Practicum." It takes more work with the transcripts to discover three-credit versions of physical education activities courses for which other students in the same institution received only a half credit, or course titles that obviously masked other realities—a "Field Research" course for a physical education major, for example.

There are a number of ways to describe the college curricula of varsity football and basketball players. To begin with, we can refer to their comparatively weak high school preparation and ask the extent to which they took remedial courses in English and math in college. The results, drawn from transcript entries for developmental writing, speech and reading, and precollegiate math courses, are displayed in Table 3.7. They should surprise no one.

The curricula of varsity athletes can also be described in terms of specific courses that accounted for the largest proportion of the athletes' total earned credits. How did the NLS-72 athletes— compared to other groups of students—use their academic time? What we find (see End Table 3A) is that, other than performing arts students (particularly music majors), varsity basketball and football players had the most concentrated common curriculum. That is, they did more of their undergraduate work within the boundaries of a relatively small number of *courses* than students in any of the other groups under examination. This phenomenon reflects the "clustering" of athletes in courses by their academic advisers (Adler and Adler, 1991). In comparison, performing arts students took more of their undergraduate work within a smaller number of *fields*

Table 3.7. Varsity Athletes and Others Who Took Remedial
Courses in College, 1972–1984.

	Remedial English	Remedial math
Varsity athletes (major sports)	32.9%	35.6%
Varsity athletes (minor sports)	17.3	29.9
Performing arts students	18.2	25.9
Intramural sports participants	14.6	20.4
Nonathletes	13.5	19.2
Everybody else	24.7	32.2
All groups	20.3	27.1

than any other group in this analysis. Indeed, it is apparent that, compared with varsity athletics, the performing arts are far more co-curricular than an extracurricular activity. After all, one can major in performing arts, whereas it is hard to major in football—even though it can be (and no doubt is) done.

Undergraduate Major

The analysis of course-taking patterns for any group of students must take account of undergraduate major. And when one compares the curricula of varsity football and basketball players with those of performing arts or intramural sports participants, for example, major tells much of the story.

End Table 3B presents the undergraduate majors of those in this study who earned bachelor's degrees. It appears that varsity football and basketball players majored far more heavily in education and engineering/computer science than others. But the figure for engineering is an anomaly, a by-product of the extremely small universe of varsity football and basketball players and a visible representation of the Air Force Academy and West Point among the schools attended by those players.

The aggregation of the data on majors masks other important distinctions. For example, 22.6 percent of the varsity football and basketball players who earned bachelor's degrees majored in fields bearing directly on their extracurricular work: 17.8 percent majored in physical education, and the balance in recreation or allied health sciences. Of those who failed to earn a bachelor's degree, three out of four had no major at all. It is thus not unexpected to find that, as a group, varsity football and basketball players earned 15 percent of their undergraduate credits in sports-related fields such as applied anatomy, personal health, kinesiology, recreation, and physical education activities. That is, roughly one out of every seven academic credit hours accumulated by varsity football and basketball players who earned bachelor's degrees was in this de facto sports curriculum. Of course, this is an average. The range was 4 to 73 percent.

In contrast, "seniors" in the AIR study show a mean of 6 to 7 percent of earned credits in the combined curricular categories of physical education (activities), physical education (theory/coaching), sports management, and sports medicine/physical therapy (American Institutes for Research, 1989b, p. 24). But no doubt other sports-related credits in the AIR sample are buried in some of the very general categories used—for example, "Biological Sciences" or "Professional Occupations." (It is also not clear whether recreation, the standard anatomy and physiology service course, sociology of sport, and "leisure studies" fall in the AIR taxonomy at all.)

In addition, varsity football and basketball players spent, on average, 4 percent more of their undergraduate time on basic skills and the kind of vocational courses usually not associated with baccalaureate degrees than did other students. The skills/vocational and sports curriculum courses add up to 26.7 percent of the undergraduate credits of all varsity football and basketball players, whether or not they earned any degrees. In addition, this group earned a higher percentage of credits (15.2 percent) in *introductory* humanities and social sciences courses than was the case for any other subgroup. Despite this undemanding curriculum, though, varsity football and basketball players in the class of 1972 performed less well in college than they did in high school (though among students who earned a bachelor's degree, the grade-point average of varsity football and basketball players compares somewhat more favorably), as illustrated in Table 3.8.

Table 3.8. Grade-Point Average of Varsity Athletes and Others,
1972–1984.

	Mean for all students	Mean for bachelor's degree recipients
Varsity athletes (major sports)	2.65 (.57)	2.86 (.45)
Varsity athletes (minor sports)	2.89 (.51)	3.00 (.46)
Performing arts students	3.07 (.44)	3.14 (.43)
Intramural sports participants	2.69 (.70)	2.85 (.46)
Nonathletes	2.74 (.76)	3.06 (.46)
Everybody else	2.80 (.55)	2.95 (.45)
All	2.79 (.63)	2.98 (.46)

Note: Standard deviations are in parentheses.

Varsity Athletes at Age Thirty-Two: An Economic Success

The most frequent criticism of big-time college sports is that they exploit athletes, using them to entertain without providing them with an education that will help them succeed after college. The popular image is one of the former college athlete, barely able to read, barely existing on skid row. In opening a series of Congressional hearings on intercollegiate athletics in 1991, Representative Cardiss Collins of Illinois reflected this image when she said that "the saddest victims [of the transformation of college sports into "big business"] . . . come from the poorest neighborhoods in our country. Lured by dreams of being the next Michael Jordan, many leave their university after 4 or 5 years, unemployed, without even a decent education" (Committee on Energy and Commerce, U.S. House of Representatives, 1992, p. 1).

The NLS-72 archive allows us to evaluate that image with fairly hard data. If we look at basic economic outcomes through such variables such as unemployment, home ownership, and earnings, it is obvious that the varsity football and basketball players of the NLS-72 were rewarded handsomely for the time they spent in higher education, whatever they did with that time.

This success is a major finding that bears repeating: at least in the first decade of their work lives, those who played varsity football or basketball in college do very well economically, thank you, whether or not they earned a college degree, whether or not, in Representative Collins's words, they received "a decent education." There have been case studies demonstrating similar outcomes for athletes at particular colleges (see, for example, Sack and Thiel, 1979), but the NLS-72 archive is the only long-term portrait that provides national validation of this phenomenon.

Only 39 percent of varsity football and basketball players experienced any unemployment between ages twenty-five and thirty-two. This figure compares with 56 percent for performing arts students and 48 percent for the entire sample. Among students who received bachelor's degrees, the proportion of football and basketball players experiencing any unemployment dropped to 34 percent, and the gap between them and others widened. The only other subgroup with a similar level of unemployment experience was that of the intramural sports participants, a group with a higher proportion of science and engineering majors.

In addition, the average annual earnings of former varsity players in big-time sports were comfortably above the mean for students who attended four-year colleges (Table 3.9). Using a slightly different, though contemporaneous universe (Cooperative Institutional Research Program data for entering college freshmen in 487 four-year schools in 1971), Long and Caudill (1991) found similar results. Nine years later, the men in this group who were varsity athletes in all sports held a 4 percent earnings advantage over their peers.

As befits those with higher incomes, the NLS-72 athletes also tended to become home owners at a higher rate (77 percent) than all students in the other groups (63 percent). Given the fact that a higher percentage of the football and basketball players than students in other groups came from families in the lowest SES quartile (in Representative Collins's words, "from the poorest neighborhoods"), there seems to be some relationship between participation in varsity sports and economic mobility. I say "seems," because other analyses indicate that, for the entire universe of this study, there are no differences in home ownership rates at age thirty-two by parents' SES or students' gender or SAT scores, whereas there *do* appear to be differences by race/ethnicity, high school class rank, and college varsity status.

Table 3.9. Mean Annual Earnings for Varsity Athletes and
Others, 1984 and 1985.

	1984	*1985*
Varsity athletes (major sports)	$22,720 ($249)	$24,029 ($920)
Varsity athletes (minor sports)	28,170 (447)	29,319 (666)
Performing arts students	13,602 (282)	15,709 (295)
Intramural sports participants	24,835 (198)	26,370 (340)
Nonathletes	19,555 (272)	20,517 (326)
Everybody else	20,785 (165)	21,895 (175)
All groups	20,578 (123)	21,720 (130)

Note: The universe includes all students in the study sample who participated in the 1986 follow-up survey. $N = 5,841$. Standard errors are in parentheses.

In contrast to this economic story for athletes, performing arts students evidenced the highest incidence of unemployment, the lowest earnings, and the second lowest rate of home ownership of all student groups in this study. Given the fact that they tended to come from higher-SES brackets, they experienced downward economic mobility. This outcome should not be surprising in light of the labor market for performing arts talents. At least would-be professional athletes are sorted out of the market at a comparatively young age. Would-be professional actors and musicians can carry their dreams and efforts for decades. Can it be said that performing arts students, and not varsity athletes, are the truly exploited?

"Exploitation" is a strong judgment, and the strength of that judgment depends, in large part, on both its reference point and the intention of its subjects. Is the reference point current status or future status? Is it economic, social, and/or spiritual? Does it take informed individual preference, choice, and consent into account? What promises or expectations play a role in the judgment? If we promise varsity football players that if they will only spend from thirty to sixty hours a week in season entertaining us for four or five years of their lives, we will see to it that they get a degree of some kind, make sure that they do not worry about finances along the way, and teach them how to use their own status as varsity athletes to leverage stable jobs and a decent salary, have we exploited them— particularly if they could not get those jobs and that salary any other way? Have we exploited even those who aspired to be professional athletes? I, for one, do not think so. And if the stable job and decent salary are all the individual sincerely wants, then the trade-off may be fair. Higher education in the United States has come to an unspoken quid pro quo with its athletes: they are basically (though modestly) paid for providing the rare occasions on which a diverse community can unite behind a common goal. The athletes know the rules and choose the game. This, too, is not a new story: it has been going on since the late nineteenth century (Sears and Gilley, 1986).

Varsity Athletes at Thirty-Two: Another Shadow Falls

Usually, however, people want more than basic economic benefits from life and reason that an investment of four or five years at a college or university should provide that something more. And in this respect, our judgments of the success of varsity athletes in the class of 1972 must be tempered.

For example, varsity athletes were the only group that claimed to work less with ideas than people or paper at age thirty-two. Given an economy whose future will run on ideas and information, this factor may put former varsity athletes at a disadvantage. Given their academic records, however, it is not surprising that they work less with ideas. Indeed, their job stability and early career earnings may mask future difficulties. As the data in End Table 3C demonstrate, varsity football and basketball players experienced a greater degree of deflation in their occupational expectations at age nineteen by the time they were thirty-two than had at least three comparison groups. A higher proportion of the athletes assumed lower SES-positions (clerical, crafts, operative, labor) than did the other students. While job stability and wages in those occupations may compare favorably to other occupations at age thirty-two, there is less mobility, and comparisons with other groups would probably be less favorable at age forty.

A degree of realism may have set in among varsity athletes in recent years. The AIR study found that football and basketball players in the late 1980s expected to have lower-SES jobs at age forty than other groups of students in the study sample. The NLS-72 data suggest that those lower expectations are in line with reality.

Promises Made But Not Kept

The story told here by the NLS-72 about one group of students is ultimately about the promises we make in higher education to all students, and even beyond that, about the integrity of the educational enterprise. It is also about the benchmarks by which we measure the fulfillment of those promises.

A great deal happens to individuals after they leave college (with or without degrees) that is beyond the control of the institution(s) they attended. But essential to the basic promise of higher education is the human capital ideology described in Chapter Two: higher education leads to higher payoffs—economic, social, cultural, spiritual—and the more, the more. The correlate of this promise is that the payoff does not happen by osmosis; it requires student effort in college-level academic work and student involvement in the life of a college community. This correlate also concerns the credentialing function of colleges and the relationship between academic work and degrees. There is not a college in the country that promises to award degrees without academic work. The basic promise and its correlate, whether implicit in popular conception or explicit in college catalogues, are matters of trust. When the promise and its correlate are publicly promulgated, they are matters of *public* trust.

It was for that reason, in part, that the original, and very narrow, version of what was called in Congress the Student Athlete Right-to-Know Act became the much broader Student Right-to-Know and Campus Security Act (P.L. 101-542) in 1990.[5] The primary sponsors of the original bill were two ex–professional basketball players, Senator Bill Bradley and former Representative Tom McMillan. After the bill was dropped in the Senate hopper, nobody wanted to hear anything about data demonstrating comparatively high long-term graduation rates for athletes. Indeed, during Congressional testimony after the act was passed, McMillan and I got in a testy argument over the question of whether the nation should care more *that* people graduate than how long it takes them to do so (Committee on Energy and Commerce, U.S. House of Representatives, 1992). He admitted, after a time, that he knew some basketball players who came back and finished college after they were thirty, but he would not otherwise budge from the position that varsity athletes are exploited.

Anecdotes, you see, play very well as propaganda. Even though we live in a statistical century, they play a lot better than numbers. Consider: 1.1 million graduates of the high school class of 1972 attended one or more of 1,200 four-year colleges by the time they were thirty. Some of them, both men and women, played varsity sports along the way. But the fact that there are varsity athletes at such places as Towson State, Prairie View A&M, the Air Force Academy, and Carleton, and that these athletes play hard at swimming or wrestling or lacrosse or tennis, is something that people who live by anecdotes do not want to admit. As far as public iconography is concerned, college athletes exist playing football or basketball at thirty or so Division I NCAA schools with scandals. The symbol comes to wag the dog of public policy.

Truly *national* legislation such as the Student Right-to-Know Act is *not* about thirty (or even all 291) NCAA Division I institutions out of 1,800 four-year colleges and universities in the United States. National legislation is *not* about the relatively small number of college students who play varsity football or basketball in the 291 NCAA Division I institutions. National higher education legislation is about everybody, and whatever form that legislation takes, it should remind colleges of their normative function in our society and their ethical responsibility to keep the promises they make to students.

As the Knight Foundation Commission report (1991) noted, colleges are not keeping promises to athletes in terms of providing the same educational opportunities and education as they do for other students. But both common sense and the repeated observations of journalists make two other features of collegiate athletic life and culture perfectly clear.

First, nobody who is on the road three or four days a week in season or in practice for the equivalent amount of time is really going to school unless the courses he or she is taking carry such titles as "Field Internship," a euphemism for not going to school. Second, it is equally clear that some varsity athletes in major sports, however much they may express an interest in education, have no real commitment to it and do not choose where to attend college on the basis of graduation rates (rather, on the reputation of a coach and a program). As Adler and Adler (1991) point out, this may not be the athletes' fault: it is a product of the way role expectations play out for people with athletic talent, and in this respect, former Representative McMillan's defense of the exploitation hypothesis is justified. From the time athletic talent is identified, no one expects these students to contribute anything else to the life of their high schools, their colleges, or their communities. Solemn words, let alone NCAA rules, on the importance of education in the life of college varsity athletes constitute one of the many charades in which our society engages for the sake of safeguarding its own entertainment. The athletes who succeed in the face of that charade are true survivors.

Lousy Propaganda

When the material in this chapter was first published, it was covered extensively on both the sports and op-ed pages in the winter of 1990–91 and caught the attention of black higher education interests. At the annual Forum on the Black Athlete at Howard University in 1991, and in testimony for Representative Cardiss Collins's House Subcommittee on Commerce, Consumer Protection, and Competitiveness (Committee on Energy and Commerce, 1992), I tried to stress the idea that if the first question we ask about African Americans in college is about athletes, we make a big mistake. For what we do with that question is to announce that the only way young black men, in particular, can "be somebody" in college, let alone afterward, is by putting a ball through a hoop, and we discourage the hundreds of thousands of young black men who cannot put a ball through a hoop any better than I can. And when colleges take scholarship funds from black students of academic promise who are not athletes and give those funds to what NCAA's rules call "partial qualifiers" (Sperber, 1990), they announce to young African Americans that learning doesn't count.

This is lousy propaganda. It results in despair and cynicism. The nation loses. At the Howard forum, a number of speakers noted that we must pay attention to black athletes because young black males need role models, and that's what they are going to see on television. The idea that young people are likely to invest in themselves according to what they see succeed in the televised version of U.S. society is an odd economic notion. As a cultural notion, though, it is not so odd: entertainment has created a reality in which "success" is measured by fame and fortune—big fame, big fortune. But how many of the class of 1972 became famous by thirtysomething? How many of them, or of any cohort, made fortunes? As actor Henry Winkler reflected in 1976 on the fame business that colors the dreams of too many adolescents, "It takes skill and dedication, but you also have to be dealt a very good hand, and then know how to play it" (p. 11).

Most people who study music, for example, come to realize that they are not going to make it to Carnegie Hall or Blues Alley or the Regal (and if they make the Regal, it is amateur night and the clown will take the microphone away after twelve bars). But they also realize that they have learned something from the serious study of music that they can take into other aspects of their careers. Among the music majors in the NLS-72, for instance, only 6 percent wound up as "entertainers" at age thirty-two. That's less than a thousand people, and less than that number were making a steady living from music.

Young adults learn. The godfather of black athletic consciousness, Harry Edwards, did an estimate a decade ago that bears updating with 1990s figures (Edwards, 1983). If there are 32 million African Americans, about 8,500 of them earn their living, pay their bills, and raise their kids while working for athletic organizations. And of the 8,500, perhaps 1,600 (or one five-hundredth of one percent of the total African-American population in the United States) are professional athletes. And of the 1,600, the majority play the equivalent of third base for the Durham Bulls for $25,000 per season. There is no big show for most mortals.

I remember all the men who got up at the Howard forum to talk about the potential of sports business careers for black college athletes. The speakers were earnest, dedicated, and, from all appearances, successful. They spoke about finance, marketing, public relations and advertising, and international arenas for manufacturing and sales of sporting goods products and sporting events. Yes, there is a big industry out there, and it exists in every country. But what I did not hear was the kind of curriculum college athletes of any race would have to pursue in order to participate and succeed in that industry. I did not hear about math and accounting, advanced writing skills, foreign languages, international studies, or sports medicine other than basic "movement science" courses. I did not hear about the curriculum we do not see on the transcripts of varsity athletes. The knowledge content of work is no less important here than it is in other industries. In fact, it is probably more important to athletes, who need greater flexibility in career paths than we observed of the athletes in the class of 1972.

We cannot disparage the ability to entertain—on the court, the field, the stage, the concert hall. The world has valued entertainment since the dawn of civilization, and every culture on every continent honors its most talented players. But every culture on every continent also knows that play and players are peripheral—not central—to its economic life and well-being. Play does not put food on the tables of the masses. You cannot export play with any measurable dent in an economy. Health, production, transport, and communication are all more important, and all of these require a high level of education. Nations do not establish schools and colleges to produce play and players.

It was a tough message to bring to a Forum on the Black Athlete and to a Congressional hearing, but the history of the class of 1972 not only teaches but emboldens. When work forces become globalized, when companies can hire the most talented and educated workers without regard to national boundaries, our country will be left in the dust if we cannot offer first-rate computer programmers, first-rate production control managers, first-rate teachers. And if our standard of living goes down in the future because we have been more concerned with providing a safety net for varsity football players than with supporting mere mortal students of academic dedication and promise, we know who will be hurt the most: the disadvantaged in our society, among whom African Americans are tragically overrepresented.

Notes

1. S.580 (1989), dubbed the Student Athlete Right-to-Know Act, was predicated on the assumption that prospective varsity athletes will select a college on the basis of their prospects for graduation. Those prospects, then, were to be indicated by the graduation rates of varsity athletes who had previously passed through the institutions being considered. The basic provisions of this proposed bill were incorporated as Section 104 of the Student Right-to-Know and Campus Security Act, a more comprehensive law that also calls for reporting of graduation rates for everyone at a college, of campus crime statistics, and of campus security policies.

2. First, the NCAA data define "graduation rate" as the percentage of students who enter a school over the course of two successive academic years (for example, 1983–84 and 1984–85) and who graduated within six years (the benchmark used to be five

years but has been expanded to accommodate changing patterns of college-going for all students). The calculation does not pay any attention to precise dates of entry or graduation. It is thus possible for the period of attendance to range up to seven full years. Second, the only athletes for whom this "graduation rate" is reported are "*recruited* student-athletes" [emphasis added], and it is not clear at all what percentage of students who wind up on varsity teams are recruited. Third, the graduation rates for "recruited student-athletes" are compared to the graduation rates for "all students"—which is not the right comparison (nor is it clear whether the "all students" category includes "recruited student-athletes" along with everyone else). Fourth, only when graduation rates are presented by sport is the denominator of the basic equation expanded to include transfer students, and even then, some transfer students are not included. It is thus not clear whether the basic graduation rate applies to athletes who attended one and only one college.

The virtues of the current NCAA data (National Collegiate Athletic Association, 1989), however, are that they differentiate by geographical region, institutional control, and institutional size. In this respect, they are a significant improvement on previous NCAA-sponsored studies (see, for example, Chelimsky, 1985).

3. The differences in the classification and numbers of students between the AIR transcript sample and the NLS-72 transcript sample, which makes up the universe for this chapter, are considerable. The NLS-72 sample of 8,100 is nearly four times the size of the AIR sample and includes a general student population of 6,500 and a group of 250 Hispanic students. The AIR sample has neither of these features, and 75 percent of its students are varsity athletes.

4. "Red-shirts" (freshmen who practice but do not play with a team) are still eligible for four years once they begin playing. It is thus possible for graduate students to be members of varsity teams, and indeed, there were a few such cases in both the NLS-72 group and the AIR study. "Red-shirting" is a risk-free nurturing strategy, a common practice whereby an athlete's skills

and strength are improved without his or her losing a year of actual playing time.

5. However sincerely motivated, the law focuses only on institutional graduation rates for first-time, full-time students. It makes it difficult to account for students who attend more than one institution, particularly if significant gaps of time exist between enrollments and if the institutions are located in different states. As noted in Chapter One, 32 percent of all NLS-PETS students attended more than one institution as undergraduates, and 44 percent of those for whom the bachelor's was the highest earned degree by age thirty attended more than one institution. Under the Student Right-to-Know Act, true institutional graduation rates will not be the same as national graduation rates.

End Table 3A. Percent of Total Credits Earned in Sample of Courses Taken by Varsity Athletes and Others, 1972–1984.

Courses	Student category					
	Varsity athletes: major sports	Varsity athletes: minor sports	Performing arts students	Intramural sports participants	Nonathletes	Everybody else
Physical education (activities)	3.5%	3.3%	1.1%	0.7%	—	2.0%
English composition	3.4	2.9	2.9	3.1	3.4%	3.6
Physical education (education)	2.9	1.1	0.1	0.3	—	0.6
U.S. history surveys	2.6	1.4	1.3	1.7	1.4	1.9
General biology	2.0	2.2	1.4	1.8	1.9	2.2
Introductory economics	1.7	1.9	0.5	2.6	1.9	1.6
General psychology	1.6	2.1	1.7	2.0	2.2	2.1
U.S. government	1.6	1.0	0.8	1.2	1.0	1.2
Introductory communications	1.4	1.2	0.9	0.9	0.8	1.1
Introductory sociology	1.4	1.2	0.9	1.3	1.5	1.5
Varsity athletics	1.4	1.4	—	—	—	—
General chemistry	1.4	2.3	0.6	2.4	2.2	1.9
Calculus	1.3	2.0	0.7	2.7	2.6	1.6
Introductory acccounting	1.2	1.4	0.3	1.6	1.3	1.1
World/Western civilization	1.1	1.0	1.1	1.1	1.2	1.4
Introductory physics	1.0	1.8	0.4	2.1	1.8	1.3
Spanish: elementary/intermediate	1.0	1.4	1.0	1.0	1.0	1.1
Introduction to literature	1.0	1.4	1.1	0.9	1.0	1.1
Health practices	0.9	0.4	0.3	0.1	—	0.5

Bible studies	0.9	0.7	1.0	0.4	0.4	0.6
Introductory geography	0.8	0.7	0.6	0.7	0.7	0.6
Advanced accounting	0.8	1.6	0.2	1.5	1.1	0.9
French: elementary/intermediate	0.7	0.2	1.1	0.7	1.0	0.7
Business law	0.7	0.9	0.2	1.0	0.7	0.7
College algebra	0.7	0.4	0.3	0.6	0.7	0.7
Art history	0.7	0.3	0.6	0.6	1.0	0.8
Kinesiology	0.7	0.6	<0.1	—	—	0.2
Anatomy and physiology	0.7	0.5	<0.1	0.2	0.4	0.4
Music performance	0.2	1.2	18.0	0.1	0.5	0.4
Organic chemistry	0.4	1.0	—	1.0	0.9	0.7
Statistics (math)	0.5	0.8	—	0.9	0.8	0.6
Introduction to management	0.6	0.7	—	1.0	0.7	0.6
Music theory	0.2	—	6.0	0.1	0.2	0.1
Drama: acting and so on	0.5	—	4.0	0.2	0.3	0.2
Music history: general	0.4	0.2	2.1	0.3	0.3	0.4
Musicianship	0.3	0.4	1.1	0.3	0.2	0.4
Stagecraft	0.3	0.3	1.0	0.1	0.2	0.1
German: elementary/intermediate	0.2	0.7	1.0	0.4	0.5	0.4
General geology	0.6	0.5	0.7	0.9	0.6	0.6
General zoology	0.6	0.4	0.2	0.6	0.4	0.5
Humanities: general	0.3	0.2	0.4	0.5	0.4	0.4
Electrical engineering	0.5	0.1	0.1	0.5	0.6	0.3
American literature	0.5	0.5	0.6	0.6	0.8	0.7
Total percent of credits:	45.2%	42.8%	56.3%	40.6%	37.6%	39.7%

End Table 3B. Bachelor's Degree Majors of Varsity Athletes and Others, 1972–1984.

Undergraduate major	Varsity athletes (major sports)	Varsity athletes (minor sports)	Performing arts students	Intramural sports participants	Nonathletes	Everybody else
Business	16.0%	21.6%	3.5%	26.9%	16.3%	15.4%
Education	29.3	15.6	26.6	3.0	5.7	21.8
Engineering/computer science	11.7	2.5	0.2	7.5	7.2	3.9
Physical sciences/math	3.9	—	2.9	4.6	4.8	4.1
Humanities	5.3	9.6	8.7	2.9	9.0	5.1
Arts	4.5	1.0	36.7	2.2	5.4	2.1
Social science	11.9	20.8	7.1	26.6	19.5	16.5
Biological sciences	3.7	13.1	1.4	7.3	9.0	5.6
Applied sciences/services[a]	6.9	5.8	3.1	8.4	11.6	11.8
Other applied fields[b]	5.4	8.4	5.6	6.6	8.8	10.3
Other	1.5	1.5	4.3	4.1	2.9	3.4

Note: The universe includes all students in the study sample who earned a bachelor's degree at any time between 1972 and 1984. $N = 5,127$. Weighted $N = 732,511$. Because of rounding, not all columns total 100%.
[a]Includes agriculture, natural resources, nursing, allied health, clinical health sciences, science technologies.
[b]Includes communications, home economics, library science, recreation, protective services, social work, public administration.

End Table 3C. What Did Varsity Athletes and Others Plan to Do At Age Thirty When They Were Nineteen? What Did They Actually Do When They Were Thirty-Two?

Occupation	Varsity athletes (major sports)		Performing arts students		Intramural sports participants		Nonathletes	
	Planned	Did	Planned	Did	Planned	Did	Planned	Did
Clerical worker	2.8%	12.1%	1.0%	14.0%	1.4%	7.3%	4.6%	15.3%
Craftsperson	4.7	12.4	1.1	2.1	3.6	8.7	2.6	5.5
Operative	—	1.8	—	3.4	—	2.5	0.3	3.0
Laborer	—	3.0	—	0.9	0.5	2.2	0.1	0.9
Manager/proprietor	15.4	14.2	5.7	13.3	14.3	21.6	8.8	6.2
Professional 1[a]	23.7	18.0	42.1	28.0	32.6	27.1	34.4	30.5
Professional 2[a]	27.3	8.1	19.1	8.2	29.1	12.6	24.6	9.2
"Buy/sell"[b]		11.8	0.2	5.1	1.0	6.8	1.4	6.6
Schoolteacher	14.6	11.2	25.9	18.2	6.4	2.9	9.5	5.1
Other	11.5	7.4	4.9	6.8	11.1	8.3	13.7	7.7

Note: The universe includes all students in the study sample who answered the question on expected "kind of work . . . when you are 30" in the 1973 follow-up survey, participated in the 1986 follow-up, and provided information on their occupation in 1985. $N = 5,312$.

[a]These are classifications I constructed to render different surveys comparable. In 1973, Professional 1 included accountants, artists, nurses, engineers, librarians, writers, social workers, actors, and athletes. Professional 2 included clergy, physicians, lawyers, scientists, and college professors. In the 1986 follow-up survey, a more elaborate occupational coding scheme was used and scientists wound up in the Professional 1 category and librarians in Professional 2.

[b]This is also an occupational category I constructed to aggregate occupations that primarily involve commercial transactions. The occupational categories of the 1973 survey do not match those of 1986 perfectly. For example, the 1973 category "Sales" covered (among other occupations) insurance agents. The 1986 category covers both sides of commercial transactions but does not include insurance agents. Instead, they are in a category with accountants and stockbrokers that is included here in Professional 1.

Chapter 4

The Way We Are:
The Community College
in Our Lives

Three decades ago, as the distinctive U.S. phenomenon then known as the "junior college" was on the verge of transformation as a type of organization, Burton Clark offered a challenging description of its role in our society (Clark, 1960a, 1960b). In his analysis, the junior college had a "cooling-out" function. That is, with my hyperbole added, it took whoever entered its doors and tracked them out of the mainstream of social mobility in the United States. It froze their ambitions. It chilled their minds. It iced them with remedial courses. It cut them off from the economic benefits of a society that paid well not only for a bachelor's degree but especially for a bachelor's degree from the right schools that provided the right connections. All this happened not by the design of junior college administrators and trustees, but as a by-product of both the higher education system and the advisement process in two-year schools. Clark later revisited and revised his assessment, acknowledging that he focused too much on the internal workings of community colleges and not enough on their effects on the lives of students (Clark, 1980). But his initial assessment was insightful and credible at the time it was made.

When the Higher Education Act was passed in 1965, there were 654 two-year colleges in the United States, 30 percent of the

124

total number of institutions of higher education. A quarter century later, there were 1,350 two-year colleges, constituting 40 percent of all institutions of higher education. Few were called "junior colleges" any more. In 1965, these institutions enrolled 20 percent of all students at all levels of higher education, including graduate and professional school, and 24 percent of all first-time college freshmen. In 1990, the figures were 38 percent and 50 percent, respectively (Snyder, 1992, pp. 170, 181). These are official approximate numbers. When a social institution grows that rapidly in a specific economy or market, its identity and role are likely to change. The climate may even become somewhat warmer.

Most of the growth in the community college sector of U.S. higher education took place in the first decade following passage of the Higher Education Act. The class of 1972 graduated from high school toward the end of this steep trajectory. Their use and experience of the community college over the following decade, I propose, can serve as a thermometer measuring the warming of the internal processes of the community college and the kind of institution it has become. And to the extent to which people from the NLS-72 sample who attended community colleges are representative of all high school graduating classes in the first half of the 1970s, their experience may be emblematic of the ways we Americans use other normative institutions such as those of religion and the arts. If so, the account laid forth in this analysis may say much about the way we are.

The Questions and the Method

This analysis asks a series of questions about a large group of individuals who chose to associate themselves with a particular type of educational institution and, through that choice, about the role of that institution in our culture. To be sure, this is a limited definition of institutional role. It does not account for the service roles these institutions play in local communities or the economic roles they play in regional labor markets. Despite appearances, this definition also precludes accounts of the economic efficiency of community colleges (Nunley and Breneman, 1988). The stories in this book, though, start with people and their choices, not abstractions.

Thus, too, this account is not framed in terms of the long-standing arguments, deriving from Clark's cooling-out thesis, over whether community colleges promote or hinder access to higher education, whether their principal role is to prepare students for transfer to four-year colleges, or whether they act as self-interested institutions more than responsive institutions (Folger, Astin, and Bayer, 1970; Karabel, 1972; Alba and Lavin, 1981; Cohen and Brawer, 1989; Grubb, 1988; Richardson, 1988; Brint and Karabel, 1989). These issues will inevitably arise, but only after we read the record.

The problem with the traditional arguments about the role of the community college is that they subordinate the experience of people to larger constructs of social class and status or economic power. These arguments assume that our lives are characterized by order and continuity and that whatever happens to us has a clear origin, hence an absolute cause. Details, differences, disorder, and discontinuities are not part of this structuralism and are often swept under the rug. The possibility that individuals and groups can use institutions in the course of making their own history is not admissible. The possibility that patterns and textures of human experience could tell us more than origins and causes is unthinkable to those for whom the superstructures of class and status are all powerful.

But what if an archaeologist of the twenty-fifth century stumbled on the ancient binary remains of the NLS-72? Watching individuals leave their traces on this archive over and over again, like a palimpsest, what could that archaeologist say about the community college as an institution? And what could that person say about people who attended community colleges and the patterns and textures of their relationship to the institution? I am trying to anticipate that archaeologist, so patterns and textures govern this account, not superstructures, despite the socioeconomic vocabulary of "earnings," "occupation," and "educational attainment" that are built into such government-sponsored surveys as the NLS-72.

The record the archaeologist would discover, of course, is hardly complete. One of the principal artifacts on which I rely—a set of college transcripts—contains limited information about what students do in an institution. The transcripts do not record extracurricular activities or nonintellectual aspects of maturation that we all hope result from participation in postsecondary education. In this case, transcripts also tell us little about the environment of community colleges (see London, 1978), the changing attitudes of community college students (deArmas and McDavis, 1981), the commitments community college students make to their institutions (Stage, 1988), or the student involvement that Alexander Astin (1984) defined as the amount and quality of effort students devote to learning—though all these factors influence student progress and attainment to various degrees.

In these contexts, however, transcripts provide a strong link between the circumstances of individuals and groups prior to postsecondary education and their circumstances, activities, and attitudes after postsecondary education—not cause, but link. The transcripts reflect, too, the links between individual choice behavior and both the constraints and possibilities of the institution.

Many other researchers have used the NLS-72 surveys to analyze the careers of community college students (Breneman and Nelson, 1981; Anderson, 1981; Velez, 1985; Pascarella and others, 1986; Tinto, 1987; Velez and Javalgi, 1987; Cohen, 1988; Nunley and Breneman, 1988; Grubb, 1991). But the differences between the survey and transcript data are so significant as to call all these analyses into question. For example, if the survey says that 825 out of the 22,652 members of the NLS-72 sample enrolled in community colleges immediately after graduating from high school in 1972 (Cohen, 1988) and the transcript file shows 2,429 enrolling in community colleges in September alone, the surveys cannot be trusted.

Who used the community college?

When did they attend (at what distance from high school graduation, for how long, and in relation to attendance at other types of postsecondary institutions)?

What did they study?

What credentials did they earn both from the community college and other institutions (and when)?

What happened to these people in the labor market?

These are the basic questions I ask of the data into which we are about to plunge.[1]

To make full sense of these questions, it is important to include in the analysis those who did not continue their education at all after high school. Unlike the other chapters in this book, then—let alone studies produced on both sides of the cooling-out debate—this study pays attention to what journalistic shorthand calls noncollege youth.

Temperature Readings

Let's proceed through the data, take the temperature readings, and then step back and ask what those readings say about the way we are.

The question of who attends community colleges in our society—like the question of who goes to church or to museums—is not simple. The question of who attends cannot be divorced from an understanding of *how* they attend, and I have rarely met a study that addressed this issue in any terms other than full-time/part-time or completed/dropped out. There are at least two other ways of describing community college attendance patterns. The first includes only those people who continued their education after high school and uses community colleges as the principal reference point. Let's use the term *community college attendance patterns* to describe this framework. The second encompasses all students who were seniors in high school in the spring of 1972 and uses credentials earned as its principal reference point. For purposes of convenience, let's call this second framework the *general postsecondary attendance patterns*.

Community College Attendance Patterns

The college attendance of students whose postsecondary transcripts indicated any earned credits fell into ten patterns that can be described with reference to the community college:

1. *Transfer, with two degrees (3.4 percent).* Students in this group earned both an associate's degree from a community

college and a bachelor's degree from another kind of institution (four-year college, theological school, four-year technical college, school of art or design, and so forth) and earned the associate's degree before the bachelor's.

2. *Transfer, with one degree: the bachelor's (3.3 percent).* Students in this group earned more than ten credits from a community college but no associate's degree and earned a bachelor's degree from a four-year college. They also attended the community college prior to receiving the bachelor's degree.

3. *Transfer, with one degree: the associate's (1.7 percent).* Students in this group earned an associate's degree from a community college and more than ten credits from a four-year college but did not complete the bachelor's degree.

4. *Terminal associate's degree (5.7 percent).* Students in this category earned an associate's degree from a community college. The few who also attended a four-year college (before, concurrently, or subsequently) earned ten or fewer credits from that institution, so, at best, they were incidental four-year college students.

5. *No degree, nonincidental two-year and four-year (2.7 percent).* These students attended both community colleges and four-year institutions and earned more than ten credits from each type but never earned any degrees—associate's or bachelor's. They were nonincidental attendees at both types of institutions. Slightly more than half of these students attended the community college before enrolling in a four-year institution and, technically, are also transfer students. The balance are known in the community college literature as *reverse transfers*—that is, they entered the four-year college first and subsequently enrolled in a two-year college.

6. *No degree, nonincidental, two-year only (15.6 percent).* These students earned more than ten credits from a community college but no associate's or bachelor's degree. If they also attended a four-year college, they earned ten or fewer credits from that institution—that is, they were nonincidental community college students and incidental four-year college students.

7. *No degree, incidental, two-year (7.6 percent).* Students in this

category earned ten or fewer credits from a community college and no degree. Only 4 percent of them attended other kinds of institutions, too, but they earned ten or fewer credits from those institutions as well.

8. *No two-year college, but four-year college (49.3 percent).* This large slice of the NLS-PETS consists of students who attended only four-year colleges. Within this group, there are six other patterns of attendance and degree attainment.[2]

9. *No two-year college, no four-year college (6.7 percent).* Almost all these students attended proprietary trade schools, area vocational-technical institutes (AVTIs), or specialized institutions such as hospital schools of nursing, radiological technology, and so forth.

10. *Other patterns (4.1 percent).* This is a residual category for cases that do not fit in the previous nine categories. Some students in this category, for example, earned associate's degrees from institutions other than community colleges and may also have earned bachelor's degrees. Some earned bachelor's degrees but took a course or two at a community college, either before or after the degree. Some earned an associate's degree after the bachelor's.

The reader will notice the implicit definition of transfer in the first three attendance patterns. It is a restricted definition with two components: an earned degree (associate's, bachelor's, or both) and an earned credit threshold (more than ten). I have previously used the "more than ten credit" threshold (Adelman, 1990a, 1990b) to describe those NLS-72 students who made a commitment to postsecondary education of at least one semester or its equivalent over a period of twelve years. The threshold was derived from analyses of credit production for the entire NLS-PETS and is applied to commitment at any one type of institution. Under this definition of transfer, it is insufficient merely to enroll: you have to make a go of it. A transfer is thus not a transfer unless the student made a sufficient (nonincidental) commitment to both types of institutions.

When this definition of transfer is loosened by not requiring an earned degree, some students in attendance pattern 5 (no degree, two-year and four-year, nonincidental) can be included, namely, those who entered the community college before they enrolled in a four-year college. A comparison of the effects of the restricted and loosened definitions is reflected in Table 4.1, which shows the total percentage of NLS-PETS students transferring over the twelve-year period between 1972 and 1984. While transfer is a major concern of community college mission statements, it is treated here as an ideologically neutral umbrella term for textures of attendance involving two different types of institutions. Depending on how one defines the universe of students, the term can cover up to roughly 30 percent of community college attendees. The transfer patterns are significant but hardly exhaustive.

I will refer to the ten community college attendance patterns frequently throughout this analysis and its tables. But they are somewhat difficult to follow—and not always enlightening—when we consider questions broader than community college attendance.

General Postsecondary Attendance Patterns

Particularly when comparing community college students both to four-year college students and to those who did not continue their education after high school, we need a second way of describing attendance patterns. The seven-category configuration that follows can be applied to everybody in the high school class of 1972:

1. *Transfer, bachelor's degree (3.7 percent).* These students attended both two- and four-year colleges, entering the two-year college first and ultimately earning a bachelor's degree. They may or may not have earned an associate's degree along the way.

Table 4.1. Transfer Rates Calculated Two Ways, 1972–1984.

Universe	Restricted transfer	Loosened transfer
All NLS-PETS (N = 12,599)	8.1%	9.5%
Community college attendees (N = 5,708)	18.9	22.2
Attendees earning more than ten credits from community colleges (N = 4,115)	25.3	29.5

2. *Terminal associate's degree (4.2 percent).* Students in this group earned an associate's degree from a community college but no higher degree. Some 22.7 percent of the people in this group also earned more than ten credits from four-year colleges.

3. *No degree, nonincidental (10.1 percent).* These students never earned any degree but attended two-year colleges, where they earned more than ten credits. Some 14.3 percent of this group also earned more than ten credits from four-year schools.

4. *No degree, proprietary/vocational and/or incidental two-year (7.8 percent).* These students either attended proprietary/vocational schools only *or* enrolled in two-year colleges but earned ten or fewer credits from those institutions. The rationale for putting these two groups together is that, compared with other groups, they both spent very little time in postsecondary institutions: 65 percent of the proprietary/vocational school students and 61 percent of the incidental community college attendees were enrolled for less than six months over a twelve-year period.

5. *Four-year/other, bachelor's degree (19.1 percent).* This pattern covers students who either attended only four-year colleges *or* whose postsecondary attendance patterns are not accounted for by the other patterns. Both groups earned bachelor's degrees.

6. *Four-year/other, no bachelor's degree (11.3 percent).* These students met the conditions of pattern 5 but did *not* earn bachelor's degrees. Some of them earned associate's degrees from four-year colleges or specialty schools.

7. *No postsecondary education (43.9 percent).* To the best of our knowledge, these students did not enroll in any kind of postsecondary institution between high school graduation in 1972 and the fall of 1984, when they were thirty or thirty-one years old.

Tables 4.2 and 4.3 display the demographics of the NLS-72 people who continued their education after high school and who fit the various attendance categories described under both the community college attendance patterns and the general postsecondary attendance patterns. The data confront a number of common perceptions about community colleges and the populations they serve. What do

Table 4.2. Ten Basic Community College Attendance Patterns, by
Race/Ethnicity and Gender, 1972–1984.

Attendance pattern	Race/ethnicity			Gender		
	White	Black	Hispanic	Male	Female	All
Transfer, associate's degree and bachelor's degree	3.6%	1.1%	2.9%	3.8%	2.9%	3.4%
Transfer, bachelor's degree	3.4	2.7	2.1	3.7	2.8	3.3
Transfer, associate's degree	1.8	0.9	1.3	1.7	1.7	1.7
Terminal associate's degree	5.9	3.7	6.7	5.1	6.4	5.7
No degree, non-incidental, two-year and four-year	2.5	3.0	5.0	2.8	2.5	2.7
No degree, non-incidental, two-year only	14.9	18.3	26.9	15.8	15.5	15.6
No degree, incidental, two-year only	7.1	10.8	12.7	7.3	7.9	7.6
No two-year, but four-year	50.2	47.8	30.8	50.7	47.9	49.3
No two-year, no four-year	6.5	8.5	8.0	5.6	7.8	6.7
Other patterns	4.2	3.1	3.6	3.6	4.8	4.1

Note: The universe includes all NLS-PETS students whose records show any earned credits. N = 12,332. Due to rounding, columns may not total 100.0%.

these data tell us? First, despite the greater ethnic diversity of the community college student population compared to the four-year college population, blacks from the class of 1972 were far less likely to use the community college in their postsecondary education than Hispanics and no more likely than whites. This is hardly a new observation (see Alexander, Holupka, and Pallas, 1987; Cohen, 1988). Yet somehow the popular mythology persists that a majority of black students attend community colleges. That simply was not true for the NLS-72 cohort. Nor does it appear to be true for more recent cohorts (Alsalam and Rogers, 1991). The reason seems obvious. Some 53 percent of the black college students in the NLS-PETS graduated from high schools in the seventeen-state Southern

Table 4.3. Seven Basic Postsecondary Attendance Patterns, by Demographic Background, 1972-1984.

Demographic background	Attendance patterns						
	Transfer, bachelor's degree	Terminal associate's degree	No degree, noninci-dental two- or four-year	No degree, proprietary, vocational, and/or incidental two-year	Four-year only, bachelor's degree	Four-year only, no bachelor's degree	No post-secondary education
Socioeconomic status							
Lowest quartile	1.8%	3.1%	8.4%	8.4%	7.4%	8.2%	62.6%
Middle quartiles	3.6	4.6	10.8	8.5	15.0	11.2	46.4
Highest quartile	6.1	4.5	10.5	5.7	39.5	15.4	18.2
Race/ethnicity							
White/Asian	4.0	4.4	9.9	7.6	20.6	11.2	42.3
Black	1.8	2.2	10.0	9.1	11.1	13.8	52.1
Hispanic/ Native American	2.3	3.5	13.8	9.1	6.7	8.9	55.8
Gender							
Men	4.3	3.9	10.7	7.7	20.1	11.8	41.4
Women	3.1	4.4	9.5	7.8	18.0	10.9	46.3
Language background							
Non-English-speaking	4.0	3.6	11.2	7.9	18.1	12.8	42.5
English-speaking	3.7	4.2	10.0	7.8	19.1	11.2	44.0
All	3.7	4.2	10.1	7.8	19.1	11.3	43.9

Note: The universe consists of all NLS-72 participants. $N = 22,652$. Due to rounding, not all rows total 100.0%.

region (versus 27 percent of all students in the sample), and most of the historically black colleges and universities (HBCUs)—almost all of which are four-year schools—are in that seventeen-state region. It has been demonstrated previously that blacks residing in the South prefer to attend HBCUs (Astin, 1982).

Second, students from second-language backgrounds exhibited attendance and degree attainment patterns similar to those for students from English-speaking households. Our prejudice is to associate second-language background with (1) poverty and (2) Hispanic populations. Given the propensity of Hispanic students to attend community colleges, we thus expect students from second-language backgrounds to exhibit different patterns of college attendance and attainment. Our prejudice is just that—flat wrong. Only about a third of the Hispanic students came from non-English-speaking households. And although students from the lowest SES quartile were overrepresented among college attendees from second-language backgrounds, 75 percent of these people were white or Asian, and these groups do not attend community colleges to the same extent as do Hispanics.

Third, women who attended community colleges were more likely than men to earn terminal associate's degrees and less likely than men to use the community college as a way station on the road to the bachelor's degree. As demonstrated in Chapter Two, women in the NLS-72 generation were less likely than men to continue their education after high school, but among those who did continue, women were more likely than men to earn credentials.

Fourth, community colleges served a higher proportion of NLS-72 students from low and (particularly) medium socioeconomic backgrounds than did four-year colleges but a lower proportion than did proprietary and trade schools (see Table 4.4). In fact, in terms of SES, it was the medium-range student in the class of 1972 who was most likely to attended a community college. However, there is no question that the critical community college attendance categories encompassing students who earned no degree and terminal associate's degree students house a higher proportion of people from low-SES backgrounds than do other attendance patterns (see End Table 4A).

The basic demography (race/ethnicity, gender, and SES), then, both challenges and confirms popular mythology. This demography may turn out to be slightly different for the next major group in the U.S. Department of Education's longitudinal studies program, the high school class of 1982, but in ways that only reinforce the basic trends noted above. National surveys of total enrollments (Snyder, 1990, 1992) show that, by 1986, a majority of minority students attended community colleges, but this came about principally from further increases in the percentage of community college students who were Hispanic, a dramatic increase in the percentage of community college students who were Asian Americans (a group that was too small to disaggregate in the class of 1972), and a corresponding drop in the proportions of both whites and blacks. Such cross-sectional enrollment surveys, however, tell us nothing about attendance patterns. We have no idea what kinds of enrollments these may turn out to be. "Enrollment" is not some unchanging abstraction: people make enrollments, and they do so over time.

At what ages did the members of the class of 1972 typically attend community college? The answer must be inferred from first and last dates of attendance (where known), assuming an age of eighteen in 1972. It turns out that well over half the community college attendees in the NLS-72 had come and gone before they were twenty-two, but 26 percent (and a slightly higher percentage of women) were enrolled at some time between the ages of twenty-five and thirty. It may be that community colleges serve significant numbers of "older" students, but if so, a large proportion appear to be enrolled in noncredit or continuing education programs rather than degree programs. The NLS-72 archive provides survey data on school attendance and status through age thirty-two (as opposed to age thirty for the transcripts). Some 16.5 percent of the entire sample indicated enrollment in some kind of school between the ages of thirty and thirty-two (1984–1986). Of this group, 30 percent attended community colleges. Of this latter group, in turn, 39 percent classified themselves as special students and 31 percent indicated no degree objectives. Those are large pieces of a small group.

Time of Attendance

The last of these demographic observations leads us to consider the points in their careers at which the members of the class of 1972 used the community college. There are a number of ways to approach the time factor. The first is somewhat limited in coverage but strong as a benchmark: the distribution of associate's degrees by year of receipt. Approximately three-quarters of the NLS-PETS people who earned associate's degrees by 1984 did so within 4.5 years of graduation from high school—that is, by the end of 1976. Thus, those who used the community college for purposes of acquiring academic credentials did so at comparatively early points in their lives.

A second way to consider the time spent by students in community colleges is to look at what happens between the dates of first and last enrollment. Incidental attendees (those who earned ten or fewer credits) get it over with quickly: 61 percent were in and out of the community college in less than six months. (It is not surprising that, at age twenty-six, they were the least likely of all students to say that they were tired of school.) At the other extreme, approximately one-third of the nonincidental community college attendees (including associate's degree recipients) were enrolled in community colleges for a period of forty months or more. That does not mean that they enrolled every semester or that they enrolled full-time. It simply means that these students came back to the institution time and time again. We might call this phenomenon "continual use."

A third way to think about the time factor is in terms of the date of entry to postsecondary education. As Knepper (1989) has demonstrated, delayed entry does not affect the time it takes to earn a bachelor's degree for those who earn it. But delayed entry does lessen the likelihood that the degree will be earned at all. The NLS-72 transcript data indicate that, even over a twelve-year period, there is a direct correlation between when people enter community colleges and their ultimate educational attainment. In this respect, it bears noting that only among incidental community college students do we find a significant percentage (39 percent) who delayed entry to postsecondary education by more than 2.5 years. For the class of 1972, the later in life one entered a community college, the more incidental one's use of the institution.

In addition, students who were on active military duty at any time between 1972 and 1976 (6.5 percent of the transcript sample) not only attended community colleges in higher proportions than the entire transcript sample (55 percent versus 42 percent), but also, as one would expect, tended to delay entry to community colleges for two years or more after high school graduation; hence they were less likely to earn degrees.[3] Among the military personnel, patterns of attendance by race/ethnicity were the same as for the general population: blacks were less likely than the PETS group as a whole to use the community college, Hispanics more likely.

Time of entry is also affected by a student's plans to transfer. Two-thirds of all those who attended community college by the time they were thirty or thirty-one years old had entered postsecondary education (in any kind of institution) directly from high school, and 80 percent entered within eighteen months of high school graduation. But that percentage varied with attendance pattern and in direct relationship to the level of degree(s) earned: 75 percent of the transfer students who eventually earned bachelor's degrees entered community college directly from high school, and 90 percent entered within eighteen months of graduation. This phenomenon suggests that students on the transfer tracks had a fairly good idea when they were seniors in high school that they would transfer, hence did not unduly delay postsecondary entry.

Role of Aspirations and Plans

Entry to postsecondary education in terms of both time and place involves many choices. Among the conditions for and constraints on those choices are the student's own aspirations and plans for further education. Previous analyses invoking the aspirations of NLS-72 students who attended community colleges (for example, Levin and Clowes, 1980; Velez, 1985; Velez and Javalgi, 1987; Nunley and Breneman, 1988) were concerned principally with predicting the attainment of the bachelor's degree and were based wholly on survey data. But with reference to the transcript data, the distinction between aspirations and plans is complex and revealing. This distinction is presented in End Table 4B.

In the initial questionnaire administered to them as high school seniors, the NLS-72 participants were asked two questions: "What is the highest level of education you would like to attain?" and "What is the highest level of education you plan to attain?" The differences in their responses to those questions are directly related to entering postsecondary education directly following high school graduation.

The data in End Table 4B illuminate the differences between aspirations and plans for students grouped by demographic and ability characteristics. As one would expect, there is a continuous downshifting from aspirations to plans, but the extent and distribution of the shifts are irregular. For example, 54 percent of all NLS-72 students *aspired* to the bachelor's degree. This figure drops to 43 percent when the terms of the question are *plans*. Where did the difference go? What did that 11 percent group *plan* to do if their bachelor's degree option was removed?

Roughly a quarter of the students in that 11 percent group shifted their plans to community colleges, but nearly half dropped their plans for postsecondary education altogether. As the data in End Table 4B demonstrate, this pattern differs somewhat by race/ ethnicity and SES. For example, Hispanics in the NLS-72 had consistently lower aspirations than either blacks or whites (43 percent of Hispanics, 52 percent of blacks, and 55 percent of whites aspired to the bachelor's degree). When the question shifts to plans, Hispanics lowered their targets by a more significant amount (14 percent) than either blacks (10 percent) or whites (11 percent). Likewise, with the shift from aspirations to plans, the community college gains among whites and Hispanics, but not as much among blacks. This phenomenon is consistent with the demography of community college attendance noted earlier.

The data on aspirations and plans in relation to SAT/ACT scores demonstrate a greater degree of downshifting among students in the lower bands, indicating that the low-scoring students are not oblivious to their own general learned abilities. To the extent to which students scoring above 975 refocused from aspirations to plans, the trade-off was largely between graduate school and the bachelor's degree alone.

What should be obvious from this analysis so far is that the community college did not loom large in either the aspirations or plans of the NLS-72 high school seniors. Only 12.3 percent of the entire cohort planned to attend a community college, and only 8.5 percent of the entire cohort (and 14.2 percent of those who actually attended postsecondary institutions) planned to earn the associate's degree (the principal credential awarded by community colleges) as their highest credential. Another 8.2 percent (and 15.4 percent of those who actually attended) planned postsecondary vocational or technical education. While it is true that some proprietary and vocational schools award the associate's degree, the NLS-72 high school seniors knew the difference between a trade school and a community college.

Not only was the benchmark credential of the associate's degree but dimly visible in the plans of the NLS-72 cohort; it was also a weak force. Only 26 percent of the people who initially planned to earn an associate's degree actually got it, even in twelve years, while 55 percent of those who planned to get the bachelor's degree actually received it. Not only that, but 30 percent of those who initially planned an associate's degree never attended a community college at all, and another 15 percent were incidental attendees.

Community colleges award certificates in addition to associate's degrees, but only 4 percent of the NLS-72 community college attendees received such certificates. The recipients tended to be white women who did not earn any other credential or degree, and the most common fields for certificates were secretarial (14 percent) and allied health/nursing (24 percent).

What is at issue in this discussion is the general credentialing function of community colleges in the educational careers of high school graduates of the early 1970s. To what extent were associate's degrees or certificates awarded by community colleges primary goals of students? To what extent were they consolation prizes? Were the credentials relevant at all to the education of this generation? The transcript data strongly suggest that people attended community colleges principally for purposes that had little to do with earning credentials and that the credentialing role of the community college is, in fact, a minor aspect of its mission.

Do the ways in which students use community colleges in this respect speak more accurately about the way we are than the popular perception of a credential-hungry society? Does our economic life demand credentials—or something else—from education? These are questions worth pondering as we learn more from the NLS-72 archive.

Background and Ability of Community College Students

To appreciate what the community college does for its students, it is helpful to consider what those students bring to the community college in terms of previous education. In addition to providing baseline information against which to set community college course-taking patterns, general educational attainment, and basic labor-market outcomes, these academic background variables can further refine our understanding of community college attendance patterns.

The data on high school class rank (Table 4.4), and SAT/ ACT scores (Table 4.5) present a complex portrait of community college attendees. It is obvious, first, that those who never continued their education after high school had the weakest backgrounds, no matter what measure one uses. Community colleges may be open-door institutions, but a significant proportion of high school graduates aren't prepared to walk through that door—and aren't interested in walking through.[4] However, the gaps between the high school performance of the weakest group of postsecondary students (those who attended proprietary/vocational schools and incidental community college attendees) and the NLS-72 seniors who did not enter postsecondary education through age thirty are not great, either. In their high school course taking, for example, 56 percent of those who never went to any kind of college took less than three semesters of math, compared to 51 percent of those who either attended proprietary/vocational schools or were incidental community college attendees. Substituting science for math in the same comparison yields figures of 62 percent and 56 percent, respectively.

Table 4.4. Community College Attendance Pattern, by High School
Class Rank, 1972–1984.

	Class rank in quintiles				
Attendance pattern	Highest	2nd	3rd	4th	Lowest
Transfer, associate's degree and bachelor's degree	36.6%	23.5%	20.1%	15.3%	4.3%
Transfer, bachelor's degree	30.6	27.6	23.9	14.0	4.0
Transfer, associate's degree	23.4	28.7	22.2	15.8	9.7
Terminal associate's degree	20.1	25.0	26.7	18.8	9.3
No degree, nonincidental, two-year and four-year	23.1	25.8	23.4	19.2	8.6
No degree, nonincidental, two-year only	13.9	19.3	25.3	23.7	17.9
No degree, incidental, two-year only	11.2	18.9	21.8	26.9	21.3
No two-year, but four-year	40.7	26.2	17.6	11.3	4.3
No two-year, no four-year, proprietary/vocational only	16.2	19.6	23.3	25.1	15.7
Other patterns	40.1	28.4	17.6	10.0	3.9
No postsecondary attendance	9.0	16.8	22.5	26.0	25.6

Note: The universe includes all NLS-72 students for whom high school class rank could be computed. $N = 19,641$. The N for those in the NLS-PETS who met this condition and earned any postsecondary credits is 11,017. Because of rounding, not all rows total 100%.

The weakest group of postsecondary students, then, was marginal, indeed.

The few highly talented students in the NLS-72 simply did not attend community colleges, regardless of socioeconomic background. These data will no doubt surprise many who have contended that high-ability students from low-SES backgrounds are shunted into community colleges and do not earn bachelor's degrees (Folger, Astin, and Bayer, 1970; Karabel, 1972; Brint and Karabel, 1989; Grubb, 1989, 1991; Educational Testing Service, 1991). Part of the problem lies in the definition of "high ability" or "high talent" (Karabel and Astin, 1975) or "high resource" (Alexander, Holupka,

**Table 4.5. 1972 SAT/ACT Scores by Highest Degree Earned to 1984
and by General Postsecondary Attendance Pattern.**

Highest degree and attendance pattern	SAT/ACT scores		
	Mean	Standard deviation	N
All PETS	951	204	7,642
Highest degree			
No degree	884	190	2,851
Associate's degree	869	163	565
Bachelor's degree	995	194	2,933
Bachelor's and less than ten graduate credits but no graduate degree	1012	198	356
Master's	1047	198	569
Doctorate/first professional	1167	181	228
All NLS-72	934	207	9,197
Attendance pattern:			
Transfer, bachelor's degree	919	188	561
Terminal associate's degree	877	159	465
No degree, nonincidental, two-year and four-year or two-year only	844	170	936
No degree, proprietary/ vocational and/or incidental two-year	839	172	464
Four-year/other, bachelor's degree	1029	196	3,487
Four-year/other, no bachelor's degree	916	195	1,713
No postsecondary education	836	197	1,457

Note: The universe for the highest degree earned includes all NLS-PETS students who took either the SAT or ACT *and* earned any post-secondary credits, 1972–1984. N = 7,642. The universe for the attendance patterns includes all NLS-72 students who took either the SAT or ACT. N = 9,197). ACT scores were converted to the SAT scale.

and Pallas, 1987). Surprisingly, most of these analyses use a single aggregate measure of ability or talent, and few of them tell us where the "cut score" for high ability or talent lies. That's not fair.

The definition of "high-academic resource students" used here involves three measurements, each of a different kind. First, we take the top quartile of performers on a special ability test (a mini-SAT) given to most NLS-72 participants as high school seniors.

Second, we use high school class rank and again take the top quartile. Third, we use high school records and draw in anyone who took more than five semesters of math, *or* more than five semesters of science, *or* more than five semesters of foreign languages (that's a fairly flexible formula). A "high–academic resource student" must be in *all three* measurement groups (high mini-SAT, high class rank, and high coursework in one of the three areas). Only 5 percent of the entire NLS-72 sample, and 8 percent of those who continued their education after high school, met all three criteria.

Table 4.6 lays out who these high–academic resource students were and what happened to them. The group is small, so the standard errors of measurement are sometimes large and the comparisons are not always statistically significant. Nonetheless, the vast majority—nearly 80 percent of them—never set foot in a community college. Only 7.5 percent of the entire group of high–academic resource students came from the lowest SES quartile—versus 53.8 percent from the highest SES quartile—and the principal sorting criterion was not the ability test, but the curricular thresholds. No matter how generous the formula, the results demonstrate that low-SES students are far less likely then others to take one of the three major elective pieces of a college preparatory curriculum in high school.

What distinguishes the low-SES and high-SES groups here is whether they continued their education after high school at all, not where they went to school or what degrees they earned. Some 13 percent of the high–academic resource/low-SES students—versus about 6 percent of the high–academic resource/high-SES students—did not enter any kind of postsecondary institution by the time they were thirty years old. That turns out to be a statistically significant difference. Some 72 percent of the high–academic resource/low-SES students earned at least a bachelor's degree; 80 percent of the high–academic resource/high-SES students did so. That turns out *not* to be a statistically significant difference. In other words, there was no difference in the bachelor's degree achievement rate of low-SES and high-SES students of similarly strong academic preparation and ability!

For the entire NLS-72 sample, those who eventually earned degrees of *any* kind brought a stronger background to postsecond-

Table 4.6. The Fate of High-Ability Students: Socioeconomic
Status, Attendance Patterns, and Degree Attainment, 1972-1984.

Attendance pattern and degree attainment	Socioeconomic status in 1972			
	Lowest quartile	Middle quartiles	Highest quartile	All
Attendance pattern of all high–academic resource students[a]				
Transfer, bachelor's degree	5.1% (1.1)	6.5% (.51)	3.2% (.15)	4.6% (.23)
Terminal associate's degree	4.3 (.22)	3.8 (.39)	2.1 (.30)	2.9 (.21)
No degree, nonincidental, two-year and four-year, or two-year only	3.6 (2.5)	4.7 (.47)	2.6 (.21)	3.5 (.24)
Proprietary/vocational and/or incidental two-year	2.2 (1.3)	3.2 (.45)	0.7 (.19)	2.2 (.21)
Four-year/other, bachelor's degree	57.9 (2.7)	54.8 (1.2)	72.7 (.72)	64.3 (.55)
Four-year/other, no bachelor's degree	14.2 (1.4)	16.1 (.79)	13.0 (.50)	14.3 (.42)
No postsecondary education	12.8 (1.8)	11.0 (.82)	5.7 (.34)	8.3 (.41)
Highest degree earned by high–academic resource students in NLS-PETS[b]				
None	18.5% (2.9)	23.8% (.89)	16.4% (.60)	19.3% (.48)
Certificate/license	2.6 (.13)	3.5 (.13)	0.8 (.02)	2.0 (.05)
Associate's	7.3 (1.4)	5.7 (.81)	2.3 (.31)	3.9 (.34)
Bachelor's	49.7 (2.7)	49.1 (1.0)	52.9 (.87)	51.2 (.54)
Graduate	22.0 (1.9)	17.9 (.84)	27.6 (.65)	23.6 (.44)

Note: Standard errors in parentheses. Due to rounding, not all columns total 100%.

[a] N = 1,117.
[b] N = 1,020.

ary education than those who never earned degrees, and that is no surprise. A higher percentage of transfer students who eventually earned bachelor's degrees took the requisite college preparatory curricula in math and science than did students who attended only four-year colleges and never earned a bachelor's degree. Those who earned terminal associate's degrees brought higher SAT/ACT scores, class ranks, and science and foreign language backgrounds to the community college than students who earned more than ten credits but failed to earn an associate's degree.

Failure to earn a degree, however, was due neither to poor

academic performance in the community college, nor, as Karabel (1972) darkly hinted, to a plot by community colleges to flunk out unpromising "transfer track" students: no one who earned thirty or more credits from a community college but no degree had less than a C average. Since the no-degree attendance patterns, taken together, cover the largest group of community college attendees, since the time frame for degree completion was twelve years (a substantial period), and since common sense would indicate that lack of financial aid is not a major cause of withdrawal from low-cost, open-door commuter institutions, we ought to advance some other hypotheses as to why these students did not finish a degree program.

This inquiry will take us directly into the curricular experience of community college students. I propose that there are two distinct curricular patterns of those who attend community colleges but earn no degree. The first pattern involves about 75 percent of the students who receive no degree. It is a pattern of coursework with no distinct focus. Grubb (1991) calls this phenomenon "milling around." While for some, "milling around" constitutes a de facto completion of high school, for others there is no such goal. And when students have no goals, it is easier for them to disengage.

The second curricular pattern involves a sufficiently distinct course of study (usually occupational in nature) for students to prepare for a specific niche in the labor market. The formal credential is not a concern; the subject matter is. Goals apply here, but they can be stated in terms of "sufficient knowledge"—that is, what the student thinks is enough. If this hypothesis holds, it will reinforce my previous contention that the credentialing function of the community college is not one of its principal missions, and that the way we are has more to do with learning than with pieces of paper.

Indeed, the NLS-72 students who attended community college demonstrate that learning without the currency of credentials drives us more than we think. While that learning may not pay off as much as the credential (as we will see), it appears to drive us nonetheless. When I read through the NLS-PETS transcripts, I often found myself imagining stories that would explain the stark entries of courses and dates. The following hypothetical pattern is probably archetypal: the student who enrolls in community college right after high school to take three courses in computer hardware and programming so she can work in Uncle Al's computer shop. Five or six years later, Uncle Al plans to retire and wants her to take over the business, so she goes back and takes accounting, business law, and marketing. The business expands, she starts working with Mexican producers, and she returns again to the community college for a year or so of Spanish. This is not milling around, even though she never earns a degree.

Course Taking: The Community College as Provider of Knowledge

The tendency to turn to the community college for knowledge of immediate use in the workplace, and without regard to credentials, is illuminated by Table 4.7. This table answers the following question: How much more likely were NLS-72 students to take a particular course within an attendance pattern largely limited to community colleges versus an attendance pattern involving both community colleges and four-year colleges? To illustrate the reading of Table 4.7: a student who attended community colleges in either an incidental, no-degree, or terminal associate's degree pattern is roughly four times more likely to have taken technical mathematics than a student who transferred to a four-year college.

The list of courses with high ratios in Table 4.7 is dominated by subjects of workplace utility (technical drafting, data processing, office machines), remedial courses in math and English (which are prerequisites to everything else), and courses in the standard curricula of nursing (anatomy and physiology, health sciences), or the police academy (law enforcement). In the latter connection, we should remember that the period during which the NLS-72 cohort went to college was one in which institutions of higher education received federal "capitation grants" for nursing students, and the Law Enforcement Assistance Act provided plentiful funding for postsecondary police training. Those occupational training support systems are no longer as generous.

Disequilibrium in the Provision of Knowledge

Some 22 percent of all course enrollments for the 12,332 NLS-PETS students who earned any credits over a period of twelve years were

Table 4.7. Course-Taking Differentials by Community College
Attendance Pattern, 1972–1984.

Course	Ratio
Stenography	6.75
Secretarial (general)	6.60
Office machines	4.68
Technical mathematics	4.19
Business math: arithmetic-based	4.17
Nursing (general)	2.93
Remedial reading	2.86
Law enforcement (general police training)	2.78
Arithmetic	2.76
Technical drafting (general)	2.65
Remedial English (general, writing)	2.58
Data processing	2.50
Office management/supervision	2.35
Business administration (general)	2.27
Business English	2.23
Interpersonal skills	2.14
Precollegiate algebra	2.07
Anatomy and physiology	1.92
Freshman orientation	1.91
Introduction to accounting	1.75
Drawing	1.67
Self-awareness, human potential	1.66
Social sciences (general)	1.65
Health services and sciences (general)	1.64
Human nutrition (home economics)	1.63

Note: As noted in the text, the table answers the following question: How much more likely were NLS-PETS students to take a particular course in an attendance pattern largely limited to community colleges versus an attendance pattern involving both community colleges and four-year colleges? The answer is expressed in a ratio reflecting the fact that there are 2.86 times as many students in the first pattern as in the second. Only courses taken by 100 or more NLS-PETS students are included. The list covers the twenty-five courses with the highest ratios.

in community colleges (versus 29 percent for doctoral degree–granting institutions, 36 percent for comprehensive colleges, 6 percent for liberal arts colleges, 3 percent for trade schools, and 4 percent for specialized institutions). I assume this distribution of enrollments across institutional types to be an empirical equilibrium. It is a reasonable assumption, I think, because we have never had a long-term, national data base on postsecondary course taking until the

NLS-PETS. There are 1,037 course categories in the data base, none of which will show the perfect distribution—or equilibrium—of the whole. It is inevitable that enrollments in some course categories, such as advanced courses in less commonly taught foreign languages like Arabic or modern Greek, will be found almost entirely in one category of institution. You can wager—successfully—that trade schools will capture the majority of enrollments in automobile body repair, that specialized institutions will corner the market in optometry, and that comprehensive colleges will hold the edge in a variety of specialized teacher education courses. The trail to these cases is that of commonsense empiricism.

But the distribution of enrollments within most course categories in which all institutions are represented is not so obvious, particularly when the number of enrollments is substantial (exclusive of physical education activities and English composition, 86 course categories in the NLS-PETS recorded more than one thousand enrollments each). In these courses, the measurement of disequilibrium uses the mean distribution as its benchmark. For example, the courses in which the community college share of enrollments was substantially greater than 22 percent tell us precisely where the community college was a disproportionate provider of knowledge to this generation of students. This measurement is important from a labor-market perspective. If we assume that the knowledge content of work is determined by the learning people bring to the workplace, the measurement enables us to identify the dysfunctions in work-force preparedness that can be traced to prior education and to target our educational improvement efforts more precisely. We can also better match exiting college and community college students to the labor market by referring to what they studied. If we need X, we will know better which type of institution is the principal provider; if we need a better X, we will know which provider to target for improvement efforts.

In Table 4.8, I explore an approach to this issue through the concept of enrollment differentials. I took some illustrative fields of study and selected, from within those fields, heavily enrolled courses typically offered by *both* two-year and four-year colleges but in which the community college share of enrollments in the course was at least 25 percent higher than the average community college

Table 4.8. Sample Fields in Which Community Colleges Were and
Were Not Disproportionate Providers of Knowledge.

Community college dominance		Contrasting case	
Course	Percent of all enrollments that were in community colleges	Course	Percent of all enrollments that were in community colleges
Bookkeeping	77.0	Court reporting	17.8
Commercial art	61.8	Graphic/printing communications	16.7
Data processing	56.2	Introductory computer science	17.2
Business administration (general)	49.1	Production management	9.6
Retailing	43.8	Marketing research	4.1
Engineering physics	42.3	Engineering mechanics	8.9
Introductory accounting	37.8	Tax accounting	13.3
Anatomy and physiology	37.7	Embryology/developmental biology	4.4
Landscaping	34.7	Horticulture	19.0
U.S. history surveys	34.5	European history from 1789	7.3
Photography	34.4	Film arts (general)	17.4
Technical writing	32.5	Creative writing	16.6
Real estate	31.3	Insurance	13.2
Child development/care	30.6	Family relations	18.8
Business law	30.1	Corporate finance	5.9

Note: Only courses with a minimum of 100 enrollments in the NLS-PETS are
included.

share for all enrollments. For each of twenty such examples, a con-
trasting case is offered: another course, in the same general field, for
which the community college is a less significant provider. For
example, if one were looking for a technical writer, one would more
likely turn to the universe of community college students than one
would if the job involved creative writing. Likewise for real estate
agents as opposed to insurance agents, child-care specialists as opposed to family relations counselors, and so forth.

Not all courses, to be sure, are so occupationally specific.
Some, however, are clearly tied to occupational curricula—for example, the engineering physics course to the engineering technol-

ogies programs offered in community colleges versus the engineering mechanics course frequently taken by engineering majors in four-year colleges. But within traditional arts and sciences courses, the community college is a principal player only at the introductory and general level. There is nothing wrong with this: for most of us, the knowledge received through formal education in all areas except our specialization is general and introductory. It's part of the way we are.

Labor-Market Outcomes: The Emphases of Work

What happened in the labor market to those students from the high school class of 1972 who attended community colleges? Given the rich data from the 1986 follow-up survey, there are many ways to approach that question and many labor-market variables on which we could draw, such as earnings, unemployment rates, and industry. At this point, however, I want to focus on an unusual connection between curricular experience and work.

The most interesting group in terms of the way the community college functions in our society are the terminal associate's degree holders. Even though credentialing may not be one of the principal roles of the community college and the associate's degree a weak force in the aspirations and plans of students, that degree, nonetheless, is the basic credential for the U.S. community college. Furthermore, we can be sure that people who earned an associate's degree from a community college experienced as full a range of community college curricula as the benchmark requirement of sixty-credits allows. In other words, this group had maximum exposure to community college curricula without being "contaminated" by curricular experience at another type of institution.

The 1986 survey asked NLS-72 respondents the degree to which they worked with ideas, people, paper, and things in their present or most recent job. Most of the responses fit commonsense empiricism. Majors in "protective services" need to work with the law (ideas) as well as people, for example. Those in business support services work far more with people than with ideas. A general match thus appears to exist between curriculum and work role.

In terms of aggregate rankings, respondents worked mostly

with people, followed by paper, ideas, and things, with the spread between people and ideas being 21.4 percent. But what happens if we focus the same questions only on those in the 1986 survey who said that they used their postsecondary education a great deal in their work? Within this group, the proportion who said they worked "a great deal" with ideas is 20 percent higher than that for the entire universe of associate's degree holders.

What this variation implies is that a community college curriculum dominated by ideas is far more occupationally relevant, has far more actual workplace utility, than the curriculum experienced by the majority of those who study in community colleges. In fact, the proportion of associate's degree recipients for whom education was very relevant to work *and* who worked a great deal with ideas is higher than that for bachelor's degree recipients who never attended a community college (70 percent versus 63 percent).

College, Church, Museum: Pragmatic Patterns of Use

We have been swimming through a great deal of data, though perhaps not enough. So far, what this account says about the role of the community college in the lives of a generation confirms previous analyses or imputations from national data bases such as the Current Population Surveys of the Bureau of the Census or the old Higher Education General Information Surveys of the former Office of Education. But the transcript data both augment and depart from previous analyses in ways that should encourage us to reconfigure the language we use to describe the mission of the community college, and in at least two ways.

Occasional Institutions

First, the community college seems to function in a variety of what I would call "occasional" roles. It serves individuals for ad hoc purposes. While there are regular churchgoers and museum habitués, the attendance patterns at those institutions are more likely to resemble attendance patterns at community colleges. An institution capable of an occasional role must be flexible, tractable, and accessible. That does not mean that the institution is friendly, efficient, or effective. In the case of community colleges, it does not necessarily mean that the institution provides quality instruction or guidance or that it keeps its promises to students. It simply means that the institution easily accommodates individuals' decisions to engage in intentional learning within a formal organization. Governed by the culture of credentialism and its timetable, four-year colleges are less accommodating.

The students whose records we see in this archive are adults, and their choices to use a particular institution for a particular purpose at a particular time in their lives are intentional, even if that purpose is "milling around." What the community college does is to canonize and formalize the many decisions we make as adults to engage in learning for either limited, highly focused purposes or for general purposes. The community college is thus neither a terminal institution (Karabel, 1972) nor a transfer institution. Beyond the "value" of learning (the normative aspect of its existence), its purpose and role are not so easily fixed (Zwerling, 1986). The same can be said of such institutions as churches and museums that speak a language of values (the normative) but that serve us in practical, utilitarian ways.

A qualitatively different version of this theme is that the community college functions as an intermediary institution. It is a way station or stepping-stone or gap filler for individuals in transit from one status to another—for example, adolescent student to labor-market adult, working adolescent to adult student, and so forth. The universes of the labor market and baccalaureate education, however complex, place far more definite boundaries, rules, and expectations around the lives of individuals than does the community college. While it is hard to infer student motivation from transcript data, it appears that students in all attendance patterns (including "incidental") knew that the community college would do something for them, would help them get from here to there. Even if they were constrained by geography, family circumstances, poor academic preparation, or low SES, they seemed to make of the community college what they wanted to make of it. They used the institution for a time and then moved on.

Yet another version of this theme casts the community college in the role of testing ground. That is, the institution provides individuals with the chance to test their tolerance for and interest in postsecondary education. More than half of those whose educational aspirations as high school seniors were limited to the high school diploma eventually attended community colleges, but a third of those people decided that postsecondary education was not for them and became incidental students.

These variations on the "occasional-use" theme reinforce Grubb's (1988) observation that labor-market conditions and anticipated rate of return are not the most powerful factors in motivating students to enroll in community colleges. The concept of occasional use also calls into question the notion of attrition or dropping out of community colleges.

From their days as seniors in high school through age thirty, NLS-72 students had a vague image of the community college. This lack of a clear image most likely resulted from the community college's minimal role in credentialing and from the amorphous nature of the associate's degree. For some students, particularly those whose associate degree "majors" can be described only as general studies or liberal arts and sciences, the associate's degree was just an advanced high school diploma, serving as a warranty, so to speak, of general learning. There is nothing wrong with that. In fact, given the well-documented decline of the quality of learning in U.S. secondary schools, such programs are necessary, and the community college is one of their principal providers.

The Proximate Institution

The second way we ought to reconfigure our ideas of the community college's mission involves the populations served by the community college. Thanks to its occasional role, minimal cost, and ease of access, the community college can reach a broader spectrum of Americans than other types of postsecondary institutions. From the 1970s onward, this reach has been augmented by the sheer number and geographical distribution of community colleges.

While recent (1990) data show that the proportion of minority students who are U.S. citizens is higher in community colleges (23.3 percent) than among undergraduates in four-year institutions (17.7 percent), for reasons of proximity to one's primary residence, the community college inevitably will serve the majority more than minorities (Snyder, 1992, p. 203). Outside the South and parts of the Southwest, for example, rural America is heavily white, and the principal postsecondary education presence in rural areas is either a community college or a state college. In 1970, the highest ratios of community college enrollment to total undergraduate enrollment were in California, Florida, Washington, Arizona, Mississippi, and Illinois (Medsker and Tillery, 1971), and most of the community colleges in those states were located outside central cities. As Grubb (1988) pointed out with respect to more recent trends, the highest enrollment rate in community colleges in 1990 was in the state of Washington (22.9 percent of the eligible population)—a state in which over 90 percent of the population is white and in which there are twenty community colleges *outside* the metropolitan areas of Seattle and Spokane.

The NLS-72 data can demonstrate an old rule of elasticity of supply: when the only provider is X, X provides both to (in this case) the dominant ethnic population and to students of all ages. So if the community college, considered nationally, serves an older population as well as a younger one, it is the result of elementary economics. For the same reasons, the community college winds up serving a higher proportion of white, Hispanic, and Native American students than black students (who will make extra efforts to attend a historically black college). We also know that rural populations are more likely to be classified in the low- and medium-SES ranges than metropolitan populations. So for those who select postsecondary institutions on the basis of proximity, as many students do (Astin, Green, and Korn, 1987), community colleges will inevitably be the principal providers. Hence they will wind up serving a higher proportion of low- and moderate-SES students than will other types of educational institutions.

In this respect, the community college is not like our religious or cultural institutions. Its "liturgy" (curriculum) is nonsectarian; thus there is no need for more than one community college in a town (or county, or city district). From another perspective, while there are variations in that liturgy, they do not depend on visiting exhibits or performers: they are resident. Indeed, the curricular liturgy of the community college is fairly consistent. We can infer what the community college offers from what students take. What the NLS-72 transcripts suggest is that it offers a combination of specialized curricula in three major occupational fields (allied health sciences/ services, business and business support services, and engineering technologies), and a general studies curriculum dominated by the social sciences. Students interested principally in the sciences or the humanities either do not attend community colleges at all or transfer out of them quickly. Common sense would conclude that there is no way these institutions could offer enough depth in the basic sciences or the humanities to reach the knowledge "trapgates" of these fields. The transcripts confirm such a hypothesis.

Defenders and Critics: Reflections on an Old Debate

Having read a good deal of the NLS-72 record together, and having reflected briefly on the nature of the community college as both an occasional and proximate institution, let us go back to the debate between the functionalist defenders of the community college and what Dougherty (1987) calls the "class reproduction school" of community college critics. Simply put, the functionalists say that the community college is the best vehicle for equal opportunity in postsecondary education; their opponents counter that the community college does nothing but perpetuate existing inequalities in our society. Both schools may now select what data they wish from the transcripts, but I think the entire NLS-72 data base ultimately helps us transcend this unproductive debate.

Hocus-Pocus

Three points need to be raised about the research used in the work of both community college defenders and detractors. First, I am baffled by the construction of variables and estimates in most of the work bearing on this debate. Without the transcripts, for example, it is nearly impossible to determine precisely who is on a transfer-academic track in a community college and who is not. What the student writes on a survey form or tells the registrar is not necessarily what he or she actually does.[5] Without transcripts, it is nearly impossible to determine who changed from one track to another, and when.

Second, the literature on both sides evidences considerable confusion and outright naïveté concerning students' aspirations and plans with respect to the "baccalaureate degree." To use a metaphor from the nightly newscasts, the bachelor's degree is the Dow Jones Industrial Average of U.S. higher education. Everybody has heard of it. When people ask "What did the market do today?" they mean the Dow Jones, and that is the answer they get, even though it is not the real answer to their question. In the semantic shorthand of our culture, we equate Dow Jones and stock market. We do the same with "bachelor's degree" and "college degree" (and for that matter, with "bachelor's degree" and "higher education attainment"). The bachelor's degree is a culturally visible symbol with significant power in public policy, and in the language and rhetoric of the critics' discourse, "a degree" is shorthand for the bachelor's.

Conversely, the associate's degree is like the NASDAQ average of over-the-counter stocks: virtually nobody knows what it is or how to interpret it. No Congressional committee asks the U.S. Department of Education for trends in the production of associate's degrees. They do not ask for the NASDAQ average; they want the Dow Jones. And what is true for Congressional committees is even more true for eighteen-year-old high school seniors, let alone their parents.

In fact, the Higher Education Act itself defines a "first generation college student" as a student whose parents have not received bachelor's degrees or, if the student lives with or receives support from one parent, whose parent has not earned a bachelor's degree. National policy, enacted by Congress, thus says that if your parents earned an associate's degree from a community college, transferred to a four-year college but did not complete a bachelor's degree, and came back to a community college and earned another associate's degree, they have never been to college! If you then follow in the footsteps of your parents, national policy will insult your efforts as well. When national policy so demeans the associate's degree, it becomes invisible.

So, when we look at students' aspirations for degrees, we are looking at attachments to culturally visible and powerful symbols, even if this symbolism is vaguely understood. Those of us who have administered the Cooperative Institutional Research Program (CIRP) survey to entering college freshmen know that a significant proportion do not understand what various degrees either mean or require. Furthermore, the intensity of students' aspirations ranges widely, from casual dreams to deep commitments (Alexander and Cook, 1979). When we look at students' plans, on the other hand, we get closer to an individual's sense of his or her realistic options, and these seem to rely less on the most visible and powerful symbol of postsecondary educational attainment in our society. Inheriting their constructs from Clark's (1960a) initial "cooling-out" thesis, none of the defenders or critics bothers with this distinction.

Third, when it deals with the economic outcomes of education, the critical literature is often bizarre. The most notable and persistent of the critics (Karabel, 1972, 1986; Pincus, 1980; Pincus and Archer, 1989; Brint and Karabel, 1989) perform hocus-pocus analyses of secondary sources. They take other scholars' studies, state system studies, institutional studies, and census data—all with different samples, different populations, different years (both boom and bust), and different definitions of variables—utter an incantation, and pretend that the studies are comparable and make sense. When the picture they draw does not make sense, they challenge their opponents, the defenders of community colleges, to prove that it does make sense. The defenders, in turn, are even more helpless because, as the critics correctly point out, the defenders are trapped by the propaganda machines of organizations that seek increased federal, state, and local funding for community colleges. When there is money on the table, no one will admit to either flaws or ambiguity in institutional performance. And no one wants to look directly at unobtrusively obtained national data.

Measuring Mobility

The debate between community college critics and defenders also relies heavily on the effects of community colleges, principally in terms of students' social mobility. But the debate takes place in a comparative vacuum of meaningful effects. With the exception of Monk-Turner's work (1983) based on the National Longitudinal

Surveys of Labor Market Experience (see Resource D), none of the studies analyzed by Dougherty (1987) have truly long-term employment, occupation, or earnings data, let alone family formation, home ownership, or any other information that would allow comparison of the SES of children to that of their parents. With the 1986 follow-up survey, the NLS-72 archive provides such data, at least through age thirty-two or thirty-three. So let us examine some variables that could be used in constructing SES ratings for the NLS-72 students at thirtysomething.

Occupational Plans Versus Occupational Realities

There are a number of ways to consider the occupational distribution of community college attendees in their early thirties. The NLS-72 data show that the routes we take from schooling to work are not always linear. In fact, contrary to the claims of both defenders (for example, Roueche and Baker, 1987) and critics (for instance, Pincus, 1980, 1986), attending a four-year college does not straighten the line between education and work any more than does attending a community college.

To demonstrate what I mean, let us look at the occupational distribution of students in the NLS-72 cohort at age thirty-two with reference to their plans at age nineteen. This particular portrait, set forth in Table 4.9, brings us flush against the contention of community college critics from Clark (1960a) to Brint and Karabel (1989) that community colleges, far more than four-year colleges, frustrate the ambitions of their students. Early critics such as Clark never had the large-scale, long-term data of the NLS-72, particularly with its transcripts as a sorting mechanism. The later critics seemed to ignore such data or used them without the transcripts. In neither earlier nor later analyses were the kind of data arrayed in Table 4.9 considered.

What can we see in these data? First, as a rule, the hopes of youth exceed the realities of age. That's the way we are. No matter where people go to school or what degree they earn (if any), they wind up at age thirty-two doing something other than what they had planned at nineteen, and what they wind up doing tends to have less "status." Does this surprise anyone? As teenagers, we dream of becoming Nobel Prize winners or the equivalent; by thirty-

Table 4.9. Occupational Aspirations at Age Nineteen Versus Actual Occupations at Age Thirty-Two (1973 and 1986).

Occupation	Community college students				Four-year college students				Non-college students	
	Received no degree (62.6%)		Earned degree (37.4%)		Received no degree (26.8%)		Earned degree (73.2%)			
	Plan	Did	Plan	Did	Plan	Did	Plan	Did	Plan	Did
Clerical worker	12.9%	20.0%	9.4%	16.6%	5.8%	17.5%	1.5%	8.0%	14.9%	16.8%
Craftsperson	6.9	12.6	6.9	7.9	4.3	7.6	1.0	3.2	12.9	14.2
Operative	2.0	6.5	0.4	3.6	0.8	4.4	0.1	0.8	6.0	12.5
Laborer	1.4	2.5	0.7	1.8	0.2	2.9	0.3	0.6	4.9	7.1
Homemaker[a]	10.6	12.1	9.1	13.8	8.2	13.8	3.6	9.5	23.1	18.9
(Students		0.7		0.5		0.9		0.8		0.7
Managers/proprietor	10.2	13.2	10.7	10.4	11.6	15.5	9.1	16.9	7.7	9.8
"Buy/sell"[b]	2.3	5.8	1.9	5.2	1.6	6.7	0.8	5.0	2.0	3.9
Professional 1[c]	21.9	12.2	26.6	21.5	29.8	17.3	35.0	23.3	10.6	6.0
Professional 2[c]	8.5	0.7	7.4	3.7	15.6	1.7	25.4	12.5	2.1	0.5
Schoolteacher	6.7	1.1	7.6	1.3	11.7	1.9	17.6	12.1	1.4	0.7
Technical	7.9	3.0	9.9	3.7	5.8	3.1	2.4	4.0	5.4	0.9
Other	8.6	10.3	9.4	10.5	4.7	7.6	3.3	4.1	8.9	8.7

Note: The universe for community college students includes all NLS-PETS students who earned more than ten credits from community colleges, did not earn a bachelor's degree, answered the question, "What kind of work will you be doing when you are 30 years old?" in the 1973 follow-up survey, and participated in the 1986 follow-up survey. $N = 1,592$. The universe for four-year college students includes those students who never attended a community college, earned more than ten credits from a four-year college, answered the 1973 question, and participated in the 1986 survey. $N = 3,846$. The universe for noncollege students includes all NLS-72 students who are not in the NLS-PETS, answered the same occupational aspirations question in 1973, and participated in the 1986 survey. $N = 3,935$. Due to rounding, not all columns total 100%.

[a]Includes full-time homemakers, full-time homemakers who were also students in 1986, and others.

[b]The equivalent 1973 category was "Sales" and included insurance agents. For the 1986 data, insurance agents are grouped with stockbrokers in Professional 1.

[c]In 1973, Professional 1 included accountants, artists, nurses, engineers, librarians, writers, social workers, actors, and athletes. Professional 2 included clergy, physicians, lawyers, scientists, and college professors. In the 1986 configuration, scientists were classified as Professional 1 and librarians as Professional 2.

something we have forgotten Nobel's first name or how he blasted his way into history. We are happy to have steady jobs, to be respected in our work, and to pay the rent, take a vacation, and raise our children well. Is this, as the community college critics imply, a national tragedy?

In fact, when asked if they were satisfied with the progress of their careers at age twenty-six (unfortunately, this question was not asked at age thirty-two), 82.5 percent of the NLS-72 cohort said yes. Among those who continued their education after high school and who "made a go of it," the only feature of personal history that distinguished the most satisfied from the least satisfied was an earned degree of *any* kind, including a terminal associate's degree from a community college.

Second, people who do not earn degrees are more likely to wind up in "lower-status" occupations than they originally planned than are those who did earn degrees. Does this surprise anyone? What may surprise some is that this phenomenon *applies equally* to community college students, four-year-college students, and students who never went to college. For example, a higher percentage of NLS-72 community college students who earned terminal associate's degrees wound up in professional occupations (26.5 percent) than four-year-college students who did not earn a bachelor's degree (20.9 percent).

Third, the stage on which most occupational life plays out is commerce, an area that is vast and unknown to the typical nineteen-year-old. The cohorts represented by the NLS-72 were more likely to take places on this stage by the time they were in their early thirties—as managers, administrators, salespersons, and buyers—than they ever imagined, and less likely to invest the considerable time, effort, and energy in the additional schooling to become professional workers.

The literature that criticizes community colleges for thwarting the aspirations of their students often views the occupational category of "manager" as a privileged class. Given the number of people who call themselves managers in any survey, the occupation hardly represents an elite. As an occupational category, "manager" covers vast territories, from CEOs to the proprietor of the local dry cleaning establishment to the administrator of the county recreation department's evening programs. It sounds somewhat strained to call the people who inhabit this territory a privileged class. In general, as the data in Table 4.9 show, a higher percentage of people in the class of 1972 wound up in this category than originally aspired to it, whether they went to a two-year college, a four-year college, or no college (the only exception involves terminal associate's degree holders).

The category of professional is also misused in the critical literature. If at age nineteen I say I want to be an actor, am I aspiring to a profession in the same sense as a would-be lawyer or college professor? Given the wages at dinner theaters and regional theaters, is acting an elite occupation? The literature critical of community colleges for thwarting the aspirations of students to become professionals never tells us what it means by "professional" nor justifies the putative professions as elite classes. Are schoolteachers members of a profession? I would say so. Are they a privileged or elite class? Tell that to the 2.5 million schoolteachers in this country! As Table 4.9 demonstrates through three explicit categories of professionals (including teachers as a separate category), even if one defines professions as occupations requiring a *post*baccalaureate degree, community college attendance had no greater negative impact on occupational aspirations than four-year college attendance. In fact, in both types of institutions, the more significant determinant of whether a student's aspirations to become a professional were fulfilled was whether or not the student earned a degree. This phenomenon should also surprise no one: to a great extent, what makes professions professional is that they require certified, specialized knowledge, and the certification is reflected in the degree.

Earnings and Home Ownership: No Clear Picture

As components of SES, earnings and home ownership constitute important variables. There was no clear-cut pattern in the 1985 earnings data that would lead us to conclude that community college attendance is a drag on earnings, at least through age thirty-two or thirty-three. The highest-paid group attended community colleges, and the lowest paid group did not. For women who attend community colleges, earning a degree had a greater impact on earnings at thirtysomething than was the case for men. Overall, terminal associate's degree holders earned less than those who were nonincidental attendees but never earned any degree. This is not a new observation (see, for example, Pincus, 1980; Nunley and Breneman, 1988). This earnings differential happens, in part, because the nongraduate has more years of job experience. It also happens because a higher percentage of the nongraduates wind up in business-related occupations that, at age thirty-two, pay better than occupations in health care fields dominated by terminal associate's degree holders. And it happens even more because women are a majority of the terminal associate's degree holders, and women are unquestionably the victims of inequities in the labor market that have nothing to do with educational attainment (see Chapter Two).

One also cannot conclude that community college attendance either hinders or advances the chances of home ownership. If we focus on students who were in the lowest SES quartile at age eighteen, hence least likely to come from families that owned their homes, the highest rates of home ownership by thirtysomething were among those who attended community colleges and whose highest degree was the associate's (64.5 percent). The lowest rates of home ownership among this group were for people who attended community colleges, transferred to four-year colleges, and subsequently earned a bachelor's degree (45.2 percent). Even NLS-72 students from the lowest SES quartile who never went to college had a higher rate of home ownership (59.1 percent) than that, and not much lower than all students in the cohort (63.3 percent).

General Economic Mobility

But in terms of economic mobility, the critics have a point that is strongly borne out by the NLS-72 data. Table 4.10 looks at 1985 earnings, unemployment, and job experience by both postsecondary attendance pattern and SES in 1972. The data in the table indicate the patterns of postsecondary attendance most likely to minimize unemployment, maximize earnings, and move an individual from a lower to a higher SES category.

As Jencks and others (1979) observed, SES has a lasting impact on economic status. It takes a lot of work to override one's

Table 4.10. General Postsecondary Attendance Patterns and Economic Mobility, 1972–1985.

Socioeconomic status in 1972	Mean 1985 earnings	Mean years job experience, 10/76–2/86	Mean years unemployment, 10/76–2/86
Lowest quartile			
No postsecondary education	$15,440 ($195)	7.4 (.04)	0.84 (.03)
No degree/proprietary/vocational and/or incidental two-year	14,138 (247)	7.2 (.06)	0.98 (.05)
No degree, nonincidental, two-year and four-year or	14,913 (713)	7.9 (.14)	0.68 (.10)
two-year only	16,904 (829)	7.5 (.13)	0.80 (.10)
Terminal associate's degree	15,609 (1,122)	7.9 (.19)	0.65 (.13)
Transfer, bachelor's degree	17,845 (1,181)	7.1 (.24)	0.78 (.14)
Four-year only/other	19,952 (494)	7.8 (.07)	0.44 (.04)
Middle quartiles			
No postsecondary education	18,191 (283)	7.6 (.03)	0.68 (.02)
No degree, proprietary/vocational and/or incidental two-year	16,225 (294)	7.3 (.05)	0.87 (.04)
No degree, nonincidental, two-year and four-year or	16,902 (617)	8.0 (.10)	0.68 (.07)
two-year only	20,145 (590)	8.1 (.07)	0.59 (.05)
Terminal associate's degree	18,072 (728)	7.8 (.13)	0.71 (.08)
Transfer, bachelor's degree	21,003 (852)	7.9 (.09)	0.43 (.05)
Four-year only/other	21,104 (340)	7.8 (.04)	0.44 (.02)
Highest quartile			
No postsecondary education	22,051 (285)	7.7 (.03)	0.54 (.02)
No degree/proprietary/vocational and/or incidental two-year	18,998 (747)	7.8 (.11)	0.66 (.07)
No degree, nonincidental, two-year and four-year or	20,686 (1,379)	7.5 (.17)	0.52 (.11)
two-year only	21,059 (868)	8.0 (.11)	0.56 (.07)
Terminal associate's degree	18,785 (1,214)	7.7 (.17)	0.63 (.11)
Transfer, bachelor's degree	24,433 (935)	7.6 (.10)	0.42 (.07)
Four-year only/other	23,258 (401)	7.7 (.04)	0.51 (.02)

Note: The universe includes all NLS-72 students for whom SES in the base-year or 1973 follow-up surveys could be determined, who also participated in the 1986 follow-up survey, and who indicated both an occupation and earnings for 1985. $N = 9,265$. Standard errors are in parentheses.

initial circumstances, whether one starts out in the lowest or the highest brackets. In the NLS-72 cohort, those students who did not continue their education after high school are in exactly the same economic positions fourteen years later. But even with no postsecondary education, as initial SES rises, wages rise, mean years of job experience rise, and unemployment drops. While the standard Pearson correlations based on initial SES are not consistent for all patterns of postsecondary attendance in terms of years of job experience (.06) and unemployment (-.08), the correlation between initial SES and later earnings is consistent and mildly positive (.18).

Nonetheless, the only postsecondary attendance pattern that consistently overcomes initial economic circumstance is that of four-year college attendance, whether or not a bachelor's degree was earned. Low-SES students who attended four-year colleges only, for example, had, at age thirty-two, higher earnings, more years of job experience, and less unemployment than all students who were initially in the middle SES quartiles. Students from the middle SES quartiles who attended four-year colleges only had higher earnings, more years of job experience, and less unemployment than most (though not all) groups who were initially in the highest SES quartile.

This is an unfortunate aspect of the way we are. It is unfortunate in terms of the community college role because so many community college students in the NLS-72 sample seemed to use the institution for genuine purposes of learning, without regard to social outcomes. Their behavior seems to say that intentional learning is ingrained in us, whether that learning is incidental or continuous, whether it is general education or occupationally oriented, whether it is undertaken for enlightenment or the acquisition of specific skills. It is an article of our faith that learning ought to be rewarded, and that is one of the major normative messages of educational institutions.

There may be a brighter side to this matter, however, that the account given in these pages does not reach. The most significant work to date on these data (Conaty, Alsalam, James, and To, 1989) uses the transcripts to demonstrate that, with few exceptions, *what one studies* has a greater impact on earnings at age thirty-two than where one attended college. To be sure, the subjects of this 1989 study were the NLS-72 bachelor's degree recipients, but if the relationships between course taking and earnings (after controlling for college major, SAT scores, SES, and so on) are significant, we ought to examine those relationships among community college attendees before we conclude that the normative message of community colleges remains unfulfilled.

Is Life So Cold? Concluding Thoughts on the Way We Are

Roughly one-quarter of the NLS-72 generation attended community colleges in different ways, and this large fraction represents a more typical segment of the population of high school graduates than any other group in the class of 1972, including those who never continued their education. They clustered around the averages of just about everything and gave every indication that they were among those who would come to occupy what Leonard Kriegel (1972, p. 50) called "life's middle ground." For that reason, perhaps, the mainstream media did not notice this story in 1992 when it was first published. Unlike the other populations represented in this book, this one was too undefined, too general, too—well—typical. Like a suburban strip, the population has no imagibility.

But the population of people who take courses at community colleges must be as rich with stories as any subgroup of this generation. Their behaviors are highly variable. Their world is ad hoc. Other than what I have called the incidental students, they illustrate five proclivities of the American character, and of the character of their generation, that should leave us fairly upbeat.

First, we use major normative institutions for utilitarian purposes and that our relationships with those institutions are more occasional than otherwise. We recognize the value of education, but once schooling ceases to be compulsory, we tend to go to school only on our own terms.

Second, we are more interested in learning, in acquiring new skills, and in completing our basic general education than in acquiring advanced credentials, even if those credentials yield greater economic rewards. At the same time, to the extent to which we acquired strong academic backgrounds in the course of our compulsory schooling, we are more likely to complete postcompulsory schooling of any kind, academic or occupational.

Third, while we are genuinely committed to lifelong learning, we nonetheless concentrate formal learning at early stages of our lives. We are children of time and its conventions. We do not easily break from cultural traditions of when to do what. Perhaps we know that the more distant we are from formal education, the more difficult it is to recapture both knowledge and the discipline of schooling.

Fourth, our general knowledge is just that—general and introductory. The time we typically allow for schooling does not permit depth. So we grasp for something particular, something we perceive as related to current or future work. The result is that we may know more about what we do for a living but are less adaptable to changes in the conditions or opportunities of work. If there is a just complaint about what community colleges allow individuals to do, it lies here (Pincus, 1986). That is, community colleges are too willing to take in bodies for fragmented pieces of education. Their culture does not insist on completion of the associate's degree with a general education component as much as it should. If the associate's degree is to be duly honored as a known currency, this culture must change.

Finally, our youthful aspirations and hopes exceed what actually happens to us, no matter what we do in between. Does that mean we should abandon them? If life itself is a cooling-out process, does that mean we should spend most of it moping about what could have been or blaming the system for what did not happen to us? Do we adopt the position that only the 1 percent of the population at "the command posts of the American occupational structure" (Karabel and Astin, 1975, p. 389), only the movie stars, succeed in our society and that everyone else fails? That everyone else is a victim? That everyone else doesn't count?

Aspirations and hopes usually translate into effort, and effort makes something better than what it otherwise would have been— for individuals, groups, and the nation. We all gripe about our lives and fortunes, but if that is all we do, we freeze ourselves out of efforts to improve the lives and fortunes of our children. The class of 1972 did not throw in the towel. We cannot afford to, either.

Notes

1. When one uses transcripts to take a census of community college students, the key to accuracy is, in large part, how one defines a "community college," a "public technical institute," and a "private vocational school." In the cleaned version of the NLS-72 transcripts, the status of each college or school was reviewed in light of the 1975 Carnegie typology and the nature of credentials actually awarded to NLS-72 students. I invented a new "Carnegie" code for what Grubb (1991) calls "public technical institutes" (generally, area vocational-technical institutes) and distinguished them from public technical colleges (which I retained in the community college universe). And, with few exceptions (each handled case by case), no institution that awarded degrees higher than the associate's to students in the NLS-PETS was classified as a community college.

2. For those NLS-72 students who attended four-year colleges *only,* the weighted percentages in each of the six attendance patterns, 1972–1984, were:

    > Earned bachelor's degree, attended only one four-year college: 36.9 percent
    >
    > Earned bachelor's degree, attended more than one college: 24.2 percent
    >
    > No bachelor's degree, and earned more than fifty-nine credits: 12.4 percent;
    >
    > No bachelor's degree, and earned eleven to fifty-nine credits: 18.3 percent
    >
    > Incidental four-year, earning fewer than eleven credits: 5.2 percent
    >
    > Other four-year pattern: 2.9 percent

3. There are a number of ways to identify NLS-72 participants who served in the military. One way is to use a special file created in 1986 that merged the records of the NLS-72 with the comprehensive data of the Defense Manpower Data Center (DMDC), at least through 1979. Since DMDC keeps records on everyone who ever applied to, enlisted, or otherwise served in

the U.S. military, this procedure sounds like an unassailable unobtrusive way of identifying these people. The merged NLS-DMDC data file, however, does not include women, and up to 1976, it confuses applicants and actual "accessions" (Kolstad, 1987). A second method, employed here, is to use the NLS-72 surveys, which asked questions about military service through 1979.

4. At various points in the NLS-72 surveys, respondents who did not continue their education were asked why they did not continue. Of those who never entered any kind of postsecondary institution by age thirty, 24.7 percent had said when they were nineteen that they didn't continue at that time because they "didn't like or need school."

5. An example underscores the misinterpretation that can occur in classifying students if one does not use transcripts. Here are the courses taken by an associate's degree recipient who listed "engineering technology" as the "major":

Microbiology	Marriage and Family
Games and Exercises	Psychology of Adjustment
Calculus I	Principles of Economics
History of the United	Social Problems
States	Architectural Drawing
Texas Government	Organic Chemistry
Engineering Drawing	Introductory Sociology
Principles of	Business Communications
Accounting	Basic Technical Drawing
Introduction to Business	
Calculus II	

This is not the record of someone with an occupational major, especially in engineering technology, though there is no question that the individual has probably developed an employable skill through three courses in technical drawing.

**End Table 4A. Socioeconomic Status and Community College
Attendance, 1972–1984.**

	Socioeconomic status		
Attendance pattern	*Lowest quartile*	*Middle quartiles*	*Highest quartile*
All students	17.7%	47.1%	35.2%
All community college attendees	19.5	51.7	28.8
By race/ethnicity			
Black: in community college	56.3	36.4	7.3
in any college	54.0	37.4	8.6
Hispanic: in community college	51.3	39.1	9.6
in any college	53.2	36.7	10.1
White: in community college	14.0	53.9	32.1
in any college	12.6	48.5	38.9
By community college attendance pattern			
Transfer, associate's degree and bachelor's degree	11.4	49.3	39.3
Transfer, bachelor's degree	14.6	46.1	39.3
Transfer, associate's degree	10.7	51.8	37.5
Terminal associate's degree	21.3	55.5	23.2
No degree, nonincidental, two-year and four-year	14.6	44.0	41.4
No degree, nonincidental, two-year only	22.6	54.3	23.1
No degree, incidental, two-year only	25.9	53.3	20.9
No two-year, but four-year	13.8	42.1	44.1
Proprietary/vocational only	32.8	53.1	14.1
Other patterns	9.1	43.2	47.7

Note: The universe consists of all NLS-PETS students. N = 12,599. Not
all rows total 100.0%.

End Table 4B. Educational Aspirations Versus Educational Plans of High School Seniors, 1972.

Highest educational level	Aspired to	Planned
All		
High school graduate	13.1%	23.9%
Postsecondary vocational	23.0	20.6
Two-year college, associate's degree	9.6	12.4
Four-year college, bachelor's degree	25.9	30.6
Graduate/professional school	28.5	12.5
Gender		
Women		
High school graduate	15.2	27.4
Postsecondary vocational	24.4	21.0
Two-year college, associate's degree	10.8	13.2
Four-year college, bachelor's degree	24.5	29.1
Graduate/professional school	25.1	9.3
Men		
High school graduate	11.1	20.4
Postsecondary vocational	21.5	20.2
Two-year college, associate's degree	8.3	11.6
Four-year college, bachelor's degree	27.2	32.1
Graduate/professional school	31.9	15.7
Race/ethnicity		
White/Asian American		
High school graduate	13.2	24.2
Postsecondary vocational	22.2	19.5
Two-year college, associate's degree	9.5	12.4
Four-year college, bachelor's degree	26.2	31.3
Graduate/professional school	29.0	12.6
Black		
High school graduate	11.0	19.0
Postsecondary vocationa	28.1	28.4
Two-year college, associate's degree	9.4	11.1
Four year college, bachelor's degree	23.9	27.8
Graduate/professional school	27.6	13.8
Hispanic/Native American		
High school graduate	17.4	29.9
Postsecondary vocational	27.6	26.0
Two-year college, associate's degree	12.1	15.2
Four-year college, bachelor's degree	23.7	21.3
Graduate/professional school	19.3	7.6

**End Table 4B. Educational Aspirations Versus Educational Plans
of High School Seniors, 1972, Cont'd.**

Highest educational level	Aspired to	Planned
Socioeconomic status		
Lowest quartile		
High school graduate	20.6%	38.2%
Postsecondary vocational	32.9	27.0
Two-year college, associate's degree	9.9	10.4
Four-year college, bachelor's degree	20.1	18.3
Graduate/professional	16.5	6.2
Middle quartiles		
High school graduate	14.1	25.5
Postsecondary vocational	24.9	22.6
Two-year college, associate's degree	11.0	14.2
Four-year college, bachelor's degree	25.2	28.0
Graduate/professional	24.8	9.7
Highest quartile		
High school graduate	4.0	7.2
Postsecondary vocational	9.5	10.5
Two-year college, associate's degree	6.5	10.6
Four-year college, bachelor's degree	32.8	47.6
Graduate/professional	47.3	24.2
SAT range		
700 or less		
High school graduate	7.3	11.7
Postsecondary vocational	18.7	19.9
Two-year college, associate's degree	13.1	19.8
Four-year college, bachelor's degree	35.4	38.0
Graduate/professional	25.5	10.6
701–975		
High school graduate	3.1	6.1
Postsecondary vocational	10.2	11.8
Two-year college, associate's degree	8.2	14.1
Four-year college, bachelor's degree	40.0	53.2
Graduate/professional	38.5	14.8
976–1148		
High school graduate	1.2	2.3
Postsecondary vocational	4.4	5.3
Two-year college, associate's degree	3.7	7.2
Four-year college, bachelor's degree	31.1	59.8
Graduate/professional	59.6	25.4

End Table 4B. Educational Aspirations Versus Educational Plans of High School Seniors, 1972, Cont'd.

Highest educational level	Aspired to	Planned
1148+		
High school graduate	0.8	1.6
Postsecondary vocational	2.0	2.3
Two-year college, associate's degree	1.0	2.6
Four-year college, bachelor's degree	21.6	47.0
Graduate/professional	74.6	46.5

Note: The universe includes all NLS-72 students who answered questions on educational aspirations and plans in either the base-year or supplemental survey. $N = 21,106$. For those with SAT/ACT scores, $N = 8,862$. ACT scores were converted to the SAT scale. Due to rounding, columns may not total 100%.

Chapter 5

Tourists in Our Own Land:
Cultural Literacies and
the College Curriculum

"Education and culture are not yet on speaking terms in our country," wrote Frank Lloyd Wright in *The Living City* (1970, p. 205). A lifelong curmudgeon, Wright had a knack for encapsulating social criticism in a sentence and for offering what appear to be flippant observations that nonetheless endure.

Current arguments in the United States over what students should know about various aspects of our culture and how that knowledge should be provided can be enlightened considerably by the records of the NLS-72. These records are complete enough to show that, on one level, Wright may still be right. If we define *culture* in terms of a narrow conception of the humanities disciplines, that culture has not spread too far through formal educational channels. But when the definition of culture is cast in terms that admit of history and its materials as well as anthropology and other social sciences, the diffusion of knowledge is more encouraging.

Diffusion of Culture

My purpose in this chapter is to explore the role of higher education in this diffusion of cultural information to a generation, or, more accurately, to that half of the generation that went to college. In the

process, I will pay particular attention to undergraduate enrollment, courses completed, and credits earned by the class of 1972 in
three clusters of courses:

- Western culture and society
- Non-Western culture and society
- Ethnic and gender studies

This exploration is framed by some notions concerning language and society, and also about higher education as an information system. This approach, with empirical transcript data at its
core, should shed a different kind of light on debates about curriculum and culture that have persisted in various forms for the past
twenty years but that have recently become especially dim and acri-
monious. Ultimately, this account, like the others in this book, is
an "economic" study because the diffusion of cultural information
provides students with currencies to access the world.

This Topic Has Become Contentious

The subject of the diffusion of cultural information and knowledge
sounded fairly neutral when I first embarked on this inquiry. To be
sure, there were intense debates that marked the introduction of
women's studies, ethnic studies, and Third World studies courses
and majors in the U.S. higher education in the late 1960s and early
1970s. And intense debates followed the calls of national commis-
sions for more coherence and/or attention to tradition in the college
curriculum in the mid 1980s (Bennett, 1984; Association of American Colleges, 1985). But the more recent forms of these arguments
have become vituperative at times, initially as a result of the mass
marketing of two very different books that were perversely yoked
together in many reviews and commentaries simply because they
were both published in 1988: Allan Bloom's *The Closing of the
American Mind* and E. D. Hirsch, Jr.'s *Cultural Literacy: What
Every American Needs to Know*. The newspapers put these books
on the front pages and editorial pages, thus guaranteeing a continuing public audience for what, a decade or two earlier, would have

been arguments largely restricted to academic circles (Todorov, 1989).

Bloom's book is a philosopher's lament for a lost past. It is filled with anecdotes and fragmentary analyses of contemporary cultural phenomena such as college students' favorite books, feminism, and rock music; it contains a less fragmentary exposition of the origins of relativism in nineteenth- and twentieth-century intellectual history. It also rails against modern science and social science (particularly in "serious universities"), spins tales of student radicalism at elite universities in the 1960s, and briefly pleads for the study of "great books." As befits a rationalist's polemic, there are no references or data. But there are some eloquent paragraphs. The book was a best-seller.

In contrast, Hirsch's *Cultural Literacy* is an empirically based, future-oriented analysis focused on the process by which individuals learn to read. It is specific and detailed in its recommendations for improving the curriculum in primary and secondary schools in all subjects and for all students (not just those who are likely to attend "serious universities"). It does not lament a lost anything, does not enter special pleas for "great books," and insists that, in the United States, "cultural revision is one of our best traditions" (p. 101). Hirsch's book is radically different from Bloom's, more constructive, and far more relevant to formal education.

Since 1987, the very idea of cultural information has been wrapped up in sloganistic notions of "cultural diversity" and "multiculturalism" that often mask discordant realities. College faculty and school officials are calling each other names that most folks do not understand, doing so in journals that most folks do not read, and tying themselves in rhetorical knots over what Wayne Booth (1981, p. 13) once called "fake polarities." The mainstream media, reporting on all of this, focus more on the polemical writings and speeches of the combatants, their tenure status and salaries, and their organizational affiliations than on what is taught, and hence, diffused, in real classrooms. When the personal becomes the political, temperatures are bound to rise. They are bound to rise even further when the arguments are tied up with campus speech codes, campus hate crimes, discrimination suits, and affirmative action policies. At that point, most commentators have lost touch with the issue.

One reviewer of a draft of this chapter asked whether it is valid to try to illuminate the current darkness with data generated by a group that went to college between 1972 and 1986. I think yes. For both the books and commission reports that have played prominent roles in these arguments over cultural knowledge were themselves grounded in observations of trends in mass culture and education of an earlier period. For example, Bloom's touchstones of the decline and shallowness of U.S. culture and education in *The Closing of the American Mind* include the rise and "fade" of Mick Jagger, the film *Kramer v. Kramer* (1979), and Woodstock (1969). None of these occurred last week or last year, and all are within the formal schooling years of the high school class of 1972. In a similar vein, former Secretary of Education William Bennett's essay on the state of the humanities in higher education, *To Reclaim a Legacy* (1984), used high school curriculum trends from 1969 to 1981, college curriculum trends from 1966 to 1983, and degrees conferred between 1970 and 1982 as foils in its presentation and argument. Finally, in 1982, on the basis of dissatisfaction with the fragmentation of undergraduate education during the previous decade, the Association of American Colleges formed the committee that produced *Integrity in the College Curriculum* (1985).

All of these reference points overlap or coincide with the data examined in this chapter. Yes, the tone and terms of the argument may have changed over the years, but what we may feel is a long period is but a moment on another scale. To say that there is a conflict between a 1985 observation and 1979 data is, from the perspective of history, silly.

Cultural Information

What is cultural information? It is information that reveals or conveys to us the mental habits, attitudes, prejudices, values, moral commitments, aesthetic preferences, and aspirations—in addition to constitutional arrangements, political histories, social customs, publicly accessible technologies, and economic organizations—of particular societies (Weintraub, 1966). It does not include the technical information of basic science for which special languages are necessary (Levin, 1967) or the specifics of vocational practice that are generally inaccessible to nonpractitioners. The former is transcultural; the latter tend to be arcane.

So defined, cultural information is *not* confined to artifacts and activities subject to aesthetic judgment, nor is the diffusion of cultural information the sole province of the humanities. When one thinks of how the vastness and complexity of this information are conveyed, our institutions of formal education come instantly to mind. How, then, could Frank Lloyd Wright possibly be right, for education and culture must be on speaking terms to get the job done? What could he possibly mean?

Let us take one simple case—perhaps too simple—from the high school records and college transcripts in the NLS-72 archives. Let the study of foreign languages represent a formal conveyance of cultural information and the study of basic science represent a formal conveyance of information that, in essence, is more transcultural than cultural. Table 5.1 displays the percentages of the 732,500 high school graduates from the high school class of 1972 who earned bachelor's degrees by the time they were thirty or thirty-one years old and who managed to get through *both* high school and college (1) without studying any foreign languages, or science,[1] or (2) with studying a minimum amount (no more than one year in high school and one year in college) in both areas.

This table itself conveys cultural information in that its data say something about what we value as a society: what our educa-

Table 5.1. Bachelor's Degree Recipients Who Did Minimal Coursework in High School and College in Foreign Languages and Science, 1972–1984

Number of college credits in foreign languages or science	No courses in high school		Only one year in high school	
	Foreign languages	Science	Foreign languages	Science
0	14.3%	0.7%	16.1%	2.6%
1–4	1.9	0.9	2.5	3.7
5–8	1.8	1.9	2.5	5.2
Total	18.0	3.5	21.1	11.5

tional institutions have allowed students to choose, and what, in fact, the students of the NLS-72 did choose. Over the course of at least eight academic years, some 39.1 percent of the people who earned bachelor's degrees in the United States did minimal to no work in a language other than English. Over the same period of time, 15 percent of credentialed students did minimal to no work in basic science. These ratios would be unthinkable in other advanced industrial countries.[2]

The issue is not whether we should be pleased or upset at the percentages in this half-empty glass (I could have inverted the table and shown the half-full glass), or whether, for example, one year (five to eight credits) of college-level laboratory science is sufficient for nonscience majors. Rather, the hypothesis that emerges from the data is that our system of education values scientific knowledge more than cultural information about societies that do not share our language.

In a world less conscious of its complexity—the world in which Wright lived and worked—simple presentations such as that in Table 5.1 might have been sufficient to make his case. But the issue of the diffusion of cultural information through formal education is both more complex and of a different order: it is about language, reading, and memory. Before I count heads of who studies what at the college level, it will be helpful to review these relationships.

Culture, Language, and Memory

Wright, who died in 1959, obviously did not read Hirsch's *Cultural Literacy* or ponder the implications of its widely publicized list of over five thousand terms, names, and phrases that, he contends, literate Americans should know. But in that volume, Wright would find a rationale for his judgment. Hirsch's work is grounded in serious scholarship concerning how we learn to read, how national languages are formed and sustained, and how the cultures of six continents ensure their continuity by transmitting stocks of information to their young. *Cultural Literacy* also rests on research demonstrating that "part of language skill is content skill" (Hirsch, 1983, p. 164).

Supradialects and Language Stores

Hirsch's list was seen by many as an attempt to standardize the basic
elements of the shorthand we use to communicate, and, hence, what
knowledge should be utilized in school and college instruction.
Hirsch would say that the list simply reflects what is empirically
present in a national vocabulary used every day in newspapers and
on television without explanation. A random dozen terms from one
portion of the list provide typical examples:

> sink or swim
> Sioux Indians
> Sirens, the
> Sistine Chapel
> Sisyphus
> sitcom (situation comedy)
> sit-ins
> sit on the fence
> Sitting Bull
> skepticism
> Skinner, B. F.
> skin of your teeth [p. 204]

Hirsch advocates that schools make sure, in their own ways, that
their students can read the newspapers in which such phrases,
terms, and names appear. In the hot debates that followed publication of *Cultural Literacy,* both critics and defenders assumed that
the list would have considerable impact on education.

　　What Hirsch was doing might be understood better through
a sociolinguistic analogy. It has been pointed out that, in the process of its development, any nation will come to accept one form of
language spoken within its borders as a "supradialectical norm"
(Ferguson, 1968). Where there are minority language cultures and
a mainstream culture that requires unification and efficiency
through a common language, as Joshua Fishman (1971) observed,
the mainstream culture and its language have historically prevailed
in most nations where that situation existed. In describing these
cases, Fishman (1976, p. 49) points out that people learn "the lan-

guage of their functional polity" while maintaining "the language of their intimacy." This paradigm exists in the United States, where national language policy, implicit in dozens of statutes, seeks to protect and preserve minority languages and cultures as supplements to the supradialect (Grant, 1978). Critics who described Hirsch's goal as promoting "the nationalization of knowledge" (Ross, 1989, p. 13) or "American facts" (Kohl, 1989, p. 50) might think again if they looked at the history of languages. From that perspective, Hirsch is simply illustrating a supradialectical norm in an unquestionably multidialectal society. The supradialectical norm consists of more than the language system of American English. It involves particular words, phrases, names, and numbers that are commonly used to access key concepts of the material and spiritual life that surrounds us. Our economy does not function without this norm. The same analysis holds for other countries in which more than one language or dialect is spoken. Every polity has a "national vocabulary" that has been determined by its history, and that is maintained by the necessity of economic transactions, broadly speaking. We are not alone.

Our arguments over curriculum relate directly to this concept of the supradialectical norm. The question we debate is a normative one: out of the vast universe of knowledge, what *should* a person know? Our answers are grounded in a net of expectations. We expect our colleges, more than our primary and secondary schools, to open up the full range of that universe of knowledge to students who can choose a large part of what they study. We know that the process of learning—in whatever corners of the universe of knowledge college students choose—rests on the store of language students bring to the learning situation. We expect education to expand that store of language, and through the expansion, to enable individuals to participate more fully in our society, culture, and economy. We expect of college graduates as full a participation as possible and know that in our time, that participation must transcend our own national borders.

Expanding our stores of language requires that we master the "supradialectical," including its accessible scientific and technical territory, and that we include other "dialects" in our learning. Cultural literacy involves the expansion and use of those stores of language so that we become more efficient producers, disseminators, and users of knowledge. It is an advanced form of language learning. Hirsch's work reminds us how this happens, and how it could happen better. While it stresses the empowerment of the individual, it also echoes Fritz Machlup's (1980) more utilitarian ideas of knowledge production as an economic activity: the more people who possess a large store of language, the more knowledge we can produce, and the more knowledge we can produce, the wealthier our society. In his earlier work on knowledge production, in fact, Machlup (1962, p. 107) advanced the notion that the learning of high school students and college students represented "implicit earnings" that should be added to official computations of the gross national product. The extent of those implicit earnings, we might say, is dependent on the acquisition of an appropriate store of language.

Schemata and Scaffolding

But let's think about the issue for a moment simply in terms of empowering individuals the way learning *any* language would empower them. The ideas informing *Cultural Literacy* derive from a school of research on reading that emphasizes structures or "schemata" by which our memory organizes and stores massive amounts of information. These structures, collectively, have been called *scaffolding*. The scaffolding of memory enables us to build meaning when we read a text, and not merely to decode the text (Anderson, 1977). Whether the communication is written or oral, the memory structures we use to advance from mechanical decoding to full understanding contain "world knowledge" (Chall, 1983, p. 8). The more of this world information we have, the better we are able to process new information received through any medium. The more we possess, the more we can create new schemata for ourselves by "tuning" or "restructuring" what we already hold (Rumelhart, 1980).

The more world information we possess, for example, the more we can laugh at the allusive banter of late night television hosts such as Arsenio Hall or David Letterman, or of a deft film script such as Steve Martin's *L.A. Story*. People who know nothing from Shakespeare laugh less at a showing of *L.A. Story* then people who do. Comparatively and figuratively speaking, the space of their lives is a smidgen smaller. This point remains the same whatever the movie and its allusions. And it remains the same if the movie is in a language other than English and its allusions are to a different cultural setting.

Default Settings and Sirens

Yet another way of describing this cognitive phenomenon of schemata uses a computer analogy. When we are faced with unfamiliar material, we all have a stock of memory that functions like a default setting on a computer. That is, in the absence of other clues, we refer to a basic known value (Minsky, 1975). Activating this default setting is not like being prompted with a "fill-in-the-blank" task on a test or a question in Trivial Pursuit. Rather, the defaults come into play when we are faced with the challenge of organizing and comprehending a *sequence* of information, including information drawn from a task or text and from the environment of that task or text. For example, the reader of this paragraph is able to understand it, in part, because in the 1990s, the schema elicited by *default setting* has become pervasive or supradialectical enough to justify the use of the term in a text such as this. As recently as ten years ago, however, I could not have written this paragraph for a general audience. But there is now a critical, democratic mass of people in the U.S. work force, from secretaries to schoolteachers to warehouse clerks to graphic artists, who have been trained to use computers and who possess a schema for "default."

What about schemata grounded explicitly in the supradialect of American English, and not in a technological vocabulary that would be accessible in other cultures? Let's take an item from the random dozen terms I listed from Hirsch's book: "Sirens, the." Imagine a newspaper article or television commentary about any situation in which a person or group of people, confronted with a critical decision, are tempted with one or more alluring extremes. They can choose one, or, more painfully, resist the temptations. For purposes of both shorthand and dramatic intensity, the newspaper writer or television commentator refers to the temptations as "the

Sirens.'' How do we know that these Sirens are *not* police sirens or fire truck sirens? On what do we draw to understand what is being said? Would the same word, and its conceptual scheme, be used in other languages in the same situation?

There is no question, in this case, that to understand the term, we would have to draw on a story that is widely known and widely used in *Western* cultures. The word *Sirens*, with this particular cultural evocation, exists in other Western languages—German, Spanish, and French, for example. Native speakers of English, *wherever* they are found (North America, the Caribbean, Oceania, the British Isles), are not alone in being able to use the concept of the Sirens in this way, though in other languages the evocation is not always produced by a noun (in German, for example, the adjective, *sirenenhaft*, is used to mean ''bewitching'' or ''seductive''). Thus, the concept is supradialectical in a way that cuts across national boundaries and is accessible to over a billion people—no small number.

At the same time, the word does not exist with this particular cultural evocation in Arabic, Hindi, or Chinese, for example. It does not derive from a story in the core mythologies of cultures in which these languages are spoken, though I suspect there may be analogous stories in those mythologies, and hence, words that can evoke a similar schema among native speakers of those languages who know those stories. Native speakers of those languages who do *not* know those stories are in a position similar to the American moviegoer who watches *L.A. Story* knowing no Shakespeare.

Lists and Language Space

Hirsch's list is essentially a selection of defaults or schemata from the supradialect. Such a list is always a hazardous undertaking and invites contention, even when it can change and even when it does not pretend to be complete. But Hirsch's point, in part, is that our tendency to emphasize skills—rather than content—in our schools conveniently avoids any contentiousness whatsoever. When we elevate skills over content in teaching, we fail to expand our students' language space.

Understanding references in the context of a list such as

Hirsch presented, though, is not complete understanding because these references are usually encountered in the contexts of conversations, texts, and visual presentations, all of which offer other clues to help students construct meaning (Resnick, 1984). Context, in fact, underscores the difference between mere information and the higher order we call knowledge. As Wayne Booth (1989) pointed out in a critique of Hirsch's work, even in cultures that require their children to memorize large bodies of material, what is disseminated is more than information, more than what Machlup terms "disconnected events or facts." The children are immersed in a stream of stories and sagas, oral editorials and discoveries, all of which convey the touchstones, totems, and values of the societies into which they will grow. In short, there is context for the content. Without that context, there is no motivation to become engaged, to search further, to question. Knowledge is diffused in a society when people can recognize and act on innovations—that is, departures from existing patterns of experience—or when they can extrapolate ideas from the old to the new. The recognition and action depend on more than mere information, but without the information, the recognition of what is a departure, what is change, is itself problematic.

Indeed, virtually all scholars of cognitive processes in reading will acknowledge the essential validity of Hirsch's story but may regard it as incomplete. In fact, some of those who objected to his prescribed list then advanced their own rival lists (for example, Simonson and Walker, 1988) and, in the process, conceded the basic point: without an expanding stock of information, individuals do not know where to search further or what to question. One can think of a variety of words, terms, phrases—and their associated knowledge—that entered common usage during the young adulthood of the class of 1972. A good example is *ayatollah*. This word did not exist in most dictionaries that would have been used by students of this generation in high school and college. By 1980, the word was not only in the dictionaries but had become an English slang term and was firmly ensconced in anybody's lexicon of cultural literacy. More important, the wide use of the term brought us to acknowledge that there was something called Islamic law that governed 600 million people. It is almost impossible to use the word today without a host of associations born of televised knowledge of Islamic customs and social organization.

Information Systems, Colleges, and "the Canon"

In the context of higher education, these ideas take on added complexities. While the educational implications of Hirsch's work devolve principally on elementary and secondary schools, the subject of the college curriculum inevitably arises because the college curriculum assumes a basic scaffolding, assumes a plot of language space that can be cultivated, and assumes that students will use the scaffolding of their memories to search further and question. Even more important to our understanding of why college curricula look the way they look at any moment in time is the fact that colleges are responsible for discovering and preserving knowledge through research and scholarship in addition to diffusing it through instruction. The dynamics of academic work are thus key to understanding how college curricula work.

There is a difference between "the scholarly and the pedagogical canon" (Mueller, 1989, p. 24) that is important for judging arguments over what stores of cultural knowledge should be taught. The *scholarly canon* refers to the range of accepted topics or problems studied by professors in their research. That is what they were trained to do in graduate school, and that is what the bureaucracies of their disciplines reward. The *pedagogical canon* refers to the range of materials and treatments professors use in instruction, the range of course topics reflected in the transcripts of generations passing through college. The pedagogical canon derives from scholarship. What happens, as Gerald Holton (1962) demonstrated, is that just at the moment when scholarly work on a question is exhausted, the materials and methodologies of that work are established and influential enough to make their way into the college classroom and the pedagogical canon. This transformation from research to mass instruction occurs as much in the humanities and social sciences as it does in basic science.

For example, as ways of interpreting literary texts, the New Criticism, psychologism, Marxist analysis, and historicism all represent communities of scholars whose influence reached a peak when they had analyzed virtually every major text from their perspective. Each school of criticism, in its turn, became what Kuhn (1970) called *normal science* (that is, to put it crudely, the accepted way of doing things) and at that point entered the classroom as the dominant method with preferred literary texts. At that point, too, each school was challenged in the "scholarly canon" by its successor. So the pedagogical canon revealed in the records of one generation of students may be different from the pedagogical canon of the succeeding generation. In the terms of this analysis, what is true for the class of 1972 may be less true for the class of 1982 and not true at all for the class of 1992.

Of course, the organized dissemination of cultural information in colleges takes place through a great deal more than pedagogical canons. As communities, colleges provide cultural information through public television programming, drama, film festivals, literary magazines, colloquia and conferences, "unofficial" courses, and so forth. None of these involves formal course taking, and all are features of college life that have historically made campuses vibrant, although student attendance and participation do not generate any records. College students can learn a great deal about history, the arts, and literature on their own. And more and more, college student learning about cultural diversity in the United States takes place outside the formal curriculum as institutions establish discussion groups and encounters (Daniels, 1991). The larger and more complex the institution, the greater the range of potential cultural exposure. The circumstances of intentional learning (choice) are more hospitable.

However much colleges, as communities, act as cultural information systems in their everyday activities, we usually measure and discuss these matters in the lives of college students by referring to the formal curriculum. What we can learn from the NLS-72 data base, more than from anywhere else, is who chose to study how much of what, and in what kinds of institutions, with respect to various classes of cultural information. Commonsense empiricism suggests that the chances people will expand any part of their language space are higher if they successfully complete formal courses in subjects that embrace those spaces, and, in the process, develop new stores of discrete information. As Alexander Astin has frequently observed in his research on college student development, you learn what you study (Astin, 1984), and a number of investigations using the Graduate Record Examinations have supported this observation (Wilson, 1985; Ratcliff and Associates, 1990). Whether formal coursework at the college level also increases the chance that students will transform information into knowledge, search further, and question is something we really do not know. We take it on faith.

The Validity of Unobtrusive Sources

There are seven types of documents a researcher can use in estimating the nature and extent of the cultural information passed to a generation of college students through formal coursework: college catalogues, course schedules, enrollment surveys, course syllabi, tests and project assignments assessments given in individual classes, de facto national tests, and student transcripts. Each has its virtues and limitations. Because some of these documents are cited often in arguments about college curriculum, I want to spend a few pages discussing their validity as sources of information. This is more than a technical issue.

The Catalogue Rule

One of the strategies in the rhetorical firefights over the contemporary college curriculum involves the citation of college catalogue rules and their consequences. The critic's objective is often to find the most outlandish examples of what courses a student *could* take to fulfill various graduation requirements, and then to extract the more extreme, jargonistic, or convoluted portions of the syllabi for some of those courses. The following statement illustrates this technique: "A student can fulfill core requirements at Harvard by studying tuberculosis from 1842 to 1952, and distributive requirements at Dartmouth with 'Sexuality and Writing,' which analyzes 'the use of sexuality and its ramifications as symbols for the process of literary creativity, with particular reference to . . . [ellipses in original] potency and creative fertility; marriage or adultery and literary sterility; deviation and/or solitude and autobiography; prostitution and history; chastity and literary self-referentiality' " (Cheney, 1990, p. 31).

Leaving aside the point that what the fifteen thousand undergraduates enrolled at Harvard and Dartmouth study is generally irrelevant to the eleven million undergraduates enrolled in less elite institutions, the statement is derived from analyses of catalogue rules rather than student behavior. One could be more devastating by listing all the courses that satisfy physical education requirements in U.S. colleges—such as bowling, jogging, billiards, yoga, scuba diving, and fly casting—and doing so without telling the reader whether these courses carry full credits, fractions of credits, or no credits. It is easy to take advantage of catalogues for propaganda. I confess to having done my share of it.

More generally, critics seek to outrage public opinion with statistics on the number of institutions that allow their students to graduate without studying a particular field (foreign language, math, English literature, history, and so on). While counting institutions is not as convincing as counting affected students, the point is that this rhetoric, too, assumes that the college catalogue, or the dean's account of the catalogue, reflects the norms of student course-taking behavior. But we never know whether the courses listed in a catalogue were actually offered—let alone taught, whether more than a dozen students actually took them, or in the example cited earlier, whether "Tuberculosis, 1842–1952" was a case study in biostatistics, quantitative history, or demography (hardly worthy of derision in any of those cases). When he was dean of arts and sciences at the University of Texas, John Silber astutely remarked that the catalogue is the university's contribution to American fiction and ought to be placed on appropriate shelves in the library.

To be fair, catalogues do have their virtues. They are official statements of institutional intent and are very public. One can use them to mark long-term changes in curriculum, both in terms of particular fields and college graduation requirements (Dressel and DeLisle, 1969; Toombs, Fairweather, Chen, and Amey, 1989). They reflect the birth, growth, mutation, and decline of disciplines and the changing values and missions of different types of colleges.

Course Schedules

If the catalogue is not a reliable source of information on the operational status of individual courses or groups of courses, the course schedule is better. It indicates whether the courses were actually offered and how extensive and frequent those offerings were. Was the course a seminar for 15 students offered every other year, a lecture for 100 students offered only once by a visiting professor, or a twelve-section course for 300 students each semester? Was registration restricted to majors or to students who had passed through six prerequisite courses, or was it open to all? Course schedules usually include such information. The study of tuberculosis from 1842 to 1952, for example, may have been limited to students who had previously taken both one statistics course and an introduction to epidemiology. Few people have done that as undergraduates.

Course schedules, however, also have limitations. In too many cases, we never know whether the courses offered were actually taught (did enough students register to justify a "go"?), or whether more than a dozen students out of the eleven million undergraduates in the United States actually took the courses.

Surveys of Deans and Enrollment Surveys

As sources of information on what college students study, surveys of deans are probably more unreliable than catalogue surveys. Because our public discourse values the bureaucracy of the academic information system over the behavior of real students, we tend to be overly indulgent of these surveys, accepting them under the logical fallacy known as the appeal to authority—that is, if the provost says so, it has to be true.

Levine and Cureton's (1992) curriculum survey of chief academic officers is typical in its naïveté about information retrieved in this manner. I was once an associate dean and probably typical in my desire to make the college look however the college was supposed to look according to whatever survey was being taken by a government agency, academic organization, or other outside group. If the survey came to the academic vice president, I sometimes filled it out. At other times, the registrar filled it out, or the director of institutional research. It depended on who was around and had the time. But there was no faculty senate or review committee to screen our responses, as there would have been for a catalogue. I would not trust a registrar to know whether "new [multicultural] material [was] added to existing courses" (Levine and Cureton, 1992, p. 26), let alone how often, because registrars do not track syllabi. Unfortunately, data from such surveys are often presented, as they are in Levine and Cureton, as "facts" (p. 24).

Enrollment surveys filled out by department chairs fall in a similar bin. Some disciplinary groups—for example, the Association of Departments of Foreign Languages or the Mathematical Sciences Education Board—are more diligent about collecting such data than others. But the NLS-72 transcripts evidence an overall gap of 11 percent between enrollments and completions, and this gap is greater in some courses and fields than others. Some people register for a course but never show up, some show up the first week and then disappear, some stick around until the local "no-penalty" drop deadline, and others stay right to the end but fail to take the final exam or hand in the final project. Whatever the timing or reason, someone who enrolls in but does not complete a course cannot be counted among learners of that particular subject matter.

Another problem with enrollment surveys is usually acknowledged only in the fine print of footnotes that no one reads. Enrollment surveys do not count students. They count enrollments at a given point in time. This methodology results in three distortions of reality. First, the same student, enrolling in two or three courses in history, is counted two or three times. The more majors there are in a field, the more likely the enrollments in that field are high, and the more course requirements in a major, the higher the enrollments, regardless of the true number of students majoring in the field. Second, the counts usually occur in the fall semester, because that is when federal reporting under the Integrated Postsecondary Education Data System (IPEDS) is due, and fall semester enrollments are always higher than spring semester enrollments. Third, because the survey is taken at a particular point in time and double counts students, one has no idea of the percentage of students who take a course in a field at any time during their college careers. The patina of statistics in an enrollment survey pretends to tell us something, but it is difficult to determine what we are being told.

Syllabi and Assessments

A syllabus brings one closer to the empirical reality of what may actually be taught or read, and indeed, content analyses of syllabi (including texts and other course materials) in specific courses would provide grist for a history of the academic disciplines and the changing shape of received knowledge. A syllabus is the instructor's statement of intent, and in this, it is analogous to a catalogue. Its virtue lies in its detail, but the content and degree of detail in syllabi vary widely, even within the same multiple-section course. There is no nationally standardized way of writing or presenting a syllabus, and while catalogues are public and widely disseminated, syllabi are not. Often, a syllabus is submitted for the initial approval of a course, but the course may then change while the original document sits in a file drawer of approved courses and is subsequently examined (if at all) only by visiting accreditation teams. In other instances, the syllabus is not followed or the class moves too slowly to complete it. In courses with multiple sections, a core syllabus will receive different interpretations from different instructors. The document is thus both fugitive (you first have to find it in somebody's file drawer) and unreliable.

Course assessments in the form of assignments, tests, projects, papers, exhibits, oral presentations, simulations, and computer exercises would be a better indication of specific expectations for student learning, and hence, one assumes, of what was actually studied. Despite small-scale analyses of assessments in individual disciplines (for example, Tribe and Tribe, 1988; Warren, 1989), no one has ever performed a large-scale comparative analysis of assessment content, form, and practice.

De Facto National Tests

A Gallup survey that asks a sample of 691 college seniors from sixty-seven four-year colleges eighty-seven questions in a self-administered booklet during personal interviews conducted by different people, under different conditions, in an untimed situation, and in exchange for $5 can, by no responsible yardstick whatsoever, be called a national test.[3] Yet, in the matter of cultural literacy, that survey is what makes the newspapers, and with inflammatory revelations such as that 25 percent of the seniors "could not distinguish Churchill's words from Stalin's" (Cheney, 1989, p. 11), even though no such question was on the "test."[4] I am no defender of this degree of ignorance, but anyone concerned with the uses of testing cannot countenance such data being presented as valid and reliable indicators of knowledge.

The only long-term reliable data we possess on college student learning in specific disciplines come from the Graduate Record Examination (GRE) subject-area tests. These differ dramatically from the other potential sources of information on the nature and extent of student learning that I have described. Looking at student performance on individual tests covering, for example, history, literature in English, French, or political science, and using proper metrics of interpretation, one can determine general trends (long-term and shorter-term) in subject-matter achievement (Adelman, 1985; Stern and Chandler, 1988). Yet there are severe limitations to using the GRE subject-area tests to measure the flow of cultural information and its impact. Most obvious among these is the relatively modest number of college students who take the subject-area tests and the fact that these students are self-selected (Grandy, 1984). Even at the height of application to graduate schools in the early 1970s, only 125,000 people took the subject-area tests compared to 300,000 who took the GRE general examination compared to the 800,000 to 900,000 bachelor's degrees conferred annually. The samples in individual fields, even then too small for national analysis (11,500 in history, 15,000 in English, 6,100 in political science, and so forth), are smaller today, and are smaller, still, because we cannot sort out the foreign students who take the subject-area tests (whereas we can sort foreign and domestic student performance on the GRE general exam).

Less obvious but more important are some of the psychometric aspects of the GRE subject-area tests. For example, scores are reported on a scale (and no two GRE subject-area tests use the same scale); and the best a researcher can do is to obtain subtest raw scores where they are available. Even then, if you knew that 40 percent of the students who took the political science exam were correct on more than half of the 40 questions that could be grouped as a subtest in comparative political systems (out of 170 questions for the whole exam), what could you make of that knowledge? That we do not teach comparative politics well in U.S. higher education? That students do not take courses in comparative politics? That the students who took the test did not learn their comparative politics well even if they did take courses in the field? And since the field of comparative politics is cross-cultural, does the distribution of subtest scores mean that cultural information is not getting through? All those possibilities are open.

Transcripts, Again

Transcripts are another matter. In economic terms, they are neither leading nor trailing but are concurrent indicators. They constitute *general* empirical evidence of what courses were actually taken irrespective of what the catalogue or course schedules said. If there were not enough enrollees to justify a course, that course will not appear on a transcript. And while the catalogue rules may allow a student to earn a bachelor's degree without studying history, the transcript will show whether or not the student actually studied history at any time in his or her college career, regardless of whether it took four, eight, or twelve years to earn a degree. The transcript will also show the kind of history studied and whether the student completed the course, hence whether he or she can be counted among the learners of that kind of history. The transcript can show how many courses in history the student took, how many credits were earned, and when. No, it will not say what the student read, what was otherwise taught, or how. But it will show for sure what the student did and even provide a general guide, via a grade, to how well the student did it.

In her foreword to *50 Hours* (1989), an otherwise challenging proposal for a core curriculum for college students, former National Endowment for the Humanities Chair Lynne Cheney relied on a survey of institutions that indicated the percentage of four-year colleges from which it was possible to graduate without having taken a course in six areas: history of Western civilization, history, English or American literature, foreign languages, math, and "natural and physical sciences." Table 5.2 matches the survey findings (which are not to be found in detail in *50 Hours*, rather in Lewis and Farris, 1989) against the empirical evidence of the NLS-72 transcripts. The transcript data in the table show the percentage of students from the high school class of 1972 who earned a bachelor's degree at any time between 1972 and 1984 and did *not* earn any credits in four of the six fields mentioned by Cheney.[5]

However distressing the transcript data, what is obvious in all four cases illustrated in Table 5.2 is that student course-taking behavior exceeds putatively official minimums, at least among those students who received bachelor's degrees (those who earned less than a bachelor's degree could not be included in the comparison because the Cheney's criterion is graduation). The differences between minimum guidelines and maximum behavior in history, foreign language, and mathematics/statistics courses are particularly striking. Even if one expects student course taking to exceed catalogue standards, it would not be by such margins. Transcripts do not deal in possibilities, rather actualities. To be sure, some student behavior reported here antedates the data on institutional

Table 5.2. Graduation Requirements in 1984 Compared to
Course Taking, 1972–1984.

Course category	Percent of colleges from which students could graduate in 1984 without a course in the category	Percent of NLS-72 bachelor's degree recipients with no credits in the category (N = 5,127)
History	42.0	26.2
English or American literature	48.0	39.6 (32.2)[a]
Foreign languages	80.0	58.4
Mathematics	54.0	30.8[b]

[a]English or American literature plus literature in translation.
[b]College-level math and statistics courses only; no precollegiate or remedial courses included.

policies, but the differences are too large for such a comfortable analysis. Colleges do not get religion overnight.

Discovering Commonsense Relationships

Common sense tells us that general course-taking behavior will differ by student major and type of institution. Students who graduate from liberal arts colleges, for example, are more likely to take courses in history, foreign languages, and English or American literature than students who graduate from either doctoral degree-granting institutions or comprehensive colleges. At the same time, they are less likely to study college-level math or science and engineering because liberal arts colleges generally do not offer degrees in such professional fields as engineering or such occupational fields as accounting, whereas the larger, more curricularly diverse institutions do. Most U.S. undergraduates attend large institutions, and most undergraduate degrees are *not* in traditional arts and sciences fields (see the list of undergraduate majors in Resource A). The requirements for degrees in professional and occupational fields are such as to leave precious little time for anything else.

Looking at all the NLS-PETS students who received bachelor's degrees, engineering majors, for example, are the least likely to study history (see Table 5.3), foreign languages (Table 5.4), or English or American literature (Table 5.5). The same kind of analysis could be applied to majors in music education, nursing, and accounting. For instance, if one wished to major in music education (indeed, any professional degree in music), 65 percent of the bachelor's degree program is already prescribed in music and education courses.[6] And prior to 1991, a major in accounting *might* have been able to get away with only 45 percent of his or her coursework prescribed in business administration, economics, accounting, and math.[7] To blame universities or state colleges for the negative consequences of offering such degrees is aiming the arrow in the wrong direction. The "villains" are the requirements for accreditation in specialized fields.

In fact, despite calls from both sides of the barricades for new core curricula, we cannot have either fifty hours, as Cheney (1989) recommends, or more than fragments of non-Western or multicul-

Table 5.3. Bachelor's Degree Recipients Earning College
Credits in History, by Gender, Race/Ethnicity,
Institutional Type, and Major, 1972–1984.

Student characteristics	Credits				
	None	1–4	5–8	9–12	13+
All	26.2%	24.7%	26.9%	12.4%	9.7%
Gender					
Men	26.2	23.2	26.0	12.6	12.0
Women	26.4	26.4	27.9	12.0	7.2
Race/ethnicity					
White	26.9	25.2	26.2	11.8	9.8
Black	19.4	17.3	32.8	21.2	9.3
Hispanic	19.7	22.8	39.0	11.3	7.2
Type of institution attended					
Doctoral	31.9	24.1	25.7	9.5	8.9
Comprehensive	22.8	25.6	28.5	14.1	9.0
Liberal arts	19.5	26.2	21.5	15.8	17.0
Other	26.4	16.4	33.1	14.2	9.9
Major					
Business	28.2	24.9	31.3	11.9	3.8
Education	18.3	25.3	31.0	17.0	8.3
Engineering	45.9	27.0	19.8	6.5	0.8
Physical sciences	34.2	24.7	30.3	9.2	1.7
Math/computer science	31.3	26.4	29.2	9.5	3.7
Life sciences	33.9	26.9	26.6	10.6	2.0
Health sciences/services	41.9	32.3	23.0	2.2	0.6
Humanities	18.5	19.7	24.2	19.3	18.3
Fine/performing arts	33.5	26.3	27.1	10.4	2.7
Social sciences	16.6	17.7	22.2	13.1	30.4
Applied social sciences	20.9	29.7	29.5	13.8	6.1
Other	24.2	22.8	24.3	19.1	9.6

Note: The universe consists of all NLS-PETS students who received
a bachelor's degree by 1984. N = 5,127. Weighted N = 732,511. Rows may
not total 100% due to rounding.

tural studies as long as 50 percent of bachelor's degrees and 67
percent of associate's degrees are awarded in occupational fields, as
long as the accreditation/certification requirements in most of those
fields eat up as many credit hours as they do, and as long as students
attempt to assemble records that will provide them with multiple
skills and areas of knowledge for a mutable economy.

**Table 5.4. Bachelor's Degree Recipients Earning College Credits
in Foreign Languages, by Gender, Race/Ethnicity,
Institutional Type, and Major, 1972–1984.**

Student characteristics	Credits				
	None	1–4	5–8	9–12	13+
All	58.4%	12.2%	12.9%	7.2%	9.3%
Gender					
Men	64.1	11.0	10.7	7.0	7.2
Women	51.9	13.6	15.3	7.4	11.7
Race/ethnicity					
White	58.4	12.5	12.9	7.1	9.2
Black	62.2	8.8	13.2	9.4	6.5
Hispanic	45.7	9.0	12.5	8.4	24.5
Type of institution attended					
Doctoral	55.2	12.1	12.8	7.7	12.3
Comprehensive	63.5	11.5	12.3	6.1	6.7
Liberal arts	43.3	16.0	17.7	10.2	12.9
Other	67.8	13.0	9.6	8.4	1.3
Major					
Business	78.1	10.1	6.7	2.9	2.2
Education	71.7	11.4	9.5	4.0	3.4
Engineering	83.7	6.9	5.1	3.8	0.5
Physical sciences	43.9	15.2	15.5	11.9	13.4
Math/computer science	52.4	11.0	16.7	11.2	8.7
Life science	49.0	10.9	19.5	7.9	12.7
Health sciences/services	65.5	14.2	11.8	4.0	4.5
Humanities	23.7	11.5	13.4	10.3	41.1
Fine/performing arts	48.5	15.5	16.3	9.3	10.5
Social sciences	40.5	13.9	19.1	12.3	14.1
Applied social sciences	57.4	12.5	13.6	8.9	7.5
Other	35.5	23.2	19.8	11.2	10.4

Note: The universe includes all NLS-PETS students who received
a bachelor's degree by 1984. N = 5,127. Weighted N = 732,511. Rows may
not total 100% due to rounding.

Demography of General Course-Taking Behavior

A closer examination of the data on the general course taking of
bachelor's degree recipients, as presented in Tables 5.3–5.5, raises a
theme that bears pursuit: there is often a correlation between a
student's demographic characteristics and what the student studies.

**Table 5.5. Bachelor's Degree Recipients Earning College Credits
in English and American Literature, by Gender, Race/Ethnicity,
Institutional Type, and Major, 1972–1984.**

Student characteristics	Credits				
	None	1–4	5–8	9–12	13+
All	39.6%	29.4%	20.6%	5.2%	5.2%
Gender					
Men	45.6	28.4	18.2	4.4	3.4
Women	32.7	30.5	23.4	6.2	7.2
Race/ethnicity					
White	39.9	29.8	20.1	5.1	5.1
Black	33.3	23.5	30.7	6.7	5.9
Hispanic	43.9	29.9	15.9	6.6	3.8
Type of institution attended					
Doctoral	42.3	29.9	17.8	4.8	5.3
Comprehensive	38.4	28.2	23.0	5.6	4.8
Liberal arts	31.7	33.0	20.9	6.5	7.8
Other	44.9	30.7	21.3	2.4	0.7
Major					
Business	43.3	30.8	22.1	3.4	0.4
Education	31.1	30.1	28.1	6.3	4.4
Engineering	63.3	24.3	9.9	2.5	0.0
Physical sciences	51.4	32.7	10.6	5.2	0.0
Math/computer science	43.7	27.4	20.8	2.6	5.5
Life sciences	44.6	34.5	17.1	3.0	0.8
Health sciences/services	44.0	38.1	16.3	1.1	0.6
Humanities	17.4	3.4	9.4	8.5	51.4
Fine/performing arts	39.0	28.1	22.7	5.3	5.0
Social sciences	39.1	29.4	21.0	8.1	2.5
Applied social sciences	35.1	28.8	26.0	6.7	3.5
Other	35.5	25.8	28.6	6.5	3.6

Note: The universe includes all NLS-PETS students who received
a bachelor's degree by 1984. N = 5,127. Weighted N = 732,511. Rows may
not total 100% due to rounding.

These relationships are not inevitable. They are written in neither
stone nor genes. But they are observable. In some cases, they can be
explained; in others, not. For example:

- White bachelor's degree students in the NLS-72 sample were *less
  likely* (73 percent) to study history than either black (81 percent)

or Hispanic (80 percent) recipients of bachelor's degrees (Table 5.3). A partial explanation for this phenomenon is that a higher proportion of white students majored in engineering and the sciences, while a higher proportion of minority students majored in the social sciences and education (see Resource C, Table C.4). Engineering and science majors are less likely to study history than majors in the social sciences (which include history) and education.

- Black recipients of bachelor's degrees were *more likely* (67 percent) to study English and American literature than either white (60 percent) or Hispanic (56 percent) bachelor's degree students (Table 5.5). This disparity is partially explained by the fact that 65 percent of the black students who earned bachelor's degrees took a course in African-American literature. Usually, these are upper-division courses with prerequisites of at least one introductory course in English or American literature.

- Not only were women who earned bachelor's degrees *more likely* (48 percent) than men (36 percent) to study foreign languages (Table 5.5), but women were more likely to persist to advanced levels. Partial explanation: a far higher percentage of women than men took more than two years of foreign languages in high school and so were well on the road to advanced levels when they entered college.

My point in these examples is twofold—first, that student backgrounds involve academic "momentum" that carries from high school into college, and, second, that a student's major directs this momentum into certain curricular channels. This is hardly a surprising finding, yet it is strangely absent from contemporary discussions of who gets how much multicultural education (see, for example, Levine, 1991).

Culture in the Back Seat

When we use transcripts as guides to mapping the diffusion of cultural information, we learn that the majority of students' academic time is spent acquiring information and skills that are generic, psychomotor, devoid of any prima facie cultural and social information, and/or designed to produce occupational competence. The sheer amount of time the generation of the NLS-72 spent studying accounting, marketing, physical education, nursing, and basic electrical circuits, for example, absolutely dwarfs the amount of time it spent in the formal streams of explicitly cultural information—whether we define culture in terms of the artifacts and texts of the humanities or as the totality of material and spiritual life.

What is the empirical basis for this conclusion? First, we isolate all the courses taken by bachelor's degree recipients in the NLS-72 that were most likely to provide *explicit* cultural information—for example, Latin American politics, architectural history, or medieval philosophy. Then we aggregate the percentage of credits earned in those courses into larger categories—for example, "historical/political studies" or "anthropological fields." When we add the percentages, we find that the glass of higher education curriculum is filled to 31.3 percent with cultural information.

But if we reverse our perspective, the glass is largely empty. Almost 70 percent of the total academic time spent by this generation in college did not have, as its primary objective, encounter with explicitly cultural information. One can always argue that cultural information is implicit in virtually every course taught in a college, from macroeconomics to interior decorating to animal behavior to forest management. Learning how to operate a television camera, treat athletic injuries, use an air brush in graphic design, or compute tax liabilities *may* convey, in each case, some cultural information. The presence of that information in the execution of those tasks, however, is highly problematic. Yet those tasks—and others—are what the mass of students in U.S. colleges, community colleges, and universities spend the mass of their time learning. No, students do not spend their time that way at Harvard or Dartmouth or Stanford (see Resource B, Tables B.3 and B.4). But they do spend their time that way just about everywhere else, and "everywhere else" accounts for 93 percent of U.S. undergraduates. The languages learned through such curricular experience connect these students more to economic activity narrowly construed than to the contexts of economic activity broadly construed. As the data throughout this chapter demonstrate, culture takes a back seat in college.

Five Cultural Literacies

While there is a primary store of references that we use in our everyday language for shortcuts and abbreviations in communication, there are also secondary stores that allow demographic, cultural-interest, and specialist subgroups to communicate in similar ways. In presenting the postsecondary curricular experience of the class of 1972, I am proposing five stores of information that are derived from transcript evidence. One of these stores is our supradialectical cultural language, as described by Hirsch. The four others correspond to demographic, cultural-interest, and specialist subgroups. These five stores are not mutually exclusive; rather, they are competitive in the finite time of undergraduate education. More of one language store always means less of another when the full glass measures 120 credits, and when credits are proxies for time.

The five streams of cultural information in the NLS-72 archive are represented by six course clusters, because Western culture, which dominates the supradialect, is divided into two parts. These clusters are as follows:

1. Introductory studies in Western culture and society
2. Advanced studies in Western culture and society
3. Studies in non-Western culture and society (a cluster defined by academic specialist interests)
4. Minority and women's studies (a cluster defined by demographic categories)
5. General culture and society: humanities studies (this cluster includes courses that provide general cultural information and those not easily assignable to one of the other clusters)
6. General culture and society: social science studies (this group includes courses that provide general cultural information and those not easily assignable to one of the other clusters)

The content of these clusters, listed in End Table 5A, was empirically derived from a combination of literal course titles, a priori decision rules, and the revised taxonomy of the 1985 edition of the *Classification of Instructional Programs* (CIP) as described in *A College Course Map* (Adelman, 1990a). These clusters do not include basic science courses, even though a basic scientific vocabulary is part of the supradialectical literacy necessary for individuals to negotiate a contemporary culture dominated by scientific and technical questions (Miller, 1983). They do include the history of science under the Western culture and society cluster, and science, technology, and society (STS) courses under the general social sciences cluster on the grounds that such courses will include the cultural determinants of scientific theory and understanding.

Determinate and Indeterminate

The "general culture and society" course clusters are largely residual categories. Consider the cluster for the social sciences (End Table 5A, part 6). Any course in anthropology, for example, is going to expose students to a great deal of information about culture. Some of these courses are clearly either non-Western or Western in orientation. Others cover material that crosses the cultures of six continents. Others deal in ethnographic methodologies indispensable to the study of culture. Allied with anthropology in this regard are courses in human shelter and clothing offered in home economics departments, linguistics courses, and some sociology courses (for example, Rural Sociology, Sociology of Aging). And it is difficult to get through an introductory college geography course without considering the cultural and social dimensions and impacts of climate, trade routes, navigable waterways, and so forth. But it is equally hard to place any of these courses in any of the other five clusters: they transcend particular places and peoples.

The humanities cluster (End Table 5A, part 5) covers the reflective and creative provinces of culture, of ideas and theory and the modes through which ideas and emotions are expressed. One might assume that humanities course content is frequently drawn from the supradialect of Western thought, but the case is not clear. It is tough to teach a course in folklore, mythology, history of religions, history of dance, history of folk music, or political theory and stay wholly within Euro-American references. Moreover, philosophical questions in ethics, aesthetics, epistemology, or religion cannot be called "minority," "Western," or "non-Western" with any degree of certainty.

No doubt some readers will quarrel with my classification of some course categories in the two general clusters (humanities and social sciences). But if we are trying to distinguish the specific content from the indeterminate, we really have little choice. In addition, skills courses such as musical performance and studio art are not included in any of the six clusters, not only because the titles (for example, Class Woodwinds or 3-D Drawing) do not provide any hints of specific cultural content but also because the principal objectives of such courses are to perfect technique, not to acquire cultural knowledge. Does a student pick up cultural information in an introductory class piano course, for example, where the texts are standard Hanon, Blues Hanon, Jazz Hanon, or all three? That depends on how the course is taught. The case for the presence of cultural information in a music history course is far more explicit.

I do not pretend that these six clusters cover the entire range of cultural literacies. Nor do I pretend to know precisely what was taught in the courses comprising these clusters and whether it was taught in ways that encouraged active learning and engagement. We do not know, in fact, whether the students were demonstrably culturally literate as a result. And the degree of our ignorance is greatest with reference to the two general/indeterminate clusters.

However, we can make more reasonable assumptions about the content and process of student immersion in intermediate- and advanced-level elective courses than we can about broad surveys and required introductions to the disciplines: when the waters are deep, the opportunity to transform information into knowledge is greater. Hence, in the following analyses, I have selected the data principally from three of the determinate cultural literacy clusters: minority and women's studies, studies in non-Western culture and society, and advanced studies in Western culture and society.

Distinctly Labeled Courses

The course taxonomy acknowledges separate courses in various minority cultural studies in addition to courses in traditional academic departments that deal with non-Western cultures or Third World topics (for example, an anthropology course titled "Cultures of Sub-Saharan Africa" or a geography course titled "Economic Geography of the Andean Nations").[8] Though it derives from a national sample of transcripts, the taxonomy can be criticized as highlighting only cultural information that is distinctly labeled, not learning that is integrated in more general courses and curricula. The criticism has some merit, even though all specialized courses (Polymer Chemistry, Psycholinguistics, Operations Research, and so forth) are "distinctly labeled."

In light of contemporary arguments about the desirability of infusing traditional courses with multicultural materials instead of drawing boundaries around these materials by confining them to separate courses and departments, we would do well to remember that in the 1970s it was the boundaries that were favored (Sivart, 1973). It has since been argued that, in U.S. colleges, "the elevation of [ethnic] difference undermines the communal impulse by making each group foreign and inaccessible to others" (Steele, 1989, p. 48), and there is no doubt that the vast majority of the NLS-72 students taking distinctly labeled minority or women's cultural studies courses were members of the groups specified in the label. Thus, it appears that students from other groups did not experience the intensity of a focused transmission of cultural information. I admit to speculation about this, but the chances are high that students from other groups were not wholly welcomed into these distinctly labeled courses or departments. If people are not welcomed and are thus inaccessible to each other, the chances are less that they will be freed from prejudice (Geertz, 1986).

We may not be so inaccessible to each other, however. The courses in the general humanities and social sciences clusters surely included a diversity of cultural information that a transcript cannot capture. How much diversity is simply unknown. Only national samples of syllabi and assessments could overcome these limitations of a national sample of transcripts.

Who Takes What, Where, and (Maybe) Why

With few exceptions, all of them falling in the two clusters of general or indeterminate content, few people in the NLS-72 cohort completed courses in any of the three key clusters for cultural learning except the advanced studies in Western culture and society cluster, and even there, the percentages are small compared to those for the courses that seem to define the core curriculum for this generation, illustrated in Table 5.6. What is striking about this list is that it is dominated by introductions to those social science and humanities disciplines not normally taught in secondary school—that is, psychology, sociology, economics, philosophy, communications, and art history, along with mathematics courses that, if offered in secondary schools, do not usually meet college-level standards of content. In addition, unlike the courses in the cultural literacy clusters, many of the courses listed in Table 5.6 are required, and virtually all are prerequisites to something else. No wonder the

Table 5.6. Empirical Core Curriculum of Bachelor's Degree Recipients, 1972–1984.

Course category	Students taking course	Credits earned as a percent of total credits
English composition (regular)	73.6%	3.0%
General psychology	69.7	1.9
Introductory sociology	49.9	1.3
General biology	47.3	2.0
Introductory economics	44.8	1.6
U.S. history (surveys)[a]	42.1	1.6
U.S. government[a]	35.9	1.1
Introductory communications	35.8	0.9
Chemistry (general)	35.5	1.9
Introduction to literature[a]	31.1	1.0
Calculus	30.4	2.0
Western/world civilization	29.3	1.2
Introductory physics	26.3	1.5
Developmental psychology	25.6	0.8
Statistics (math)	23.3	0.7
American literature[b]	23.1	0.8
Introductory accounting	23.0	1.0
Introduction to philosophy	22.8	0.5
Art history[b]	22.2	0.8
Educational psychology	21.5	0.6
Business law	20.2	0.7

[a]These courses are included in the introductory studies in Western culture and society cluster.

[b]These courses are included in the advanced studies in Western culture and society cluster.

percentage of students taking them was high; no wonder they account for nearly one-quarter of the total undergraduate time (using credits as proxies for time) of those who earned bachelor's degrees in the NLS-72 generation.

But if roughly one out of five bachelor's degree holders studied accounting, only one out of twenty studied European history since 1789, only one out of fifty was exposed to any topic dealing with Native Americans, and only one out of a hundred studied jazz history or African-American music, then no matter how we define cultural information, no matter to which store of language we refer, its diffusion was limited. On the evidence of their coursework records, college graduates of this cohort should be far more likely to use *leveraged buyout* in a conversation (even as a metaphor) than *Waterloo, shaman,* or *riff.*

To be sure, there are course categories in the empirical core curriculum that provide students with considerable exposure to major concepts, texts, and chronicles of U.S. and European origin, and they duly appear in the cluster of introductory studies in Western culture and society. But these categories—Western civilization, U.S. government, U.S. history surveys, and introduction to literature—all cover territory previously traversed in secondary schools and usually required for high school graduation. The college-level versions of these topics may be more sophisticated, may encompass more material, or may simply be different in their approach. In these three respects, they will reinforce the store of language and references to which students have been exposed, but the only way we could determine that taking these courses would measurably expand that store would be through an elaborate and expensive national assessment. The course categories in the advanced Western culture and society cluster are far more likely to be college-level expansions of the store.

Philosophy is a different case. Assuming that an introduction to philosophy course emphasizes the logical apparatus of the discipline, it may enhance cultural literacy by enabling students to build knowledge out of information. It could teach them to take a vague collection of touchstone terms and turn them into clear frameworks for understanding. To be sure, philosophers develop analytical and deductive thinking muscles by addressing specific kinds of questions, such as whether it is better to suffer wrong or do wrong or whether words reflect or create reality. In these exercises, philosophy professors may introduce students to the ways influential thinkers or different cultures have dealt with these questions. But there is no guarantee that they will do so in an introductory course, as opposed to an upper-division course in, say, phenomenology.

The data in End Table 5A also reveal the differential effects of length of enrollment and degree attainment on exposure to cultural information. The figures demonstrate the expected: that a higher percentage of people who earned bachelor's degrees were exposed to different kinds of cultural information than those who spent less time in postsecondary education. The point of the comparison is to remind us that, in our arguments over what colleges require students to study, we often forget that not everybody who enters college earns a degree and that length of time enrolled (using credits as a proxy for time) is directly related to a generation's potential range of learning.

Enrollments: Institutional Factors

The diffusion of cultural information to a generation cannot be mapped without taking account of the nature of the institutions in which formal studies are pursued. This issue has been made particularly visible by virulent and often ignorant debates in the press over what Stanford freshmen are required to read. When one looks at the archive left by an entire generation, it should be obvious that Stanford is not where America goes to college (only 1.6 percent of the NLS-PETS students attended elite colleges), and that whether Stanford freshmen read Cicero or Franz Fanon is a matter worthy of a raree-show. If I hammer at this issue, it is because, from a *national* perspective, *everybody* who goes to college counts in this discussion. Therefore, the question to be asked is the same as one of the principal questions in Chapter Four: What types of institutions are the *principal providers* of different cultural literacies to the general college-going population? Or, to ask the same question from another perspective: In what types of institutions are students more likely to elect studies that will immerse them in different cultural literacies? Both versions of the question require us to refer to the ratios illustrated in Table 5.7.

Table 5.7. Undergraduate Course Taking by Institutional Type: Selected Cases in Three Cultural Literacy Course Clusters, 1972–1984.

Cluster and course category	Institutional type (Percentage of total enrollment in each course distributed by institutional type				
	Doctoral	Compre-hensive	Liberal arts	Community college	Other
All course categories	29.4%	36.0%	6.1%	22.0%	6.5%
Minority and women's studies					
Black studies	37.9[a]	42.1	7.6[a]	11.0	1.3
Native American studies	34.7	46.9[a]	4.2	13.8	0.4
Hispanic American studies	22.5	47.6[a]	1.5	26.9	1.5
Afro-American literature	24.7	43.8	10.3[a]	17.1	4.1
Afro-American history	21.4	45.1	7.0	24.9	1.6
Afro-American music	39.5[a]	44.2	11.6[a]	4.7	——
Sociology of race	26.9	47.8[a]	8.8[a]	15.3	1.1
Women's studies	35.9	42.3	6.2	14.7	1.0
Studies in non-Western culture and society					
Latin American studies	45.3[a]	34.3	7.7[a]	11.6	1.1
Chinese (elementary/intermediate)	49.5[a]	26.3	9.5[a]	2.1	12.6[a]
Japanese (elementary/intermediate)	62.3[a]	13.2	7.6	17.0	——
Comparative literature (non-Western)	27.7	40.4	17.0[a]	12.8	2.1
Economic development	50.8[a]	29.5	13.1[a]	3.3	3.3
African history	36.7	36.7	14.3[a]	11.2	1.0
Non-Western government	58.8[a]	32.4	5.9	0.6	2.4
Non-Western art	40.6[a]	19.8	19.8[a]	12.9	6.9
Non-Western religion	36.5	38.9	19.1[a]	4.8	0.8
Advanced studies in Western culture and society					
Russian (advanced/literature)	78.3[a]	13.2	8.5[a]	——	——
Classical literature	47.1[a]	36.3	12.9[a]	3.7	——
Shakespeare	42.0[a]	38.1	10.9[a]	8.4	0.5
Contemporary philosophy	36.1	42.2	16.9[a]	3.6	1.2
Geography of North America	35.5	48.8[a]	2.3	13.0	0.3
U.S. intellectual/cultural history	42.5[a]	35.5	13.2[a]	4.8	4.0
European government and politics	43.2[a]	45.9[a]	9.6[a]	0.7	0.7
Music history: classical	40.0[a]	36.8	15.5[a]	2.3	5.5
Bible studies	8.0	30.3	25.5[a]	7.0	29.2[a]

Note: The universe includes all NLS-PETS students who earned any credits in any kind of postsecondary institution between 1972 and 1984. N = 12,332. Because of rounding, not all rows total 100%.

[a]The share of enrollments in this course category exceeds the mean for this institutional type by 25% or more.

Table 5.7 illustrates a phenomenon similar to that observed in Table 4.8, the disequilibrium in the provision of knowledge. For each course, Table 5.7 displays the percentage distribution of all enrollments by institutional type. How do we know whether the percentage distribution for a particular course is unusual or "abnormal"? By comparing it to the percentage distribution, by institutional type, for *all* course categories. A difference greater than 25 percent means that a particular institutional type is providing and/or students in that institutional type are choosing to study in a course category at a significantly higher rate than the norm.

For example, comprehensive colleges were the principal providers of cultural information concerning African-American history to this generation of college students. Comprehensive colleges captured 45.1 percent of all enrollments in African-American history, and 45.1 percent is 25 percent above the norm (36 percent) of enrollment share for comprehensive colleges. Doctoral degree–granting institutions, however, were the principal providers of information in matters of non-Western culture and society, as illustrated by course categories in Latin American studies, non-Western government and politics, economic development, and non-Western art. These are academic specialist interests and are most easily realized in complex institutions that support a greater range of academic specialties than do other institutions. In addition, academic expertise is more an objective of specialist interests than it is of demographic or cultural interests, and the ideal of academic expertise is more firmly entrenched in doctoral institutions than elsewhere.

While liberal arts colleges were not principal providers of any category of information to the entire generation, they were significant providers in such course categories as non-Western literature in English, African history, non-Western art, classical literature, and contemporary philosophy. It is precisely because they are less complex and offer a more finite range of courses than other types of institutions that this phenomenon occurs. Because this more finite range generally excludes occupationally oriented curricula and focuses more on traditional humanities and social science fields, student course taking in liberal arts colleges will thus be overrepresented in a national measurement of enrollments in the six cultural literacy course clusters.

To be sure, these patterns reflect the missions as well as the curricular capacities of the different institutions in question. Comprehensive colleges provided the mass of degrees in teacher education for this generation, and given the preparation of teachers for work in urban schools, it is not surprising that a significant percentage of those who earned credits in minority and women's studies were teacher education majors. And community colleges are so busy providing occupationally oriented programs to two-thirds of their degree candidates that their curricula leave little space or time for culture studies. All these features of institutional type are reflected in the course-taking data.

Demography of Cultural Literacy

What kinds of students tend to engage in formal study in one or more of the three key cultural literacy clusters? Who chooses? The stock variables of student characteristics fall in two classes: demographic information (race/ethnicity, gender, SES) and educational attainment (for example, high school class rank, highest degree earned, and college grade-point average). Since we are looking principally at people who earned a bachelor's degree, the explanatory potential of the second set of variables is largely moot. And when women earn higher grade-point averages than men no matter what they study, examining grades in detail will not supply any new information. The demographic variables have more potential.

With one exception, little variation in course taking exists across these clusters by gender. As Table 5.8 demonstrates, among bachelor's degree holders, a much higher percentage of women (24 percent) than men (13 percent) took at least one course in minority and women's studies, but those percentages are still low. This obvious gender-related curricular choice is not found in any of the other cultural literacy clusters. But if we focus on individual course categories rather than clusters, considerable variations by population subgroups exist. Women comprised 80 percent of the enrollment in women's studies courses; blacks constituted 60 percent of the enrollment in African-American history, 65 percent in African-American literature, 80 percent in African languages, and 39 percent in African studies; and Hispanics accounted for nearly 20 percent

Table 5.8. Bachelor's Degree Recipients Earning College Credits
in Minority and Women's Studies, by Gender, Race/Ethnicity,
and Major, 1972-1984.

Student characteristics	Credits			
	None	1-4	5-8	9+
All	82.0%	12.9%	2.9%	2.2%
Gender				
Men	87.2	9.7	1.9	1.2
Women	76.0	16.6	4.1	3.4
Race/ethnicity				
White	84.3	12.3	2.4	1.1
Black	50.0	22.1	11.6	16.3
Hispanic	61.7	17.2	3.9	17.2
Major				
Business	91.3	6.9	1.4	0.5
Education	84.7	12.1	1.8	1.4
Engineering	95.7	3.6	0.3	0.3
Physical sciences	88.8	7.9	0.3	3.0
Math/computer science	88.1	9.6	2.3	0.0
Life sciences	90.1	7.8	1.6	0.5
Health sciences/services	90.4	7.4	1.8	0.4
Humanities	71.1	21.9	4.6	2.5
Fine/performing arts	85.6	9.2	5.0	0.3
Social sciences	64.3	22.3	6.6	6.8
Applied social sciences	71.0	21.6	3.4	4.1
Other	83.2	14.5	2.3	0.0

Note: The universe includes all NLS-PETS students who received
a bachelor's degree by 1984. N = 5,127. Weighted N = 732,511. Due to
rounding, rows may not total 100%.

of the enrollment in Latin American history. All these cases represent highly disproportionate concentrations of these subgroups in
relation to their overall presence in the NLS-72 cohort. In these
cases, demography was curricular destiny.

The SES of students who took courses in these clusters also
departs significantly from the pattern for the entire cohort. A higher
percentage of students taking courses in these clusters came from the
top 25 percent of the SES range than is the case for everyone in the
cohort who entered college. This relationship holds across all racial

subgroups. This relationship between SES and course taking in the three determinate clusters is understandable. Most of the courses in these clusters are not introductory titles. They have prerequisites and are taken more by those who have persisted to upper-division status, and people from the higher-SES brackets are more likely to persist and complete bachelor's degrees than those in the other SES quartiles (see Resource C, Table C.2).

Cultural Literacy and Undergraduate Major

Undergraduate major is a natural determinant of participation in the various clusters of cultural literacy courses. Tables 5.8 to 5.10 illustrate this phenomenon. Again, demographic subgroup interests, cultural interests, and specialist interests all play a role in interpretation of the data. Consider, for example, participation in minority and women's studies courses (Table 5.8), which is greatest for majors in education, humanities, social sciences, and applied social sciences (a category that includes social work, criminal justice, home economics, recreation, and communications). Conventional wisdom concerning the majors of women and blacks is borne out by the data: 60 percent of women and 61 percent of blacks majored in those four areas, versus 49 percent of the entire bachelor's degree population.

The non-Western culture and society cluster evidences the specialist-interest phenomenon. It is hard to major in geography, anthropology, or international relations, for example, and not encounter at least a portion of the non-Western stock of cultural and social references. It is not surprising, then, that the highest participation in this cluster is that of majors in the social sciences (see Table 5.9).

In the advanced Western culture and society cluster (Table 5.10), it is particularly noteworthy that 88 percent of humanities majors took thirteen or more credits in the fields covered by this cluster. On the one hand, given the fact that the cluster includes all period, author, and topic courses in English and American literature, all history of philosophy courses, and all advanced European language and literature courses, 88 percent is not surprising. On the other hand, there is no other case like it in any other cultural liter-

Table 5.9. Bachelor's Degree Recipients Earning College Credits
in Non-Western Culture and Society, by Gender, Race/Ethnicity,
and Major, 1972–1984.

Student characteristics	Credits			
	None	1–4	5–8	9+
All	82.1%	12.0%	3.2%	2.7%
Gender				
Men	82.4	11.9	2.9	2.8
Women	81.8	12.1	3.5	2.6
Race/ethnicity				
White	82.9	11.6	3.1	2.5
Black	74.0	14.9	5.5	5.6
Hispanic	66.3	24.9	3.8	4.9
Major				
Business	89.7	8.4	1.1	0.8
Education	89.5	8.6	1.2	0.7
Engineering	94.5	5.3	0.0	0.2
Physical sciences	83.6	14.2	1.6	0.6
Math/computer	82.7	11.0	4.5	1.8
Life sciences	86.8	10.5	1.8	0.8
Health sciences/services	92.9	5.7	0.9	0.5
Humanities	70.6	15.2	7.0	4.4
Fine/performing arts	79.6	15.2	4.5	0.8
Social sciences	59.3	21.6	8.6	10.6
Applied social sciences	83.9	12.1	3.5	0.6
Other	89.5	7.7	0.6	2.2

Note: The universe includes all NLS-PETS students who received
a bachelor's degree by 1984. N = 5,127. Weighted N = 732,511. Rows may
not total 100% due to rounding.

acy cluster. The intense concentration of humanities majors here
resembles course-taking patterns among science majors. One would
get a figure close to 88 percent if the question read, "What percentage of physical science majors earned thirteen or more credits in
courses beyond the basics in physics, chemistry, and math?" I have
added institutional type as a factor in Table 5.10 to draw attention
to the distribution of credits earned in this cluster by graduates of
liberal arts colleges. The distribution (far more instructive than a
presentation based on mean number of credits earned) demonstrates

Table 5.10. Bachelor's Degree Recipients Earning College Credits
in Advanced Western Culture and Society, by Gender, Race/Ethnicity,
Institutional Type, and Major, 1972–1984.

Student characteristics	Credits				
	None	1–4	5–8	9–12	13+
All	23.4%	23.6%	17.9%	13.7%	21.5%
Gender					
Men	26.1	24.9	17.1	11.6	20.2
Women	20.2	22.1	18.7	16.1	17.0
Race/ethnicity					
White	23.2	23.2	17.6	14.0	22.1
Black	26.6	30.5	20.9	9.2	12.9
Hispanic	21.2	22.8	23.9	15.1	17.0
Type of institution attended					
Doctoral	24.9	24.6	17.4	12.5	20.6
Comprehensive	23.2	25.3	18.0	15.3	18.3
Liberal arts	12.1	11.5	20.6	13.1	42.8
Other	36.1	21.2	14.5	10.0	18.3
Major					
Business	31.7	32.7	19.7	11.1	4.7
Education	24.0	26.6	19.9	16.7	12.8
Engineering	49.0	27.6	12.6	6.4	4.5
Physical sciences	32.2	26.2	18.7	13.4	9.5
Math/computer science	26.7	19.9	25.5	13.3	14.5
Life sciences	31.4	25.7	21.4	13.4	8.1
Health sciences/services	36.4	33.2	18.1	9.0	3.4
Humanities	1.0	0.9	3.1	6.8	88.3
Fine/performing arts	9.3	11.0	16.6	19.5	43.6
Social sciences	8.9	15.9	17.8	17.6	39.8
Applied social sciences	18.9	26.2	20.6	19.5	14.7
Other	15.9	17.1	15.0	3.4	48.7

Note: The universe includes all NLS-PETS students who received
a bachelor's degree by 1984. N = 5,127. Weighted N = 732,511. Rows may
not total 100% due to rounding.

the depth of immersion of a large percentage of liberal arts college
graduates in advanced Western cultural and social information.
This distribution reinforces my previous conclusions about the effect of institutional mission and curricular capacity on course-
taking behavior.

Western Culture and Society as the Primary Language Store

To what extent was the entire NLS-PETS group immersed in a stream of information, texts, and references *explicitly* derived from Western culture? As I pointed out at the beginning of this chapter, the answer depends on one's definition of culture, since that will determine how one defines the courses in which explicitly cultural information is likely to be encountered and the media through which students will either reinforce or expand their stock of schemata in the supradialect. If one limits the definition of culture to the life of the spirit, its expression in creative and reflective works, and its diffusion through the humanities, the percentage of total undergraduate time spent studying Western culture was limited. If one expands the definition to encompass history and other social sciences, the time this generation spent being exposed to Western culture doubles: from 5.1 percent to 10.1 percent for all students and from 7.7 percent to 15.7 percent for those who earned bachelor's degrees.

Two observations concerning these data are worth making. First, more than half of the humanities credits were accounted for by only four course categories: introduction to literature, art history, Bible studies, and American literature. More than two-thirds of the history and social science credits were accounted for by only three course categories: U.S. history surveys, world/Western civilization, and U.S. government—all of which are in the introductory Western culture and society cluster. So of the total time this generation spent in higher education, the burden of conveying cultural information from the supradialect lay on a handful of courses, most of which are introductory.

Second, the less time a student spent in postsecondary education, the lower the proportion of that time that was spent studying explicitly cultural subjects and the greater the burden on history and other social sciences (compared to the humanities) for conveying information about Western culture and society. What kind of information is this? In terms of its primary materials, history is much closer to anthropology than to literary studies. History is empirical and messy and relies on the evidence of everyday life: diaries, letters, parish registers, shipping records, newspapers, broadsides, graphic arts, paths and roads, drawings, machinery, songs, photographs, tape-recorded memoirs, motion pictures, and even college transcripts and data bases such as the NLS-72. Few of these are reflective, creative works representing the life of the spirit and designed to be pondered. Nonetheless, they are a critical part of the language of cultural information. They are artifacts from which historians extract accounts, just as archaeologists consider the products of both ordinary and extraordinary craftspeople as keys to understanding daily life, social relations, religious values, and power in ancient civilizations. Ethnographers, demographers, and geographers draw on many of these same artifacts to tell different kinds of stories, but the relationship between artifact and story line is similar.

The most accessible artifacts are texts, and the most accessible texts for U.S. faculty and students are written in English. Under such circumstances, Western cultural information will inevitably dominate the stories. Yet one out of five bachelor's degree recipients in the NLS-PETS—as well as over half of those who earned less than the bachelor's degree—had no postsecondary exposure to Western cultural and social information at all, basic or advanced. The lowest participation rates occurred among majors in engineering, agriculture, allied health, nursing, and engineering technologies. The participation rates were even lower for occupational associate's degree recipients and candidates in two-year colleges. All these students are, at best, tourists in their own land.

Immersion in the streams of language that yield Hirsch's primary cultural literacy, the supradialect, was more frequent than immersion in the streams of secondary dialects, but the cultural waters ran neither wide nor deep for the generation that is now thirtysomething. Indeed, as Chapter Six will suggest, that generation may not consist of efficient participants in the mainstream culture and economy. Given its even more limited formal study of secondary cultural literacies, the generation seems even less suited to participate in the diversity of world culture and economies.

Notes

1. In the data analysis file I created for the studies in this book, there are five configurations of college courses in science, technology, and engineering. The configuration used for this table is confined to disciplinary courses in the biological and phys-

ical sciences, clinical health science courses (for example, neuroanatomy and clinical biochemistry), and physiological psychology. Among science courses, these are most likely to include laboratory or field investigations.

2. When one examines either the *required* courses for "upper secondary" or "academic" secondary school diplomas or the courses designed to prepare students for national college entrance examinations in other advanced industrial countries, it is obvious that 100 percent of students who earn the equivalent of bachelor's degrees have taken more than minimal work in foreign languages and basic science. To be sure, we do not know what these students study at the university level because no other country has a national transcript sample like the NLS-PETS.

3. This is a real survey (Gallup Organization, 1989) commissioned by the National Endowment for the Humanities and used in the opening paragraphs of Cheney's *50 Hours* to prove, among other findings, that "25 percent of the nation's college seniors [are] unable to locate Columbus's voyage within the correct half-century" (Cheney, 1989, p. 11). It may be a survey, but it is not a "test," and the results should not be used as if it were.

4. The actual question was: "Which twentieth-century leader said, 'I have nothing to offer but blood, toil, tears, and sweat,' and 'From Stettin in the Baltic to Trieste in the Adriatic, an iron curtain has descended across the Continent'?" The multiple-choice answers, with the percentage of responses received by each, were: (1) Adolph Hitler (1 percent), (2) Winston Churchill (67 percent), (3) William Gladstone (2 percent), (4) Joseph Stalin (23 percent), (5) [No answer] (3 percent) (Gallup Organization, 1989, p. 43). The most accurate way to describe these disappointing results is to say that only two out of three college seniors could identify Winston Churchill's most famous lines as having been uttered by Winston Churchill. In order for one to conclude that students "could not distinguish Churchill's words from Stalin's," the question would have to be constructed as a "matching pair," using quotations from both Churchill and Stalin. Had the question been so constructed, the percentage of correct responses would have been higher because the "prompt" would have contained more clues.

5. The table does not cover Cheney's categories of "history of Western civilization" or "natural and physical sciences" because it was difficult to determine precisely what she was aggregating under these categories. To be persuasive, taxonomic categories should be well defined.

6. The current program accreditation standards of the National Association of Schools of Music for the Baccalaureate Degree in Music Education say that "music education degree programs typically comprise 120–132 semester hours . . . of which studies in music . . . should comprise at least 50%; general studies 30% to 35%; and professional education, 15% to 20%. . . . Student teaching is counted as professional education" (National Association of Schools of Music, 1991, pp. 62–63). If the curriculum is 120 credits, the music and professional education requirements consume 78. Given state teacher certification requirements that demand between 6 and 15 credits of student teaching, chances are high that a music education major will take more than 120 credits and that the additional credits will be in the major.

7. The 1988 standards of the American Assembly of Collegiate Schools of Business (AACSB, 1989) required accounting majors in accredited programs to devote "at least" 25 percent of their work to a "common body of knowledge in business administration" and a minimum of 15 percent to accounting. They also required, within the general education portion of a student's program, the study of "probability theory and statistics" (presumably, a minimum of one course). The 45 percent estimate is a minimum.

   In April 1991, the AACSB adopted new accreditation standards that are difficult to compare to the old, but it appears that they lower the prescribed business/accounting requirements to roughly 30 percent of undergraduate work, while tallying up to 15 credits of math and economics courses under institutional general education requirements (American Assembly of Collegiate Schools of Business, 1991).

8. When it comes to distinctly labeled courses that treat the imaginative expressions of culture, there is a raucous critical tradition that says, "If you have to label it that way, it cannot be any good." There *is* "high art" and "low art," but the difference

between the two does not refer to cultural labels. The criteria, in part, include the empirical judgment of whether the *teaching* of the art—the method of passing the art from generation to generation within a culture—has been systematized and institutionalized, and whether practitioners can tell us what they do. If these conditions are met within any cultural tradition, the art has been elevated. Music offers some of the best examples. There are folk music traditions everywhere, some of which have been adopted by religious or public ceremonies. But until these traditions are taught systematically, self-consciously, and formally, they have not been canonized by their own cultures. Fifty years ago, for instance, the blues was treated as folk music. Today, it is taught: scales, riffs, and extended forms. In part because the teaching of the blues has been systematized, because there are rules, music students know the difference between good blues and lousy blues and can illustrate with both composition and performance. Yes, tactile and aural senses play a significant role in that illustration, but the illustration is also discursive. An expert can now pass on the tradition of the blues to a student by means that go beyond mere imitation. The form has been canonized.

End Table 5A. Students Completing Undergraduate Courses in
Six Cultural Literacy Clusters, 1972–1984.

Cluster and course category	All students earning >10 credits[a]	All students earning bachelor's degree[b]	All students earning 45+ credits but no bachelor's degree[c]
1. Introductory studies in Western culture and society			
Literature (general)	20.7%	31.1%	16.7%
Poetry (general, introductory)	2.4	3.8	1.7
Fiction (general, introductory)	7.3	12.0	4.8
Drama (introductory, general dramatic literature)	2.5	4.1	1.7
Western civilization, world history, modern history	22.1	29.3	20.2
U.S. history surveys	32.1	42.1	32.4
U.S. government and politics	26.2	35.9	25.5
American civilization	4.7	6.6	4.4
2. Advanced studies in Western culture and society			
Eastern European studies	0.1	0.1	0.0
European studies (general)	0.8	1.3	0.3
Russian studies	0.5	0.9	0.2
Scandinavian studies	0.2	0.2	0.0
Western European studies	0.1	0.3	0.0
Canadian studies	0.2	0.3	<0.1
Russian (advanced/literature)	0.2	0.4	0.1
German (advanced/literature)	1.0	1.8	0.4
Scandinavian languages	0.1	0.2	<0.1
French (advanced/literature)	1.5	3.0	0.3
Italian (advanced/literature)	0.1	0.2	0.0
Portuguese (advanced/literature)	<0.1	0.1	0.0
Spanish (advanced/literature)	1.6	2.7	0.9
Classical literature	3.5	6.2	1.3
Bible as literature	0.9	1.5	0.6
Bible studies (theology)	7.9	11.6	5.8
Comparative literature (Western)	3.0	5.7	1.0
American literature	14.0	23.1	9.1
English literature	10.0	16.5	5.9
Shakespeare	3.9	7.1	1.5
Literary history/criticism	1.1	1.9	0.4
History of philosophy (general)	0.9	1.6	0.5
History of philosophy (ancient)	1.1	1.8	0.7
History of philosophy (modern)	0.8	1.5	0.4
Contemporary philosophy	1.2	2.1	0.4

End Table 5A. Students Completing Undergraduate Courses in
Six Cultural Literacy Clusters, 1972–1984, Cont'd.

Cluster and course category	All students earning >10 credits[a]	All students earning bachelor's degree[b]	All students earning 45+ credits but no bachelor's degree[c]
Religion (Christianity)	2.1	3.4	1.4
Religion (Judaism)	0.5	0.9	0.2
History of psychology	1.0	1.7	0.4
History of economic thought	0.5	0.9	0.2
Geography of North America	2.2	3.8	1.1
Geography of Europe/USSR	0.3	0.6	0.1
Intellectual/cultural history (European)	1.5	2.5	0.9
Economic/business history	1.5	2.7	0.7
History of science/technology	1.3	2.4	0.4
U.S. history topics (to 1860)	2.4	4.4	0.9
U.S. history topics (from 1860)	1.4	2.6	0.4
U.S. intellectual/cultural history	1.6	2.8	0.8
U.S. state/local/regional history	3.8	6.1	2.6
U.S. history (other topics)	3.1	5.5	1.6
European history to Renaissance	1.5	2.7	0.8
European history (Renaissance to 1789)	2.8	5.1	1.0
European history since 1789	3.7	6.3	1.9
European history (individual countries)	2.8	5.0	1.2
European history (other)	2.3	3.9	1.1
U.S. Constitutional law/history	3.4	5.6	1.9
European government and politics	1.1	2.1	0.4
Political behavior/parties	1.9	3.5	0.6
U.S. foreign policy/diplomacy	1.6	3.1	0.8
U.S. state/local government/politics	4.5	6.7	3.9
History of drama/theater	5.1	7.6	3.8
Art history (general)	15.6	22.2	13.9
History of architecture	0.9	1.5	0.6
Music history (classical)	1.3	2.3	0.6
Music history (opera/musical theater)	0.2	0.4	0.1
Classical Greek	0.6	1.0	0.3
Classical Latin	0.8	1.3	0.5
3. Studies in non-Western culture and society			
African studies	0.7	1.1	0.4
Asian studies (general)	0.6	1.0	0.2
East Asian studies	0.7	1.2	0.3
Latin American studies	1.1	1.7	0.5
Middle Eastern studies	0.5	0.8	<0.1

End Table 5A. Students Completing Undergraduate Courses in
Six Cultural Literacy Clusters, 1972–1984, Cont'd.

Cluster and course category	All students earning >10 credits[a]	All students earning bachelor's degree[b]	All students earning 45+ credits but no bachelor's degree[c]
Pacific area studies	0.2	0.3	0.0
South Asian studies	0.1	0.3	0.1
Southeast Asian studies	0.1	0.3	<0.1
African languages	0.1	0.1	0.1
Chinese (elementary/intermediate)	0.3	0.5	0.2
Chinese (advanced)	<0.1	0.1	<0.1
Japanese (elementary/intermediate)	0.2	0.3	0.2
Japanese (advanced)	0.1	0.1	0.1
Other East Asian languages	<0.1	<0.1	0.0
Arabic (elementary/intermediate)	0.1	0.2	0.0
Arabic (advanced)	<0.1	<0.1	0.0
Modern Hebrew (advanced/literature)	0.1	0.2	0.0
Indic languages	<0.1	0.1	<0.1
Comparative literature (non-Western)	0.6	1.1	0.4
Non-Western philosophy	0.5	0.8	0.3
Non-Western religions	1.1	2.0	0.4
Non-Western peoples (anthropology)	0.3	0.5	0.1
Native American (North and South) peoples	0.7	1.1	0.5
Economic development	0.5	0.9	0.3
Geography of Africa/Near East	0.2	0.4	0.1
Geography of Asia/Pacific	0.2	0.3	0.2
Geography of Latin America/Caribbean	0.3	0.5	<0.1
Asian history	1.7	2.9	1.0
African history	0.6	1.0	0.3
Latin American history	1.2	1.9	0.8
History of other world regions (for example, Oceania, Near East)	0.9	1.6	0.5
Non-Western government and politics	1.0	1.8	0.3
Third World sociology	0.4	0.6	0.2
Non-Western art	0.7	1.1	0.4
Non-Western music	0.2	0.3	<0.1
4. Minority and Women's Studies			
African-American/black studies	2.3	3.1	1.8
Native American studies	1.7	2.9	1.2
Hispanic-American studies	1.0	1.3	1.1
Asian-American studies	0.1	0.1	0.1
Other ethnic studies	0.8	1.6	0.3

**End Table 5A. Students Completing Undergraduate Courses in
Six Cultural Literacy Clusters, 1972–1984, Cont'd.**

Cluster and course category	All students earning >10 credits[a]	All students earning bachelor's degree[b]	All students earning 45+ credits but no bachelor's degree[c]
Bilingual/bicultural education	0.3	0.5	0.2
Native American languages	0.1	0.1	<0.1
African-American literature	0.9	1.3	0.8
African-American history	1.4	2.0	1.3
Sociology of race/minorities	3.1	5.0	2.1
African-American music	0.2	0.4	0.1
Women's studies	3.5	6.0	1.9

5. General culture and society: humanities studies[d]

Nonfiction prose/biography	0.7	1.0	0.5
Science fiction/fantasy	1.1	1.8	0.8
Folklore/mythology	1.1	2.0	0.4
Literature and film	0.6	1.0	0.2
Literature (other topics)	3.7	6.0	2.6
Interdisciplinary humanities	7.8	10.7	7.1
Interdisciplinary humanities and social sciences	1.1	1.7	0.8
Interdisciplinary humanities and arts	1.1	1.5	0.9
Introduction to philosophy	15.3	22.8	12.3
Ethics/moral philosophy	6.6	10.5	4.7
Aesthetics/philosophy of art	0.8	1.4	0.4
Metaphysics/epistemology	1.1	1.9	0.5
Philosophy of language	0.5	0.9	0.2
Philosophy of education	0.9	1.7	0.5
Philosophy of science	0.8	1.5	0.2
Philosophy of religion	1.1	1.7	0.8
Religion (general/comparative)	7.5	12.3	5.0
Religious ethics/morality	0.5	0.9	0.2
Religion and philosophy (other topics)	1.1	2.0	0.3
History of religion	1.4	2.3	0.9
Historiography	1.0	1.9	0.4
Political theory/ideology	2.9	5.3	1.3
Social theory	2.0	3.6	0.8
Visual and performing arts survey	2.3	3.3	2.2
Film arts/studies	3.0	5.0	1.8
Film history/theory/criticism	1.9	3.3	0.9
History of dance	0.2	0.3	<0.1
Music history and appreciation	10.9	16.0	8.9

**End Table 5A. Students Completing Undergraduate Courses in
Six Cultural Literacy Clusters, 1972–1984, Cont'd.**

Cluster and course category	All students earning >10 credits[a]	All students earning bachelor's degree[b]	All students earning 45+ credits but no bachelor's degree[c]
Music history (jazz)	1.2	1.8	0.7
Music history (pop/folk)	0.6	0.7	0.6

6. General culture and society: social sciences studies[d]

Mass communications	4.1	6.6	2.7
Public opinion/propaganda	0.6	1.3	0.2
Communication ethics/regulation	0.8	1.6	0.2
Introduction to education	4.9	7.9	3.2
Foundations of education (social, historical)	6.4	11.7	2.4
Shelter/housing (home economics)	0.3	0.6	0.1
Clothing/dress (home economics)	1.3	1.7	1.4
Linguistics	4.9	8.8	2.1
Popular culture	0.6	0.9	0.5
Science, technology, and society	2.5	4.3	1.2
Sports and leisure studies	1.1	2.0	0.4
Social psychology	10.8	17.3	8.0
General anthropology	10.8	16.6	8.4
Cultural anthropology/ethnology	7.5	11.4	5.9
Physical anthropology	2.6	3.7	2.5
Language, linguistics, and culture (anthropology)	0.4	0.5	0.2
Anthropology (readings/research)	0.2	0.3	<0.1
Anthropology (other topics)	0.9	1.6	0.5
Archaeology	1.3	2.4	0.4
Geography (general/introductory)	12.4	19.4	8.6
Cultural geography	1.7	2.6	1.2
Economic geography	1.1	1.8	0.9
Urban geography	0.6	1.1	0.2
International relations	3.5	6.2	1.7
Introductory political science	8.2	12.1	6.4
Comparative government and politics	1.9	3.3	1.1
Sociology of marriage and family	8.8	12.6	8.2
Sociology of youth, aging, death	1.9	3.2	1.3
Social change/movements	1.8	3.4	0.5
Social deviance/disorganization	10.5	15.3	9.1
Community/rural/urban sociology	2.3	3.9	1.3

**End Table 5A. Students Completing Undergraduate Courses in
Six Cultural Literacy Clusters, 1972–1984, Cont'd.**

Cluster and course category	All students earning >10 credits[a]	All students earning bachelor's degree[b]	All students earning 45+ credits but no bachelor's degree[c]
Social stratification/inequality	1.3	2.2	0.7
Urban studies	2.5	4.5	0.9

[a]The universe includes all NLS-PETS students who earned more than ten credits over the twelve-year period. N = 10,739. Weighted N = 1,540,849.

[b]The universe includes all NLS-PETS students who earned a bachelor's degree at any time over the twelve-year period. N = 5,127. Weighted N = 732,511.

[c]The universe includes all NLS-PETS students who earned forty-five or more credits but no bachelor's degree (though they may have earned an associate's degree). N = 2,948. Weighted N = 424,728.

[d]In this cluster, the course categories are either indeterminate—that is, they cannot be placed in any of the other clusters—or they cover general cultural and social material.

Chapter 6

Beyond the Paper Trail: Becoming an Adult in the 1970s

It's hard to read the gas meter in my basement. One has to negotiate through boxes and files stuffed with newspapers and stacks of magazines. There was a time, even before "The Day After," that the dreams of nuclear holocaust with which I grew up motivated me to save all this paper. I thought that if most of urban civilization perished, somewhere in a basement would lie enough history to reconstruct recent times.

Reaching for the pull string of the light, I knock over a pile of *Rolling Stones*. From the top number, dated August 29, 1971, an eleven-year-old superstar named Michael Jackson stares. Inside, Hunter S. Thompson writes about the day a Los Angeles County sheriff's deputy fired a teargas bomb through the window of a bar in the barrio and killed *L.A. Times* columnist Ruben Salazar. Inside, Joe Eszterhas writes about the morning the Hell's Angels and The Breed went at each other at a motorcycle show in the Polish Women's Hall in Cleveland: twenty-nine were stabbed, and five died. There are reviews of George Lucas's sci-fi *THX 1138* and Carol King's *Tapestry*, interviews with Al Kooper of the original Blood, Sweat, and Tears and Jack Nicholson (*Five Easy Pieces* period), and ads for Simon & Garfunkel's "Bridge Over Troubled Water" and Richard Brautigan's novel *The Abortion*.

This issue of *Rolling Stone* appeared as the class of 1972 was entering its senior year of high school. The base-year survey of the NLS-72 had already been drafted. It asked whether people read magazines, newspapers, and books that were not assigned in school, but it did not ask which ones, nor which sections, nor with what interests. It asked how much television people watched but not what programs. And in the surveys that followed the base year, this line of questioning was dropped. We never tracked where people got their information, their basic media exposure. We know a lot more about what they studied in school and college, their academic and occupational knowledge, than we do about their knowledge of their proximate lives and times.

At their twenty-fifth reunion, the class of 1972 might play a little Trivial Pursuit. They could ask what they know or remember of the following items and, just as important, where their knowledge came from:

> *The Greening of America*
> Biafra
> Earth Day
> *Future Shock*
> Pentagon Papers
> Attica
> Idi Amin
> *Bury My Heart at Wounded Knee*
> fraggings
> Lordstown
> *Supermoney*
> Arthur Bremer
> Yom Kippur War
> White House plumbers
> Saturday Night Massacre
> *Fear of Flying*
> Fanne Foxe
> petrodollars
> Symbionese Liberation Army
> *Lives of a Cell*
> the Killing Fields

the Fernwood Flasher
the Freedom Train
Ragtime
tall ships
Soweto
the Gang of Four
Gary Gilmore
Kunta Kinte
the Bakke case
"I, Claudius"
Proposition 13
Saturday Night Fever
the MX
Three Mile Island
Pilgrim at Tinker Creek

This is a selective list, drawn from the newspapers and magazines in my basement from the 1970s. The class of 1972 should love
the challenge; they came of age in the age of lists and made Trivial
Pursuit the hottest selling board game since Monopoly. By the late
1970s, when folks got bored, they made, or read, lists. *Simon's List
Book* and *The Book of Lists* were on the best-seller list in 1977. And
the celebrity surfeit of the decade that produced *People* and *US* and
similar glossy accounts of lives in the fast lanes and lost lanes is also
a form of list making. If we think of the anything-goes talk show
as the national diversion of the 1990s, the media of lists played well
in the decade or so prior to the current age.

Though the history we possess of them extends to the mid
1980s, the members of the class of 1972 became adults in the 1970s.
Events, discoveries, and creations swirled around the three million
people in that class and influenced what they did, thought about,
and came to value. And what can be said of the three million in the
class of 1972 can also be said of the three million in each of the
classes of 1971, 1973, and 1974. The Trivial Pursuit list could continue for volumes. Each item is a pebble that ripples memory and
carries its own complex of associations.

In the high school graduating classes of the early 1970s, there
are twelve million people for whom the NLS-72 participants are

standing in. That is about 5 percent of the total population and 8 percent of the adult population of the United States today.[1] That is a lot of people who became chronological adults at roughly the same time and with similar experiences.

In some cases, the members of the class of 1972 and their immediate peers were themselves the creators of the traces and artifacts that collectively are part of the spirit of the age. The accounts given in the previous four chapters are all built from these traces and suggest much about the way we are. But these accounts took place against a tapestry of events. And it may be wise to order some of the major strands of the tapestry—principally of the 1970s but also of the early 1980s—to enlighten these accounts and draw out their hidden dimensions. As I noted in the first chapter, history by the numbers is strong, but it needs external guidance to turn numbers into stories.

What is it we remember about the seventies? That we started using "911" and got rid of Green Stamps? That Sadat went to Jerusalem and the United States gave up the Panama Canal? That we were still fighting over school busing? That the Force was with Us? That *Ms.* magazine began to change our language and our perception of gender reality? That we got *Lives of a Cell, The Gulag Archipelago,* and *Ragtime?* That we bought locking gas caps, wore WIN buttons, and watched O. J. Simpson running through airports instead of the defensive secondary? These are fragments; they are not strands in a tapestry.

Economic Life

While our fragments of memory may be strong, we would strain to connect them to the information in the archive of the NLS-72. The stories told in this collection are dominated instead by themes that are broadly economic. Even the story of cultural literacy is ultimately an economic account because it views the knowledge stores being acquired and distributed as commodities and investments that help individuals negotiate the world.

How Much Did You Pay?

While our use of the term *economic* has been broader than the production and acquisition of goods and services, to flesh out the story of the class of 1972 we might reflect on its "economic" experience in the narrower sense of what happened in the nation's refrigerators and bank accounts. Table 6.1 may prod memories. Did everyone here hoard coffee and sugar in 1980? (In constant dollars, you paid less for both of them in 1991 than you did in 1972.) Did those who could afford the minimum get the fabulous 13 percent

Table 6.1. Economic Indicators During the Twenty Years of Adult Life of the Class of 1972.

Indicator	Year				
	1972	1976	1980	1985	1991
Credit (billions of dollars)					
Domestic credit	990	1438	2146	3319	4264
Consumer credit	446	660	1039	1468	1813
Interest rates					
Prime rate	5.25%	6.84%	15.27%	9.93%	8.46%
Long bond	6.2	17.61	11.46	10.62	7.86
Certificate of deposit	N.A.	5.26	13.0	8.05	5.84
Price indices (1985 = 100)					
Stocks	58.6	55.0	64.7	100.0	214.6
Consumer prices	38.9	52.9	76.6	100.0	126.6
Wages (hourly workers in manufacturing)	39.9	54.7	76.2	100.0	117.3
Industrial production	70.5	74.8	87.7	100.0	112.3
Commodities					
Coffee (Brazil/N.Y., per 100 lbs.)	$52.57	$149.48	$208.79	$148.93	$72.88
Rice (New Orleans, per metric ton)	215.87	307.91	495.12	382.50	418.15
Sugar (New York, per 100 lbs.)	7.48	11.56	28.67	4.05	8.98
Silver (New York, per 100 troy oz.)	168.4	435.4	2057.8	614.2	404.0
Average college tuition, room, and board					
Public universities	$1,668	$2,067	$2,712	$4,146	$6,057
Private universities	3,512	4,715	6,569	11,034	17,663

Source: Adapted from *International Financial Statistics Yearbook, 1992*, 1993. (Table 6.1 is a composite of several tables in this publication.)

on a certificate of deposit that year (of course, in turn, you would have been paying 15 percent on your mortgage, refinanced at half that rate in 1993)? Did you line up to sell old quarters when the Hunt brothers cornered the silver market and sent prices through the roof (and in 1992, you might as well have used those quarters in soda machines), then borrowed $1 billion to pay off their loans in the first of the megamoney scandals of the 1980s? The volatility of daily economic life was considerable.

But some trends were relentless, and the twelve million in the high school graduating classes of the early 1970s egged them on. Consumption rose as investment fell, particularly after 1980, and we were besieged with little plastic cards to carry that consumption, from CBs to CDs—and the stuff that came in between: Nintendo, camcorders, pagers, VCRs, boom boxes, cellular phones, remote control. The Census Bureau classifies this stuff in the same category with "durable toys," and census data show it was one of the most significant categories of expansion in personal consumption in the 1970s (U.S. Bureau of the Census, 1980, p. 553). By 1977, our middle-class consumerism was branded "techno-pop" (for the anti-techno-pops, we had hang gliders). Stock investments may have outscored consumer prices by a modest amount but lost out to the expansion of consumer credit (and later, to the junk bonds that were the detritus of leveraged buyouts).

In other words, we also borrowed more than we earned. In an epiphanic moment in 1977, everyone went to see the touring King Tut exhibit and bought Tut-o-Stuff courtesy of Visa, Master Card, et al. If the Hunt brothers could borrow $1 billion, what was a few hundred for Tut on plastic? Arthur Laffer, lecturing around the country in 1979 on his Laffer curve, told us it was all right. The pitch turned out to be a curve ball: the class of 1972 and its peer classes learned to borrow too well. But they were well prepared to rationalize their behavior: one out of four had studied accounting, personal finance, or consumer economics by the time they were thirty, and a nonduplicative 21 percent had studied general economics in college. The amount of financial knowledge in the households of this generation was considerable. There is no excuse for the chasm of debt.

The debt trend helped put higher education on credit cards,

too, except it was a federal credit card, and a lot of folks ran away from the debt. By 1977, student loan defaults hit $700 million, and people started to notice why the phenomenon was escalating. As one of our mass news magazines put it, "One of the largest groups of defaulting students are those who borrowed to attend proprietary, vocational, or technical schools. Although the students may have committed themselves to a large tuition payment, many lose interest after a short time, drop out, and ignore both the tuition and the loan. Federal officials say also that some operators of these schools recruit indigent students, promising them wealth and success through education" ("Study Now, Pay Never," 1977, p. 95). While I have not talked too much about them, about 3 percent of the high school class of 1972 attended proprietary and vocational schools, were far more likely to borrow than their peers, and were far less likely to earn credentials.[2] It is highly unlikely that people who do not earn credentials will pay back loans. As an antidote, though too late for the class of 1972, former Johns Hopkins President Steven Muller proposed in 1978 that we develop a universal national service program connected to federal financial aid. Sound familiar?

Inflation, of course, was the devouring monster to beat in the late 1970s and early 1980s, and real estate, everyone was told, was the way to beat it. By 1979, 57 percent of the class of 1972 owned their homes; by 1986, 65 percent. That means only 8 percent added home ownership to their economic accomplishments between the ages of twenty-six and thirty-two. The chances that anyone with children could buy a home after that point in time diminished considerably in the face of a 60 percent increase in the cost of a private college education (and a 46 percent increase for a public college education) between 1985 and 1991 alone (Table 6.1). No real estate could keep up with that.

Petromania

The biggest traditional economic story in the experience of the class of 1972 as journeymen adults was energy and its correlate, environmental consciousness. The story started in 1973 after the Yom Kippur War. Watching in the papers as various Arab states doubled the prices on crude oil, there was a day in late October when I filled a forty two-gallon drum with 44-cents-a-gallon gasoline and rolled it into a garage (you could do this in rural America at the time), fearful of being stuck without fuel at the end of an icy country road in December. This story was not confined to bizarre fuel acquisition behaviors, of course. By 1975, the word *petrodollars* had entered our vocabulary, and the news was taken up with stories of the megarich of the Middle East, who bought castles all over Europe and large chunks of big-name companies everywhere. The Shah of Iran was planning to rebuild the ancient city of Persepolis as a monument to wealth, and OPEC was the only acronym everyone knew without deciphering. But within a year, the trans-Alaska pipeline was opened, and we let ourselves fall asleep over energy (at the same time we watched one of our own states, not some Middle Eastern country, being drowned by oil money).

By 1979, we were back in the energy hole, driven there by the Shah's exile, Iranian chaos, and the Ayatollah Khomeini. We lined up for gasoline on the odd-even plan (determined by the last digit of our license plates), while we listened to that regular feature of the all-news stations, Sheik Yamani. Everyone talked investment in other sources of energy, but the Three Mile Island nuclear plant accident precluded one of the most prominent. *The China Syndrome*, filmed before the accident, became a coincidental smash hit. Demonstrators with placards that yelled "No Nukes" were not about bombs. Insulation and smaller cars sold well. Folks turned off lights, lowered thermostats, started washing clothes in cold water, and discovered heat pumps and solar panels (aided, of course, by a convenient tax credit).

Within a year, some people figured out that the only way to beat energy inflation was to find stocks in oil-related companies that would be bought out within weeks, or move to Texas, where everybody was rich. Thus began two ominous trends of the 1980s: buyouts and their related scandals, and volatility in regional economic wealth. By the mid 1980s, when oil prices had plummeted to pre-Ayatollah levels and the personal computer was becoming both an office and a household staple, the oil rigs were rusting in the Houston channels, and Boston and Silicon Valley had become the new homes of the nouveau riche.

The Actuarial Society

At the beginning of the period covered by the class of 1972 archives, the road-show cultural revolutionist, Jerry Rubin, advised everyone to *Do It!* By 1986, the last year of the archives, Jerry Rubin was just another stockbroker, and "doing it" means socking some more into that IRA. Indeed, the magazines and newspapers in my basement that chronicle the economic events of the late 1970s and early 1980s carried an inordinate amount of advertising space devoted to retirement. Banks, mutual funds, real estate agents, and insurance companies fought in hundreds of column inches over people's retirement accounts, retirement clubs, and retirement residences. The electronic waves were full of the same phenomenon. We seemed driven by the question, first raised by the Beatles, whether anyone will still need us or feed us when we're sixty-four. We became a society of actuaries, spending a disproportionate energy figuring out how long people were likely to live and orienting ourselves to the end of the life span. Becoming sixty-four was more significant to us than becoming twenty-four or thirty-four. The rite of passage was eclipsed by the rites of stasis and decline.

An economy geared primarily toward retirement and the passive investments that anticipate retirement—not the active investment years of learning life and working life—was not likely to generate real wealth for all our citizens. The secondary consequences of the dominance of retirement in our national economic consciousness was to relegate young adults to the status of producers and consumers of little more than health foods and electronic games. The actuarial society simultaneously became a society of yogurt, even if it had more calories (Hennessee, 1976). It was as if young adults were headed for Condominium City at age 34, receiving birthday greetings and a case of whatever made that 130-year-old in Armenia 130. The class of 1972 kept the yogurt but eventually tuned the actuarial society out. They tried to do better by studying more. To become a registered rep, after all, even Jerry Rubin had to go back to school and pass an industry licensing examination.

Trying to Do Better

Perhaps they were motivated to do so by the mire of recession, with big-name companies walking into Chapter 11 bankruptcy proceed-ings as if they were merely sneezing: AM International (née Addressograph-Multigraph), Braniff, International Harvester. And what corporations did, individuals mimicked. The recession that greeted the 1980s—and its aftermath—was not much kinder. The stories of forty-three exemplary corporations told in 1982 by Peters and Waterman in their best-selling *In Search of Excellence* turned out to be anything but uplifting in light of subsequent history. By 1987, twenty-nine of those exemplary companies had experienced exemplary trouble (Pascale, 1990).

One response was to figure out how to do better, irrespective of the business cycle, and Total Quality Management (TQM) became the lingering answer. By 1991, the generation of the class of 1972 was devoting more time in its nondegree education and training to courses in quality control, TQM, human resource development, and allied subjects than in any other field (see Table 6.2). In a way, this trend is a by-product of the content of this cohort's formal education. The undergraduate course-taking patterns of the generation drive toward working with paper and people more than ideas and things. At age thirty-two, 45 percent of those who had earned at least sixty college credits but no degree higher than the bachelor's[3] were working in occupations dominated (in their judgment) by people interactions, and another 16 percent were in occupations dominated by paper. Job skills (such as adaptability and supervising), attitudes (such as promptness, honesty, and loyalty), and interpersonal skills appear to be valued more than knowledge of a field in the culture of the service and distribution economy reflected in occupations such as nursing, school teaching, sales, banking, and management, in marked contrast to the culture of a primary manufacturing economy. Service and distribution industries involve more management of people, paper, and communication systems that interact with customers. The customer, we are told, is what TQM is ultimately about.

Technology in the Cottage

We can infer from the self-reports of the class of 1972 at thirtysomething that the occupations dominated by work with ideas *and* things were in science, technology, and (not so surprisingly, if you

Table 6.2. Courses Taken by Adults Aged Thirty-Six to Thirty-Nine,
Who Were Not Full-Time Students or Degree-Seeking Students, in 1991.

	Mean total class hours	Percent women	Percent of all courses	Percent of students
All students	12.0	54.8%	100.0%	N.A.
Course clusters				
Computers and software	14.9	53.1%	7.9%	15.6%
Marketing/sales	17.2	45.5	6.3	12.2
First aid/safety	8.8	51.9	5.7	12.8
Business/finance	12.9	39.8	4.4	9.9
Administrative support	10.3	60.9	3.9	9.2
Education	11.7	77.0	3.8	7.3
Health technology and services	9.6	75.7	3.5	7.6
TQM, human resource development, general management	20.0	38.6	3.4	8.1
Basic skills	5.1	63.5	2.9	7.3
Writing and speaking	6.2	61.5	2.7	5.9
Human services	7.0	69.5	2.7	5.7
Nursing	19.2	94.2	2.4	6.0
Law	7.5	38.4	2.3	3.2
Health professions/sciences	11.2	47.6	2.3	4.0
Theology/church	19.7	68.6	2.2	5.2
Mechanics/repair	14.1	3.8	2.2	3.9
Precision production	19.5[a]	14.9	2.1	3.4
Interpersonal relations	8.5	62.7	2.0	4.9
Health information	8.3	71.8	1.9	4.4
Social sciences	6.0	65.2	1.8	3.8
Self-awareness/self-improvement	7.4	61.6	1.7	3.7
Accounting	7.7	45.9	1.7	3.3
Psychology	10.6[a]	74.2	1.7	3.6
Engineering/architecture	22.7[a]	10.1	1.6	3.8
Transportation trades	11.0	24.5	1.6	3.1
Personal services	8.2	88.3	1.6	4.0
Visual/performing arts	4.9	66.6	1.5	3.7
Police/fire/military	15.5[a]	16.9	1.3	2.7
Health activities	5.5	65.4	1.2	3.1
Math (college-level)	6.0	50.8	1.2	2.7
Personal finance/career development	8.6	52.7	0.9	2.1
Humanities	3.8	69.6	0.9	2.5
Agriculture/natural resources	12.3[a]	37.8	0.9	2.0
Sciences/science technologies	8.5[a]	52.7	0.8	2.0
Construction trades	9.9	12.7	0.7	2.0
Bible studies	3.4	61.4	0.7	1.6
Foreign languages	2.8	52.9	0.6	1.5
Crafts	10.1[a]	95.7	0.6	1.0

Table 6.2. Courses Taken by Adults Aged Thirty-Six to Thirty-Nine,
Who Were Not Full-Time Students or Degree-Seeking Students, in 1991, Cont'd.

	Mean total class hours	Percent women	Percent of all courses	Percent of students
Graphics/printing/commercial art	14.6[a]	48.5	0.5	1.1
Leisure activities	6.3[a]	56.4	0.5	1.4
Other, unknown	15.3	52.0	11.4	26.9

Note: The source for this table is the 1991 National Household Education Survey.
Weighted N = 16.5 million.
[a]High standard error.

think about it) entertainment. Cometh the microchip. In 1976, word processing equipment went big time with big disks and music synthesizers began to appear on the market. Both changed their environments dramatically, as the quantity of textual and musical information stored and ease of revision increased and multiplied the effects of interactions between people and machines. The disks were gone in less than a decade, but electronic instruments have become more varied and sophisticated.

By the end of 1979, there were 400,000 computers in use in the United States. But for all practical purposes, the class of 1972 got computer religion, along with everyone else, starting in 1983, when a basic IBM system with a clunky letter-quality printer ran about $3,000 (for that price in 1993, you could buy a rocket ship with enough accessories to control a small planet). For less than $1,000, NLS-72 adults could play games at home. They learned the hardware glossaries, from *CPU* to *daisy wheel,* and they played "Frogger" while they tried to convince themselves that it was all easier than they thought.

What did it take to be ready for this? What level of education was necessary for young adults to adapt to the changes the computer wrought in the workplace and home? How friendly did the software have to be for most of the class of 1972? The people who studied real computer science (as opposed to generalized computer literacy) between 1972 and 1983 could not avoid analyses of hardware or systems software programming. They were better prepared for the advent of PCs than those who later inherited software packages that left no room for mistakes. In Table 6.3, the reader will note a skew-

Table 6.3. Percentage of Courses NLS-PETS Students Took in Selected Fields, 1972-1984.

Courses	Year									
	1972	1973	1974	1975	1976	1977	1978	1979	1980	1981-1984
All courses	11.3	20.2	17.1	15.0	15.5	6.7	4.6	3.6	2.5	3.7
Course cluster:										
U.S. government and Constitutional law	11.7	30.0	22.2	13.8	8.3	5.2	3.3	2.2	1.6	2.7
Environment[a]	8.4	18.1	18.1	19.1	13.9	7.3	4.9	3.8	2.4	4.0
Agriculture, forestry, and environment	6.3	14.5	16.9	20.4	17.8	8.6	5.3	3.7	2.3	4.2
Architecture and urban planning	4.6	11.1	15.9	17.7	18.0	11.1	6.0	4.3	4.5	6.8
Engineering	4.3	10.5	15.1	21.3	18.2	7.2	9.2	4.2	3.3	6.7
Computer Science	6.3	16.2	16.7	14.1	10.7	6.7	5.8	6.5	4.3	12.6
Education	1.9	7.0	16.8	25.2	18.7	9.6	6.1	5.0	3.7	6.0
Accounting	5.2	15.3	19.4	18.2	13.5	7.7	6.3	5.1	3.6	5.6
Psychology[b]	10.9	22.3	19.6	16.7	11.7	6.0	3.9	3.1	2.4	3.4

Note: The universe includes all NLS-PETS students who earned any credits between 1972 and 1984. $N = 12,339$. Due to rounding, not all rows total 100%.

[a]Includes environmental studies, environmental sciences, all natural resources, forestry and conservation, ecology, and marine biology/limnology.

[b]Includes both disciplinary courses in psychology and applied psychology/personal development courses.

ing in the patterns of course taking in computer science over the twelve years of college records of the class of 1972: a higher percentage of those courses was taken toward the end of that period than was the case for other fields. In light of economic history, this makes sense. It also makes sense that the trend continued across the whole population of the NLS-72. When they were asked in the 1986 follow-up survey about the fields in which they would seek further education or training, 22 percent of those responding named computer technology. That field ran second to business/accounting and far ahead of any other field. By 1991, computer and software training ranked number one among the 35 percent of the generation who took courses outside of degree programs (see Table 6.2).

The View to the East

In early 1983, Atari closed one of its major U.S. plants and moved 1,700 jobs to Hong Kong. It was a symbolic moment in a trend that combined the coming of the microchip and our consumerism, debt, and romance with the smaller as better.

At the beginning of the 1970s, our international eyes were turned uncomfortably East, exclusively focused on Vietnam. In February 1972, in the second most significant act of his presidency, Richard Nixon had tea with Chairman Mao, in Beijing. One-fifth of the globe came out of a long shadow, and our eyes adjusted with wonder to its size and complexity. Just how big a world was revealed to us when Mao died in 1976: the funeral ceremony in Tienanmen Square was attended by one million people. Just how complex a world was revealed when we forgot Vietnam but China did not and invaded in 1978, teaching that tribalism is more potent than ideology. It took until 1979 before China started to crack. At Democracy Wall, posters challenged orthodoxies, Mao was declared 70 percent right, a bourgeoisie flourished, teenagers went steady, Coca-Cola inevitably arrived in Hunan province, and a daytime TV love soap called "Five Flowers" drew more watchers than Mao reruns. Between 1972 and 1985, while the number of U.S. high school graduates declined by 11 percent (Snyder, 1992, p. 107), enrollments in high school Chinese language classes increased by 209 percent (Moore, 1992, p. 5).

In 1974, on the island of Lubang in the Philippines, the last soldier of the Japanese imperial army of World War II came out of the jungle and surrendered, but only after his former commanding officer was flown in from Tokyo with documentary proof of the official surrender. In the same year, Motorola stopped making televisions and sold its television manufacturing business to Matsushita, documentary proof of an unofficial surrender. The U.S. trade deficit with Japan was a paltry $2 billion. By 1977, it was $8 billion and headed for infinity.

Between the Saigon "baby lift" in 1975 and the end of the decade, the United Nations counted more than a million Indochinese refugees. A quarter of them had come to the United States, and more were on the way. Communities of Hmong from Cambodia sprang up in such unlikely places such as Racine, Wisconsin, and St. Paul, Minnesota, and Little Saigons began to change the face of metropolitan neighborhoods. Urban sociologists call this "invasion and succession." Of all changes to the U.S. population during the years in which the class of 1972 journeyed into adulthood, there was no more significant change than in the Asian American component. One can count the diverse people who make up the census category of "Asian American/Pacific Islander" in the class of 1972, but the number is too small to stand alone in analyses with any statistical power. In the data in this book, they are usually aggregated with whites on the grounds of similarity in schooling and educational attainment. Aggregations, however, are often deceiving. We are really not going to know much about the full diversity of this population category until the longitudinal study that began with eighth graders in 1988 (NELS-88) has run its course.

The diversity of population changes in U.S. society is the first of two reasons for citing the view to the East as a major thread in the tapestry on which the class of 1972 journeyed. Social diversity, particularly when accompanied by minority language cultures, can be a powerful educative force. In this case, we had grown accustomed to thinking that there were only three minority groups in the United States (one of which, Native Americans, lived largely in special geographical divisions) and that the world could be neatly divided and social conflicts addressed in fairly simple ways. When the landscape became more complex, it was unlikely that the education received by the class of 1972, both in and out of the classroom, was sufficient to deal with it.

My second reason for citing the view to the East is our nation's paranoid fascination with the power of the Japanese educational and economic engines, particularly when Japanese corporations replaced Middle East oil lords as the buyers of the West. In an unhappy paradox, we were willing to be beaten by oil, but we resented being beaten by organization, discipline, and education. The class of 1972 and its peers were struggling to advance in the economy at a time when, as a nation, we seemed to lose two games in a row. Throughout the 1980s, critiques of U.S. education inevitably cited Japanese performance as a benchmark. The pounding of these critiques in the media was relentless and had to have taken its toll on the self-confidence of young adults in the United States who had succeeded in education by all our traditional measures. Becoming an adult, a trajectory that involves the challenge of greater self-consciousness and self-assessment, thus involved coming to terms with public ambiguity about the strength of one's own skills and knowledge.

Social and Psychic Life

An inherited tension between self-awareness and self-knowledge, on the one hand, and social and community orientation on the other challenged young adults in the 1970s. The demands of belonging and responding in the late 1960s had been stressful. The world would not let you alone: you had to be part of something, you had to take ideological risks, and by the early 1970s, people were burned out of belonging and risks. Backing away from communities, I think, was partly a reaction to the increase of violence in social interactions. When Woodstock became Altamont, it was time for something else: a retreat first to self and the interior life, then friends, and ultimately a different way to deal with community, the ensemble.

Perhaps the class of 1972 was also numbed by violence. The 1970s started with the killing fields going to Cambodia, civil wars in Jordan and Nigeria, civil war in Pakistan leading to the birth of Bangladesh, near–civil war in Northern Ireland. The senior year of

the class of 1972 saw the despair of the last months of U.S. involvement in Vietnam: carpet bombing, heroin, fraggings. By mid-
decade, Beirut began to burn, and torture escalated in Pinochet's
Chile. By the end of the decade, we had also seen civil wars in
Nicaragua, Rhodesia, Angola, and Afghanistan. During the decade,
too, everybody shot everyone else: Arthur Bremer shot George Wal-
lace; Palestinian terrorists shot the Israeli Olympic wrestling team;
Italian terrorists kidnapped and then shot Premier Aldo Moro and
left his body in the trunk of a car; John Hinkley shot Ronald Reagan and Jim Brady; Gary Gilmore got drunk one night in Utah,
shot a motel clerk (Gilmore had killed a gas station attendant the
previous night), and asked to die for his crimes; and the Reverend
Jim Jones's followers shot Congressman Leo Ryan and three news
reporters on an airstrip in Guyana before their mass suicide by
cyanide-laced Kool Aid. Hijackings and hostages became international pastimes, and letter bombs and airport bombs at rush hour
a new form of casual terror.

Television was the messenger of this violence, and the percentage of the population getting most of its news from television
programs rose from 60 to 67 percent between 1970 and 1978 (U.S.
Bureau of the Census, 1980, p. 552). Mean TV watching time for the
entire population rose from two hours and fifty minutes at the
beginning of 1971 to three hours and eight minutes at the end of
1978, and the increase was even greater for those who had attended
college (U.S. Bureau of the Census, 1980, p. 561). The folks we saw
in the NLS-PETS, then, were increasingly exposed to blood. The
movies reinforced these news images, from *The French Connection*
through *Taxi Driver* and the first cinematic attempts to describe and
understand Vietnam in *The Deer Hunter* and *Apocalypse Now*. By
1983, the movie *Scarface* was given an X rating, not for sex, but for
violence. How did people cope?

The Interior Life

Accepting an honorary doctorate from Harvard in 1978, Alexander
Solzhenitsyn told us that our commercialism had "suffocated . . .
spiritual life." Not quite. We had reinterpreted what was spiritual
and, of course, commercialized it. From their beginnings, the 1970s

were an age of alternative interior and spiritual life. Part of what
we spiritualized and commercialized was terror. That is, we took
violence and made it so extreme in fiction that it could reside in a
mythological universe. In 1973, a disgusted Stephen King threw the
manuscript of *Carrie* in the trash. His wife retrieved it, and four
million copies later, we had a one-person industry to carry us into
more terror. To balance this terror, we created the neon cocoon of
now, disco, where *Saturday Night Fever* and Donna Summer held
us in motion-without-mind. It was the age of est, human potential,
touching your feelings in an unmediated crowd, and mixtures of
Eastern spiritualities, transcendental meditation, Rolfing, enlightenment, and serenity.

One cannot trace alternative interior life in the formal records of the class of 1972. No one taught est in colleges, and to study
non-Western religions (as only 2.1 percent of bachelor's degree students and 1.1 percent of everybody did) did not mean joining them.
The data do indicate, however, that the formal study of the Bible
in a theological (as opposed to a historical or a literary) context by
this generation was considerable. And when the National Household Education Survey of 1991 asked people what they studied,
among those parallel in age to the generation of the early 1970s,
Bible study was the fifth most cited course (out of 265 categories).[4]
As in any complex environment of spiritualism, traditional aspects
of the interior life, such as Bible study, were also very visible. And
starting in the mid 1970s, seventy million American adults learned
from our president, Jimmy Carter, what seventy million others
knew already: the meaning of the religious experience of being born
again. The meaning was more than an interior event.

Friends and Ensembles

While only 5 percent of the college students in the class of 1972 took
credit-bearing courses with titles such as "Hello, Then What?" and
"Getting to Know You," by 1986, the class of 1972 regarded "having
strong friendships" as a more important goal in life than "the ability to give [one's] children better opportunities." The research of
Campbell and his colleagues points out that while the correlation
between satisfaction with family life and satisfaction with life in

general declined in the 1970s, the correlation between satisfaction with friendships and satisfaction with life rose dramatically. What were we saying? Friends form ensembles, small communities that are like families, but without the same intimacy or permanence or purpose. The ensemble of friends may have been the mode by which individuals pulled out of or balanced their interior lives, the way they recovered from real-world violence, discomfort, and mythological terror.

Television tells our values. The 1970s gave birth to the ensemble show as smash hit: "M*A*S*H," "Barney Miller," "Happy Days," "Welcome Back Kotter," "Saturday Night Live," and even "Sesame Street" are in this genre. They led us to "Night Court," "A Different World," "Hill Street Blues," "Cheers," and "LA Law." They superseded the variety show (an artifice), the single-hero show ("Perry Mason," "Man from UNCLE"), the comedienne-in-context show ("Lucy," "Rhoda"), the pairs shows ("I Spy," "Laverne and Shirley"). The only genre that rivaled the ensemble was the staple family show (Partridge, Brady, Huxtable, and Jefferson), celebrating another kind of community. In fact, community became something accessible on television in a way that it may have not been accessible in other aspects of our lives.

Simultaneously came the 1970s version of the 1990s computer bulletin boards and on-line talk groups, the resurrection of the telephone party line via Citizen's Band radio. The nation shelled out $1 billion for 4.5 million CB units and accessories in 1975 alone (Keyes, 1976). Betty Ford was the "First Mama," voices with nom-de-frequencies arranged everything from sex to crime to rescues, and people spoke in order to belong to something, however transient.

Coincidentally arriving at a time when people needed to feel better, too, was a three-year national community block party, the Bicentennial. Tall ships were everywhere. The Freedom Train chugged around the country carrying everything from George Washington's copy of the Constitution to Hank Aaron's bat. Revolutionary War battles were refought at Bennington and Saratoga, and the eighteenth century was celebrated in festivals on the Enlightenment in Connecticut and in magic shows in New York. For those who doubted that what President Gerald Ford called our "national nightmare" was over, there was nothing like the red evening clouds behind Ella Fitzgerald and Dizzy Gillespie and the tall ships anchored off Fort Adams in the Newport, Rhode Island harbor. Everyone was your friend. People did so earnestly want to have friends.

Cultural Drama: Plumbers and Leaks

"Well, you don't look like a cop. You're not a cop, are you?"

"No, I'm an ex-convict, as a matter of fact."

"No kidding," she said, perking up. "What were you in for? I did time myself."

"I was in for trying to steal part of the Constitution" [John Dean covering the 1976 Republican convention, 1976, p. 47].

Watergate was more than a political episode of the 1970s; it was an enveloping cultural drama in the coming of age of the class of 1972. The break-in itself occurred shortly after high school graduation day. When I visited the scene a few muggy days later as an aspiring journalist/commentator to interview some minor speech-writers about politics and the American language, I thought, with everyone else, that the whole story was a cheap grade D movie. Within a year, we found out that the issue wasn't the cheap movie, but the dear cover-up. "Saturday Night Massacre," "plumbers," "smoking guns," and "eighteen-minute gaps" became metaphors, grist for comedians, and staples of the cultural literacy dictionary we can use even today. Within two years, the class of 1972 was dragging out its tag-eared or never-opened copies of the *Federalist Papers*, taking formal courses in U.S. government and Constitutional law at a disproportionate rate (see Table 6.3), and getting— along with the rest of us—a course in values education delivered live on television by Sam Ervin. In terms of "enrollment," it was the largest class in U.S. history.

Watergate started with graffiti and wound up with arcane arguments over Constitutional language on virtually every page of the newspapers. The nation saw Spiro Agnew convicted of tax evasion, Richard Nixon pardoned (as expected) by his successor, and the other figures in the case (Mitchell, Erlichman, Haldeman, Liddy, Colson) stumbling out of prisons, hospitals, and indictments. The rot of Washington began to stink. The percentage of adults cynical about government leaped from 36 percent in 1972 to 50 percent in 1974 (Campbell, 1981, p. 245). In ironic response, *All the President's Men* was a smash, and everyone in politics seemed to be running for president. Birch Bayh, Henry Jackson, Lloyd Bentsen, Terry Sanford, Fred Harris, Sargent Shriver, Frank Church, Hubert Humphrey, Robert Dole, and the two who made it: Ronald Reagan and Jimmy Carter. The level of public cynicism about government rose even further: to 52 percent in 1978.

Approaching the 1976 election, 55 percent of nonvoters said that no matter who is elected, nothing works, so why bother? Half said that candidates are all the same, and 31 percent said they did not feel qualified to vote ("The Turned-Off Voter," 1976, p. 16). The class of 1972 felt and chose differently: roughly 70 percent registered to vote during the 1970s, and 90 percent of those registered said they did vote at some time. The highest rate of registration was among African Americans, and the highest rate of both registration and voting was that of white women (Burkheimer and Novak, 1981). By February 1986, 78 percent of the NLS-72 were registered to vote, 91 percent of this group said they had voted in the previous two years, and again, the highest rate of both registration and voting was among white women. These figures are well above national averages. About a third of the group said they frequently talked about public problems with friends and/or family, and a fifth had been involved in political campaigns in ways other than donating money. These figures are difficult to judge because they come from a single age cohort, but they should set a benchmark. They may be telling us that the spirit of ensembles carries over into the larger polity.

Higher Education in the Tapestry

Higher education was a prominent thread in the tapestry of the 1970s. To be sure, we see more of it in the archive of the class of

1972 than we do of work life, but there are other, objective reasons for playing the higher education card as noticeably as the archive allows. A significant expansion of the higher education enterprise occurred in the 1970s, and with it, interior changes in higher education's substance and culture. From a strictly economic point of view, by 1984, postsecondary education had become one of the largest industries in the United States, employing 2 percent of the work force, accounting for nearly 3 percent of the gross national product, and serving nearly 10 percent of the adult population at any one moment.

The New Traditional Student

This expansion also created a class of people to whom we applied the label "nontraditional students." With images of the 1950s and 1960s dancing in our heads, it was easy to see the dimensions of this new student landscape: more female, more minority, more part-time, and older. The data in Table 6.4 clearly demonstrate the changes in the demography of higher education from 1970 to the present. But with one exception, though, the most significant changes in the representation of "nontraditional students" had all transpired by 1980. The one exception is that of minorities, for whom the immigration of the late 1970s and early 1980s from the Pacific rim and Latin America began to show up in the demographics of higher education only in recent years. In general, the cohorts of the 1970s set the benchmarks against which we must now measure a new paradigm of "nontraditional." Through choice and circumstance, they became the new tradition.

Consumers Take Over

My memories of higher education in the late 1960s are dominated by the smells of sit-ins, the colors of graffiti, the sounds of fire engines. Kent State, Cesar Chavez, the Chicago Seven, the Harrisburg Seven, Angela Davis. The placards were here and everywhere, and every week a new set. "A Day in the Life" played in the background. Beyond the physical memories were the arguments for student autonomy, the new course proposal reviews, the push for

Table 6.4. Changes in the Portrait of "Traditional"
College Students, 1970-1991.

Student category	Year			
	1970	1976	1980	1991
All students				
Female[a]	41.2%	47.6%	52.0%	55.2%
Minority[a]	11.8[b]	15.7	16.5	21.2
Under twenty-five years old[a]	72.2	63.1[c]	62.5	58.2
Over thirty-four years old[a]	9.6	12.4[c]	11.8	17.9
Graduate students	N.A.	N.A.	N.A.	36.0
First professional	N.A.	N.A.	N.A.	11.8
Two-year college	N.A.	N.A.	N.A.	23.5
Part-time	32.2	38.8[c]	41.3	43.5
In four-year colleges	26.7	29.6[c]	29.4	30.6
In two-year colleges	47.0	55.6[c]	61.2	63.3
Undergraduates only				
Female[a]	42.3[d]	48.2	52.7	55.4
Minority[a]	[b]	16.6	17.3	22.1
Under twenty-five years old	N.A.	N.A.	N.A.	64.2
Over thirty-four years old	N.A.	N.A.	N.A.	15.6
Part-time	28.4[d]	36.0[d]	39.3[d]	40.1
In four-year colleges	20.1	22.9	23.9[d]	24.2
In two-year colleges	47.7[d]	58.6[d]	62.0[d]	63.3

Note: This table was constructed from data in Snyder, 1993, pp. 174, 177, 178, 180, 187, 188, 206, and Dearman and Plisko, 1981, p. 142.

[a]U.S. citizens only.

[b]Race/ethnicity data for 1970 are not comparable to those of later years. They cannot be estimated at all for the undergraduate population.

[c]1975 data.

[d]Includes unclassified undergraduate students.

relevance, the teach-ins. A new culture would reshape society. "Wooden Ships" (Jefferson Airplane version) played in the background.

By the time the class of 1972 was hitting its stride in college, Vietnam was slipping off the radar screen, Watergate was coming on, the bad guys were losing, the student protest books were on the remainder tables in the bookstores, and the fires had gone away. Watching the deepening recession around them and cut loose from the external symbols that held political communities together, these college students made choices dictated by economic survival, both current and future, or personal need. After accounting, try psychology. In 1973, the paperback mega-sellers were *Fear of Flying* and *Jonathan Livingston Seagull,* and the Grammy Song of the Year was "Killing Me Softly."

In the late 1960s, the producers of knowledge were very much in control of curricula, defining in their own way what was "relevant." Were we concerned with the urban crisis? Everything went urban. In 1970, I was one of a group of new faculty who rescoped one of the literature/humanities survey courses at the City College of New York as "The Writer/Artist and the City." The same stuff was there as before: Blake, Wordsworth, Dickens, Balzac, Zola, Dostoyevsky, into which we threw contemporary poets (Lawrence Ferlinghetti) and minority poets (Victor Cruz), contemporary dramatists (Edward Albee) and minority dramatists (Charles Gordone), and filmmakers (Sidney Lumet). The more ambitiously interdisciplinary faculty added social theory, urban history, history of city planning, and architecture. We walked city streets and learned to look at them the way artists and poets and archaeologists would look at them. I loved every minute of it, and some of the students did, too. But by 1975, it was all irrelevant. What was relevant was corporate finance. The faculty was no longer determining what was relevant: the consumers were really in control.

The result was economic dissonance, a system in which the mass of individuals made choices about schooling (length and content) along the paths of least resistance to jobs social mythology has led them to believe would guarantee a middle-class future. This future emphasized the consumption of marginal goods and services (techno-pop bought on plastic), and as we saw in the story of the women of the class of 1972, the reward of political behavior more than productive behavior. The higher education system came to prepare students for the immediate jobs they wanted, not for long-term personal growth and contributions to national productivity.

Interviewed in the *Saturday Review of Education* in the spring of 1973, labor economist Margaret Gordon noted an increased interest in the health professions among college graduates, claiming that these were "the only fields in which we have shortages" (Gordon, 1973, p. 39). She also cited agriculture, forestry, and architecture/city planning as fields of high student interest, pointed to education and engineering as fields of declining student interest, and claimed that the small business spirit and entrepreneurism among students were on the rise on campus. It is hard to see all of that from the course-taking distribution in the records of the class of 1972, but Gordon was not wholly wrong in terms of the *degrees* eventually awarded during the 1970s and early 1980s—the period during which the class of 1972 received about all the undergraduate degrees it was going to get[5] (see Table 6.5).

Table 6.5 reflects all degrees awarded no matter when people entered college. It is not based on a single cohort, though the distribution of degrees for the modal years for bachelor's degrees in the class of 1972 (1976 to 1978) is remarkably close to what the transcripts show. Remember that the choice of a major reflected in an earned degree was made at least two years prior to the award, and in some cases, long before that. So whatever Gordon saw in 1973 turns up in 1975-76. If we had annual course-taking data (very expensive to get, and not worth it), we could predict degree distributions even better.

Some fields are more sensitive to economic conditions than others, and the case of engineering in Table 6.5 illustrates two kinds of sensitivities. Through the mid to late 1970s, engineering was a cyclical field. Following the U.S. pullout from Vietnam in 1972 and

Table 6.5. Percentage of Bachelor's Degrees Awarded to Students in U.S. Colleges, in Selected Fields, 1970–1982.

Field	1970–71	1975–76	1977–78	1979–80	1981–82
Agriculture and natural resources	1.5%	2.1%	2.5%	2.5%	2.2%
Architecture and environmental design	0.7	1.0	1.0	1.0	1.0
Nursing and allied health professions	3.0	5.8	6.4	6.8	6.7
Business/management/ accounting	13.7	15.4	17.4	19.9	22.5
Education	21.0	16.7	14.8	12.7	10.6
Engineering and engineering technology	6.0	5.0	6.0	7.4	8.4

Source: Snyder, 1992, p. 262.

1973 and exacerbated by a recession in 1973 and 1974 (when the famous sign, "Would the last person to leave Seattle please turn out the lights?" appeared), engineering was simply not an economically attractive alternative for U.S. undergraduates. But notice that the field bounced back rather quickly and entered a phase of expansion. The proportion of engineering degrees expanded right through the 1981–82 recession to peak at 9.8 percent of all undergraduate degrees in 1984–85.

Why did this happen? First, because engineering became a preferred undergraduate degree for future business careers. As adults with a chunk of labor-market experience at age thirty-two, 35 percent of everybody in the class of 1972 said that if they were to recommend how an eighteen-year-old should prepare for a career in business, they would advise "a bachelor's degree in a technical field such as engineering or computer science." That 35 percent was the highest percentage registered, by far, for any option in the 1986 survey's hypothetical guidance session.[6] The class of 1972 was being smart here—a lot smarter than the increasing percentage of undergraduates who from 1970 through 1990 thought that the best way to go into business was to major in business. The perception that engineering education can lead in more directions than narrowly technical careers removed engineering, in part, from business-cycle effects. Second, the labor market for both computer engineering and biomedical engineering grew dramatically in the 1980s (National Science Foundation, 1984, 1992a, 1992b). These became glamour fields to the media. Teenagers with talent are not immune to glamour or to the tales of fabulous fortunes made by software designers and designer gene jockeys.

The Consumers Lose, or So It Was Said

As the stories of varsity athletes (Chapter Three) and community college students (Chapter Four) reminded us, though, becoming an adult involves outgrowing the lure of media glitz. It was a tough fight in the 1970s and is perhaps an even more difficult passage today. For the mass of college students do not have the talents of future biomedical engineers and are even less immune to the lure of glamour fields with light intellectual demands and heavy mythologies about labor-market demand.

For example, college communications departments, once rest homes for speech teachers or would-be applied psychologists, in the 1970s became boot camps for batallions of future midnight deejays, ten o'clock news sports reporters, and folks who sat behind panels of little lights waving fingers to indicate that someone was on the air. Of course, they all thought they were going to be network producers. In 1975, the National Association of Broadcasters reported that U.S. higher education was about to turn out 21,000 people with bachelor's and associate's degrees in broadcasting against a total work force of 142,000 (Carlisle, 1976, p. 50). More were in the queue for graduation later in the decade. In fact, by 1986, only 1.3 percent of the associate's and bachelor's degree recipients in the class of 1972 (about 10,000 people out of 800,000) worked for the broadcasting and motion picture industries. The majority were technicians or worked in the business offices on sales, advertising, and miscellaneous management tasks. Only 166 people (out of 800,000) wound up on the air as announcers, deejays, and so forth, and an equal number were employed as writers in those industries. It would not surprise me to find that, in their most candid moments, those who now sit behind panels of little lights will tell us that they did not need a college degree to do what they do. At least varsity athletes had more sense about the potential of making it to the "big show."

Economists expended much energy in the 1970s arguing over models that showed various saturation points for college graduates (O'Toole, 1975). They also argued over case studies indicating that, with the exception of the professions and some technical and managerial occupations, the knowledge demands of jobs traditionally taken by college graduates had been dumbed down (see, for instance, Berg and Freedman, 1977; Dresch, 1975) and that the returns on the investment of time (foregone earnings) and money in higher education had fallen (for example, Freeman and Hollomon, 1975). The higher education trade press became schizophrenic, alternating articles on increased demand for higher education with those predicting decline. The latter asked, in effect, how could people possibly behave in such an irrational manner as to seek higher education once they find out that the jobs they want are not there, that the jobs that are there do not require them to make the educational effort, and that, in any event, they would lose money in the long run? The industry would go into a depression; the demand for higher education would plunge.

Fortunately, economic models based on factors such as wage equilibrium and return on investment in education are published in journals that nobody reads. I have said it more than once: the class of 1972 has reminded us that people do make choices for irrational economic reasons, and that the model best governing human capital decisions is a supply-side model, not a demand-side model. That is, whether or not the specific labor-market demand is there for the knowledge and those skills you have developed through education, you bring that knowledge and those skills to the workplace. You can change the dynamics and boundaries of whatever job you take accordingly, or add education and training to the experience in a way that enables you to find a new path.

Remixing Finite Space

Indeed, despite later pessimism, the nation entered the 1970s with a conviction of the ever-expanding boundaries of higher education. We had moved to a mass educational system, and all those who wanted to go to college—and even some folks who did not want to go—were going to go. As the class of 1972 was about to graduate, both the old U.S. Office of Education and the Carnegie Commission on Higher Education projected an increase in total postsecondary enrollments from 8.5 million to 13.2 million by 1980 (Carnegie Commission on Higher Education, 1971; Simon and Frankel, 1972). Like most projections of enthusiasts, this was an overestimate. Despite the Basic Opportunity Grants (BOGs, later Pell Grants) and Sallie Mae (Student Loan Marketing Corporation) created that year, we fell short of the projection by 1.1 million students, in part because, as a consequence of the government's shifting federal aid from institutions to students, colleges felt freer to raise tuition (Wentworth, 1972) and priced some students out. It took another decade, and a lot of waste of educational opportunities, to reach the projection.

What do I mean by "waste"? Because we gave their history a long run, the class of 1972 also taught us a lesson in education accounting (raised in Chapters Four and Five): enrollments are not students. What we see in the long term are the same people cycling and recycling themselves through the system, with or without attaining academic credentials. Waste occurs in two different ways in the course of this churning. First, there are students who earn two years' worth of credits (sixty or more) but no credential of any kind. Let us call them the "sixty-plus" group. Eight percent of all NLS-72 students who continued their education after high school fell in this bin by age thirty to thirty-one, and minority students were disproportionately represented (12 percent of all African Americans and 12 percent of all Hispanics versus 7 percent of whites and Asian Americans who went to college). Second, there are the incidental students, who earn ten or fewer credits over a decade or more. Some 2.5 percent of all NLS-72 students who entered postsecondary education earned no credits at all; their transcripts consist of nothing but withdrawals, incompletes, and failures. Another 10.2 percent earned between one and ten credits.

These two groups are like the right and left tails of a standard distribution. On the one hand are the 13 percent who could not or did not want to make it at all. On the other hand are the 8 percent who demonstrated that they *could* make it—but didn't. In the present era (the 1990s) in which higher education budgets are getting tighter, an era in which we have a stated National Education Goal devoted to increasing postsecondary degree completion, and a public accounting system that pressures colleges and community colleges to increase graduation rates, which group is the better gamble? The "sixty-plus" group may have had a weaker academic background in secondary school than those who earned bachelor's degrees, but it was stronger than that of those who earned associate's degrees.[7] The "sixty-plus" group may have had a lower grade-point average in college (2.61) than either those who earned bachelor's degrees (2.98) or those who earned associate's degrees (2.86), but nobody in that group had an average less than C-, and 42 percent were carrying averages of B or better. They were no more likely to delay entry to postsecondary education than those who earned bachelor's degrees and were just as likely to have studied college-level math, computer science, and foreign languages as bachelor's degree recipients. Their academic profile may evidence struggle, but it is not the academic profile of noncompleters. It is time to do some triage. By concentrating our efforts on this second group, we can substantially reduce the twenty-point spread in degree completion rates (both associate's and bachelor's) between whites and Asian Americans on the one hand and blacks and Hispanics on the other. We have neither the energy nor resources to help the incidental students as well.

Gerald Grant suggested a similar triage in 1972 when he urged that public policy encourage "a wider range of post–high school opportunities, lessening the pressures of a bachelor's degree as a passport to success" (Grant, 1972, p. 16). Indeed, current youth policy is moving in that direction. "Youth apprenticeships," "career academies," and other forms of school-to-work transition programs that start in the tenth grade and involve at least one year of postsecondary education will attract the kind of people who in the class of 1972 were most likely to wind up as incidental students in community colleges. These people will no longer be part of the traditional accounting system of who goes to college, but they are a small group: less than 8 percent of the class of 1972 fit the description, and only a fraction of that 8 percent would wind up in the new programs today.

Malaise and Endings

Writing in *Harper's* about the same time as Grant, John Holt (1972, p. 80) argued that higher education was falsely built on the principle of "competitive consumption"—that is, he or she who consumes more schooling, or more expensive schooling, gets an advantage in the world. The class of 1972 and its contemporaries believed in competitive consumption. But education was the one major domain of its life in which this generation appears to have been most disappointed, although we know this only by imputation from other sources of data. In the surveys that Angus Campbell and colleagues conducted in the 1970s, there was a marked decline (from 27 percent to 20 percent) of those indicating complete satisfaction with the amount of education they had received. In turn, in 1978, the correlation between amount of education and general satisfaction with life was the lowest of all major domains. We know that the generation for which the class of 1972 is standing in evidenced a unique and significant growth in pessimism in the 1970s. In the absence of being able to analyze primary data sources, I suggest—with some minor leaps of logic and faith—that their outlook was a drag on national happiness, contributed to the "malaise" that Jimmy Carter made famous, and was largely colored by disappointments in educational attainment.

Campbell's (1981, p. 45) explanation for the pessimism is intriguing and credible: "This surprising trend was contributed in large part by the increasing numbers of people who started college but did not complete a degree. . . . These people express more dissatisfaction than either high school graduates or college graduates, not only in the extent of their education but in other domains of life as well." The dissatisfaction is generalized from "bruised expectations and quirks of social comparison" (Campbell, Converse, and Rodgers, 1976, p. 137). Intriguing, credible, but, in light of the history in these archives, incomplete. Why?

National surveys and polls such as those conducted by the census or the Gallup Organization or researchers such as Campbell have been able to tell us little about education except quantity. We know how many years of schooling people have received or their level of schooling, but nothing more. Even some of these basic data are deceiving (used until 1992, the Census Bureau's category, "4 or 5 years of college," for example, is not necessarily equivalent to a bachelor's degree). What the archives of the class of 1972 have taught us is that, assuming you are something other than an incidental student, *what* you study—how and when and how well—is more important to the nation than earning a degree. It may even be more important to you, particularly in the earlier stages of adulthood.

In Chapter Four, I gave an optimist's reading to patterns of noncompletion among community college students. I said that if one looked carefully at what these students studied, they seemed to use the institution for ad hoc knowledge purposes, hence that they were more interested in learning than in earning credentials. Let me revise this interpretation slightly from the larger perspective of this chapter. I still believe that people who use community colleges but do not earn degrees are interested in learning specific knowledge, but ultimately they learn what everyone else learns about the use of credentials in the labor market. Degrees—associate's as well as bachelor's—are screening devices. They are a shorthand that saves personnel officers the trouble of assessment. They say that someone has persisted and performed at an acceptable (though undefined) level, hence that they are a better bet at sustained quality performance at work than someone who does not have a degree. In economic terms, failure to complete puts a ceiling on what you can do in the labor market. In psychological terms, a degree symbolizes an ending, and we all need signs of endings. In this respect, the most disappointed group in the class of 1972 has to be the 41 percent of those who made a go of higher education by earning more than ten credits from two- and/or four-year colleges, but never a degree of any kind. They constitute about 1.5 million people without a sense of an educational ending. They will not turn up as happy as others in surveys such as those Campbell conducted.

But should everyone who starts a postsecondary program finish a credential? Can they? Will they? Even in ten to fifteen years from the first date of attendance? The honest answer to all three questions is no. In light of public policy, it sounds heretical to say that, but history leaves us no choice. Furthermore, our state and national investments in higher education do not have, as their primary purpose, making people feel good. What the experience of the class of 1972 guides us toward is a better appreciation of the role of learning, as opposed to academic credentials, in both personal growth and national economic development. This appreciation should be a by-product of our learning about women's realism as opposed to men's fantasy (Chapter Two), about differences between what we want to be and what, in fact, we become (Chapters Three and Four), and about the potential expansion of our language space and knowledge store (Chapter Five).

Learning Choices and Wings

So this theme has turned up more than once in the accounts in this book. It is about individual choices and their collective influence on the nation. The most influential of the national reports on higher

education in the mid 1980s, reflecting on the prior decade, was suc-
cinct in its judgment about both input measures of the quality of
higher education and degree production data when it noted that
"none of [these measures] tells us what students actually learn and
how much they grow as the result of higher education," and that if
we allow "the chase for academic credentials to supersede the pursuit
of learning—all levels of education will suffer" (Study Group on the
Conditions of Excellence in American Higher Education, 1984,
pp. 15, 14). The pursuit of learning is reflected in data that identify
precisely what people study. If we know that more people in this
generation earned college credits in general personal health practices
(13.9 percent) or aerobics, jogging, and body building (9.9 percent)
than international relations (3.5 percent), international economics
(0.8 percent), or international management (0.7 percent), then we can
begin to explain some notable aspects of U.S. economic life in the
1980s: the explosion of the health club service industry and the im-
plosion of our international competitive position.

But if we also know that more people in the NLS-72 earned
college credits in ethics (15.3 percent) than in real estate (3.1 percent), more in social work (3.2 percent) than in banking operations
(1.1 percent), then we can also begin to weave another part of the
story, a slower process of outreach that indicates how much of a
caring society we can become. Of the paper trail left by the class of
1972, I once wrote—and it's worth repeating here—that "a college
generation sensitive to others is an adult generation that can come
to its senses about the relationship between academic knowledge
and the general welfare" (Adelman, 1989, p. 25). It's not a matter
of the mere accumulation of knowledge, rather a matter of our uses
of what we chose to learn—what we do and how well we can do it.
But without the initial choice, we can't do it at all.

Time and time again, the archives of this generation have
taught us how to think about metrics of choice. They have shown
us that we should be focusing on quality investments in knowledge,
not easy paths to credentials. From this perspective, it is more important that individuals use education and training (whether in
formal institutions or through employers), in measured and concentrated portions, through both traditional years of schooling and
adulthood. In this vision, credentials are serendipitous. In this vi-

sion, we have to train employers to think in ways that take them outside the box of schooling and its accounting system. The Comeback Kid of the 1970s, Muhammed Ali, once said that "the man who has no imagination has no wings." Gender reference aside, thinking outside the educational box is an act with wings.

Notes

1. In 1991, there were 16.5 million Americans between the ages of thirty-six and thirty-nine, the modal ages for the four high school classes. Some of these immigrated to the U.S. since 1975, and some are in the cohorts who never finished high school. Because it is difficult to sort these two groups out from gross population data, I leave the focus on high school graduates.
2. The NLS-72 archive confirms some aspects of this phenomenon. Proprietary/vocational school students were only 2.8 percent of all the NLS-72 high school graduates, and 6.7 percent of those who continued their education after high school. Only 35.5 percent of them completed a credential of any kind versus 55.7 percent of the others in the NLS-PETS. And their ratio of loans to all other forms of financial aid was .60 compared to .48 for the other students.
3. I choose to isolate this group (about 800,000 people in the class of 1972) so as (1) to focus on those with sufficient education to participate, if they wanted to, in an information economy, and (2) to minimize the presence of people who, because they earned graduate or professional degrees, would be more likely to be employed in occupations in which work is dominated by ideas.
4. Table 6.2 takes the 265 categories and aggregates them to 44; thus, in this calculation, Bible study does not rank as high.
5. In the National Adult Household Education Survey of 1991, only 1.9 percent of the 16.5 million adults ages thirty-six to thirty-nine (the generation of the class of 1972) claimed they were working toward a bachelor's degree.
6. The series of questions in the 1986 follow-up survey about plans for further graduate education, past experience applying for admission to graduate schools of business, and related issues was sponsored by the American Assembly of Collegiate Schools

of Business. These questions proved very helpful from a perspective broader than that of business education, and anyone who uses the archive should be pleased that they were asked.

7.   The mean high school class rank for the group that earned sixty credits but no credentials was the 59th percentile, versus the 72nd percentile for those who earned bachelor's degrees and the 56th percentile for those whose highest degree was the associate's. Mean SAT/ACT scores were 909 for the "sixty-plus" group, 1011 for the bachelor's group, and 868 for the associate's group. Furthermore, the SES distribution of the sixty-plus group was the same as for the NLS-PETS group as a whole, and they were far less likely to take out educational loans (28 percent) than those who received bachelor's degrees (38 percent).

Resource A

Definitions Used
in Tables

The following list displays the *types of postsecondary institutions awarding bachelor's degrees*. The percentage of bachelor's degrees awarded by each type of institution to NLS-72 students, 1972–1984, is shown in parentheses.

Doctoral
(40.8%)

Comprehensive
(46.3%)

Liberal arts
(9.2%)

Other
(3.7%)

Institutions classified under the Carnegie system as either research universities or doctoral degree–granting schools.
Institutions offering a broad array of academic and occupational programs. With few exceptions, the master's degree is the highest degree offered.
Institutions offering traditional undergraduate arts and sciences programs. With few exceptions, the bachelor's degree is the highest degree offered.
Specialized schools in fields ranging from design to theology to technology to music.

Three configurations of *undergraduate majors* have been used in this book. The most common configuration (with the percentage of all NLS-PETS bachelor's degree recipients for each major in parentheses) is displayed here.

Business
(17.5%)
Business administration, accounting, management, marketing, finance, specialized marketing, office support, operations research

Education
(16.0%)
Education (any kind), library science

Engineering
(6.2%)
Engineering, architecture, engineering technologies

Physical science
(3.0%)
Physics, chemistry, geology, earth science, astronomy, meteorology, science technologies

Math/computer science
(1.8%)
Mathematics, computer science, applied math, statistics

Life science
(8.4%)
Biological sciences, agricultural sciences, animal science, plant science, conservation and natural resources

Health science/services
(7.5%)
Allied health sciences, nursing, speech pathology and audiology, clinical health sciences, pharmacy, public health

Humanities
(6.0%)
Foreign languages and literatures, linguistics, English and American literature, creative writing, philosophy, religious studies, general liberal arts

Arts
(4.8%)
Art history, fine arts, graphics/design, theater arts, film, music, communications technologies

Social sciences
(17.7%)
Anthropology, economics, psychology, political science, sociology, history, geography, area

	studies, international relations, ethnic studies
Applied social sciences (8.9%)	Communications, public affairs/administration, protective services and criminal justice, home economics (textiles, nutrition, housing), social work, recreation, military science
Other (2.2%)	Interdisciplinary, theology, trades, precision production, vocational home economics

Resource B

Institutional Selectivity
and Course-Taking Patterns

The tables in this resource have, as their focus, the selectivity of the colleges attended by the high school class of 1972. Over the course of twelve years (1972–1984), the 12,599 students in the NLS-PETS group attended 2,981 institutions. For purposes of this analysis, these institutions were classified by degree of selectivity using the cell-weighting descriptions from the Cooperative Institutional Research Program's (CIRP) annual reports, *The American Freshman*, for the years 1976, 1977, 1978, and 1979. The variable had four values: highly selective, selective, not selective, and not ratable (proprietary schools, vocational-techs, hospital schools of nursing, conservatories, and so forth). Only 46 institutions out of the 2,981 proved to be highly selective.

Table B.1. Selectivity of the 2,981 Institutions
Attended by Students in the NLS-PETS, 1972–1984.

Institutional selectivity	Percent of all students	Percent of all bachelor's degrees
Highly selective	1.6%	2.9%
Selective	5.7	11.2
Not selective	84.1	81.6
Not ratable	8.6	4.3

Table B.2. Distribution of Bachelor's Degree Majors of NLS-PETS
Students, by Selectivity of Institution, 1972–1984.

Major	Highly selective	Selective	Not selective
Business	0.8%	12.4%	19.2%
Education	2.0	6.1	18.5
Applied social sciences	1.5	8.1	9.5
Health science/services	3.6	6.2	7.3
Engineering/architecture	8.4	10.2	5.5
Physical sciences	10.2	3.3	2.7
Math and computer science	7.1	1.8	1.7
Life sciences	10.5	12.8	7.2
Humanities	12.6	9.7	5.4
Arts	7.9	5.2	4.5
Social sciences	32.8	22.4	16.5
Other	2.4	2.0	2.0

Note: $N = 5,127$. Weighted $N = 732,511$.

Table B.3. Percentage of Undergraduate Credits Earned and Students Enrolled[a] in the Top Twenty Courses[b] in Highly Selective Institutions Compared to Other Institutions, 1972–1984.

	Highly selective			Selective			Not selective		
	Percent of course credits	Rank	Percent of students	Percent of course credits	Rank	Percent of students	Percent of course credits	Rank	Percent of students
Calculus	4.0%	1	50%	3.2%	1	48%	1.7%	5	27%
Introductory physics	3.0	2	43	2.2	4	37	1.3	11	24
General chemistry	2.6	3	39	2.4	2	40	1.7	4	34
English composition	1.9	4	47	2.4	3	63	3.1	1	76
Organic chemistry	1.7	5	20	1.3	8	21	0.7	24	13
Art history	1.6	6	21	0.8	21	24	0.7	22	22
Introductory economics	1.5	7	36	1.8	5	48	1.7	7	45
German: introductory/intermediate	1.4	8	25	0.7	25	12	0.5	42	8
General biology	1.3	9	26	1.6	7	39	2.0	2	49
General psychology	1.3	10	47	1.7	6	62	1.9	3	72
Math: postcalculus	1.3	11	18	0.3	63	6	0.1	112	5
French: introductory/intermediate	1.3	12	28	1.1	12	20	0.8	20	13
Music performance	1.3	13	10	0.9	16	14	1.3	10	16
English literature	1.1	14	18	0.8	18	16	0.7	23	16
Electrical engineering	1.0	15	12	0.7	26	9	0.4	53	4
Spanish: introductory/intermediate	1.0	16	15	1.1	10	19	1.1	16	18
French: advanced and literature	1.0	17	13	0.4	48	6	0.2	158	2
Geology: general	1.0	18	13	0.6	28	15	0.6	29	17
Literature: general	0.9	19	28	0.9	14	28	1.1	17	32
Humanities: interdisciplinary	0.9	20	13	0.4	51	8	0.4	52	11

Note: N = 5,127. Weighted N = 732,511.
[a] Students are those who received bachelor's degrees, 1972–1984.
[b] Out of 1,037 course categories.

Resource C

Selected Data on Educational Pathways, Socioeconomic Status, and Major Field Distributions

Table C.1 is a summary statement that covers everyone in the class of 1972. It highlights key aspects of their educational choices and work experience.

Table C.1. Eight Pathways of Education and Training and the People on Them Through Age Thirty-Two or Thirty-Three.

Student profile	Pathways							
	Four-year, bachelor's degree	Four-year, no bachelor's degree	Two-year, terminal associate's degree	Two-/Four-year, non-incidental	Two-year, incidental	Proprietary/vocational	Military	None
Population (000)	732	321	126	301	133	86	144	1210
Percent of all	24%	11%	4%	10%	4%	3%	5%	40%
Lowest quartile on ability test	7	21	22	31	38	41	53	52
SAT higher than 975	54	33	23	17	20	16	22	20
More than five semesters of high school math	53	38	30	27	19	23	21	16
More than five semesters of high school science	40	28	26	18	11	17	16	11
More than five semesters of high school business/commerce	6	11	17	17	19	18	8	23
More than five semesters of high school trade courses	3	5	8	11	12	12	23	12
No delay entering postsecondary education	88	69	74	64	39	50	22	N.A.
More than 2.5-year delay	4	15	11	17	33	27	58	N.A.
In school after age thirty	22	22	22	22	16	15	17	10
Earned higher credential after age thirty	11	19	12	19	11	7	14	7
Received financial aid by age twenty-six	66	49	49	38	19	35	23	N.A.

Table C.1. Eight Pathways of Education and Training and the People on Them Through Age Thirty-Two or Thirty-Three, Cont'd.

Student profile	Four-year, bachelor's degree	Four-year, no bachelor's degree	Two-year, terminal associate's degree	Two-/Four-year, non-incidental	Two-year, incidental	Proprietary/vocational	Military	None
					Pathways			
Took precollegiate math in college	28	21	52	39	10	21	15	N.A.
Took remedial English in college	21	16	41	32	9	16	11	N.A.
Earned more than four credits in calculus or statistics in college	38	11	15	8	0	5	0	N.A.
Years employed, 1979–1986	5.2	5.0	4.9	4.9	4.9	4.9	5.2	4.3
Unemployment ratio, 1979–1986	15%	22%	23%	24%	27%	27%	19%	44%
Works a great deal with ideas, age thirty-two	62	43	46	46	44	41	44	35
Works a great deal with things, age thirty-two	25	40	40	44	44	56	55	48
Very satisfied with opportunity to develop new skills on the job, age thirty-two	26	20	18	18	21	21	17	16
Very satisfied with opportunity to advance in career, age thirty-two	24	18	16	20	16	19	14	14

Note: The universe for each row in this table is different, and the only row on which the entire NLS-72 sample of 22,652 is based is "percent of all." But since all the data are weighted according to the conditions of these universes, they are population estimates for those who met the basic conditions for the universe. For example, only people who took the SAT or ACT are included in that row. Only people who had both jobs and earnings for 1985 and who participated in the 1986 survey are included in the data on labor-market outcomes at age thirty-two.

Table C.2. Socioeconomic Status and Highest Degree Earned by
NLS-PETS Students Who Earned More Than Ten Postsecondary Credits,
1972–1984.

Highest degree earned	Socioeconomic status in 1972		
	Lowest quartile	Middle two quartiles	Highest quartile
None	57.7%	47.9%	33.4%
Certificate/license	7.9	5.8	2.3
Associate's degree	9.5	10.4	6.3
Bachelor's degree	20.8	30.0	46.3
Master's degree	3.2	4.6	8.1
Doctoral/first professional	0.9	1.3	3.7

Note: N = 10,734.

Table C.3. Socioeconomic Status, Gender, and SAT Scores, 1972.

Socioeconomic status and gender	SAT score ranges				
	400–700	701–833	834–975	976–1148	1149+
All students	13.9%	19.7%	26.3%	25.2%	14.9%
Socioeconomic status and gender					
Lowest quartile					
Men	26.7%	23.5%	22.7%	19.1%	8.0%
Women	33.3	20.1	26.3	16.0	4.3
Middle quartiles					
Men	14.4	20.1	28.2	24.7	12.6
Women	17.3	23.8	27.2	22.9	8.8
Highest quartile					
Men	5.2	14.9	24.1	30.5	25.3
Women	9.5	18.6	26.5	27.3	18.1

Note: The universe includes all NLS-72 students who took either the SAT or ACT
exams (ACT scores were converted to the SAT scale) and for whom sufficient data were
available to construct a composite SES variable. N = 8,019.

**Table C.4. Distribution of Major, by Race/Ethnicity and Gender,
for Those in the NLS-PETS Who Earned Bachelor's Degrees.**

	Race-ethnicity			Gender		
Major	White	Black	Hispanic	Men	Women	All
Engineering, architecture	6.5	2.0	7.0	10.9	0.9	6.2
Physical sciences	3.1	1.8	5.4	4.4	1.5	3.0
Biological sciences	8.5	6.0	6.5	10.7	5.7	8.4
Math/computer science	1.8	2.0	0.4	2.2	1.4	1.8
Health sciences/services	7.5	7.2	6.8	2.8	12.9	7.5
Total science/engineering/ technology	27.4%	19.0%	26.1%	31.0%	22.4%	26.9%
Education	15.7	21.7	15.6	8.2	24.9	16.0
Social sciences	17.2	23.3	24.2	19.3	15.8	17.7
Applied social sciences	8.8	10.2	11.5	7.2	10.9	8.9
Total education/social sciences	41.7%	55.2%	51.3%	34.7%	51.6%	42.6%
Humanities	6.1	5.5	6.4	4.2	8.2	6.0
Fine/performing arts	4.9	3.0	4.3	2.9	6.9	4.8
Total humanities/arts	11.0%	8.5%	10.7%	7.1%	15.1%	10.8%
Business	17.7	16.2	11.1	24.6	9.4	17.5
Other	2.3	1.1	0.9	2.7	1.7	2.2

Note: N = 5,127. Due to rounding, not all columns total 100%.

Resource D

Other Longitudinal Studies
That Include
Educational Data

The NLS-72 is not the only national longitudinal study panel in existence, but while some of the others are stronger in areas such as labor-market data, I will contend that it is the best of them in terms of the overall richness and variety of the data in its archive, in the size and representativeness of its sample, and in the response rates of follow-up surveys. To be sure, as a federally funded project with frequent follow-up surveys, the NLS-72 enjoys an advantage over other data bases: it is much easier to maintain an accurate mailing list and find people for follow-up surveys when one is going through the exercise every two, three, or four years. Furthermore, the funding and procedures for the 1986 follow-up allowed for computer-assisted telephone interviews (CATI) for those who had failed to return questionnaires. Using CATI ensures a high response rate.

Unobtrusive measures play a large role in the virtues of the NLS-72 when compared to the other longitudinal studies. The postsecondary transcripts are unique to the federal longitudinal studies. The transcripts are expensive to obtain and code, and only large-scale national data collection can afford this step. Again, no other longitudinal study has unobtrusively obtained SAT and ACT scores, and with one exception, no other longitudinal study includes unobtrusively obtained high school records.

All these advantageous characteristics are appropriate to national archives—and that is what the NLS-72, High School and Beyond, and NELS-88 longitudinal studies are: national archives.

Each of the other major longitudinal studies has virtues and limitations. Here is a brief summary.

National Longitudinal Surveys of Labor Market Experience

The name of this series of five panels—the National Longitudinal Surveys of Labor Market Experience—is much like that of the NLS-72 data base. To avoid confusion, I refer to the collection as the *Ohio State panels,* after their university home. The Ohio State panels, sponsored by the U.S. Department of Labor, are not drawn from a single cohort but span several groups of roughly the same age. Subsamples are followed up using different means (interviews, telephone surveys, mail surveys), at varying intervals (Center for Human Resources Research, Ohio State University, 1982). For example, the New Youth Cohort is a sample of 12,700 people who were between the ages of fourteen and twenty-one in January 1979. Subsamples were surveyed annually for five years, and the data base includes high school transcripts for 6,600 of this group (whether they graduated during this period or not). These high school transcripts are more detailed than the high school records in the NLS-72, and I have found them valuable in tracking changing relationships between college admissions practices and secondary school course taking (Adelman, 1983). In addition, virtually all members of the initial panel took the Armed Forces Qualifying Test (AFQT), which is a stronger measure of general learned abilities than the mini-SAT administered to most (but not all) of the NLS-72 cohort.

Demonstrations of the wealth of information of this data base on such topics as the correlates of unemployment, the effects of high school vocational curricula, and uses of time can be found in Borus (1984). The panel to which I refer in Chapter Two included women who were between the ages of thirty and forty-four in 1967, when the panel was established. These panels (and others) also differ from the NLS-72, High School and Beyond, and NELS-

88 cohorts in that their sampling design did not depend on an individual being enrolled in school (Morgan, 1984).

The principal limitation of this otherwise enlightening archive is a paucity of reliable information on postsecondary education. Hence, the Ohio State panels do not allow us to see the consequences of educational choice and behavior and the establishment of careers as clearly as does the NLS-72.

National Bureau of Economic Research

The National Bureau of Economic Research (NBER) established a longitudinal panel under the direction of Robert Thorndike and Elizabeth Hagen in 1955. The participants were 10,000 males who had taken a battery of U.S. Army Air Force aptitude tests in 1943 and who (out of 17,000 contacted) filled out a questionnaire in 1955. Of this group, 5,100 responded to a follow-up survey in 1969. The time frame of twenty-six years is a virtue. The glaring limitation derives from the fact that the original panel, drawn from the armed forces in the middle of World War II, was all male, nearly all white, and ranged considerably in age (Juster, 1975). The NBER-Thorndike data base has no unobtrusive measures except the original aptitude test scores.

Panel Study of Income Dynamics

The Panel Study of Income Dynamics has followed 5,000 American *families* since it was established in 1968 under the direction of James N. Morgan of the Survey Research Center at the University of Michigan. The unit of analysis in this longitudinal study—a family—is obviously different from that of the others summarized here. And since the panel was a representative sample of families, it initially sampled adults of all ages and varying economic status. The purpose of the panel was to study changes in the economic progress of families, and it thus includes extensive data on changes in family composition, migration, patterns of work and leisure, and motivation and attitudes. It is particularly sensitive to major life events, such as illness, death, divorce, dislocation, and natural disaster. Education plays a comparatively minor role; it turns up in terms of school status (in or out) and total years of schooling. There have been annual reports on the progress and findings of the panel since 1974 as well as numerous exemplary studies of the fits, starts, and variability of family economic history (see, for example, Duncan and others, 1984).

Wisconsin

Perhaps the most widely known of the longitudinal study panels, this group was established in 1959 under the direction of William Sewell. All 34,151 participants were twelfth-graders in Wisconsin high schools in 1957, and nearly all were white. Follow-up surveys were conducted and unobtrusive data on employment and earnings obtained (from social security records) for 4,388 male original participants in 1964 and 1973—that is, roughly until the group was thirty-six years old (see Sewell and Hauser, 1975; Sewell and Hauser, 1976; Sewell, Hauser, and Wolf, 1980). Parental income measures were better here than for any other longitudinal study, including the NLS-72, because they were taken from state tax records, and participant income measures (for males) were also better. While the base-year data did not include high school transcripts, it did include high school class rank as taken directly from student records and the results of an aptitude test administered statewide to Wisconsin high school juniors.

Explorations in Equality of Opportunity

In 1970, a group of researchers tried to replicate the Wisconsin panel on a national scale in the study Explorations in Equality of Opportunity (EEO). They used a sample of 9,700 people who were tenth-graders in 1955 (Alexander, Eckland, and Griffin, 1975); however, this sample excluded students attending predominantly minority high schools and students attending private schools (Alexander and Eckland, 1973). While there were legitimate reasons for some of these decisions, the biases in the sample are obvious: it underrepresents racial minorities, students from large city high schools, and students likely to drop out of high school. The panel was established by the Educational Testing Service (ETS), and all students took a short basic skills test designed by ETS. ETS, in turn, followed the fates of these subjects four years later by asking their school principals whether the students had graduated and what they had done since graduation. To such basic questions, the response rate—by proxy—was 97 percent. The real, as opposed to proxy, follow-up consisted of a single survey of the students at age thirty that obtained a 50 percent response. This follow-up is further biased by overrepresentation of students from high schools in the Central states. But roughly 25 percent of the respondents were not even included in the analyses because the data they provided ranged from incomplete to scanty. There were, in fact, 2,100 usable records.

Project Talent

This data base covered 375,304 students from 1,225 schools (high schools and junior high schools) distributed across grades nine through twelve in the proportion in which they are normally found—that is, more ninth-graders than tenth-graders, and so forth (Wilson and Wise, 1975). The initial survey and an elaborate battery of tests and inventories were administered in the spring of 1960. Follow-ups were conducted for each class one, five, and eleven years later. Response rates in the follow-up surveys fell from 48.6 percent for the one-year follow-up to 22.8 percent for the eleven-year follow-up. As would be expected, response rates were highest among those who were twelfth-graders in 1960: 61.9 percent for the one-year follow-up and 27.9 percent for the eleven-year follow-up (see Wise, McLaughlin, and Steel, 1977).

The major strengths of the Project Talent data base lie in its base-year test battery and in its taxonomy of occupations. A major limitation is that at the time of the base year (1960), no one was allowed to ask questions about race, and by the time respondents to surveys could indicate their race (the five-year follow-up), two-thirds of the original sample was not responding. A second limitation lies in the fact that students themselves reported their secondary school curricula and grades. With the exception of these critical data, the sample and design for Project Talent, with particular emphasis on the eleven-year follow-up for participants who were eleventh-graders in 1960, come closest to those of the NLS-72. In fact, it was sponsored by the old Office of Education and is considered the forerunner to the NLS-72.

References

Adelman, C. *Devaluation, Diffusion, and the College Connection: A Study of High School Transcripts, 1969–1981.* Study prepared for the National Commission on Excellence in Education, 1983. (ED 288-244)

Adelman, C. *The Standardized Test Scores of College Graduates, 1964–1982.* Washington, D.C.: U.S. Government Printing Office, 1985.

Adelman, C. "On the Paper Trail of the Class of '72." *New York Times,* July 22, 1989, p. 25.

Adelman, C. *A College Course Map: Taxonomy and Transcript Data.* Washington, D.C.: U.S. Government Printing Office, 1990a.

Adelman, C. "Minorities in the Graduate Education Pipeline: Plugging the Leaks and Increasing the Flow." Unpublished background paper for the U.S. Department of Education's Task Force on Reauthorization of the Higher Education Act, 1990b.

Adelman, C. *Women at Thirtysomething: Paradoxes of Attainment.* Washington, D.C.: U.S. Department of Education, 1991.

Adelman, C. "The Changing Forgotten Half: Less Than Half; Two-Thirds Male." *Education Week,* 1993, *13*(1), 56, 41.

Adler, P. A., and Adler, P. *Backboards and Blackboards: College*

Athletes and Role Engulfment. New York: Columbia University Press, 1991.

Alba, R. D., and Lavin, D. E. "Community Colleges and Tracking in Higher Education." *Sociology of Education,* 1981, *54,* 223–237.

Alexander, K. L., and Cook, M. "The Motivational Relevance of Educational Plans: Questioning the Conventional Wisdom." *Social Psychology Quarterly,* 1979, *42,* 202–213.

Alexander, K. L., and Eckland, B. K. *Effects of Education on the Social Mobility of High School Sophomores Fifteen Years Later (1955–1970).* Final report to the National Institute of Education; grant no. OEG-4-71-0037. Chapel Hill, N.C.: Institute for Research in Social Science, 1973.

Alexander, K. L., Eckland, B. K., and Griffin, L. J. "The Wisconsin Model of Socioeconomic Achievement: A Replication." *American Journal of Sociology,* 1975, *81,* 324–342.

Alexander, K. L., Holupka, S., and Pallas, A. M. "Social Background and Academic Determinants of Two-Year Versus Four-Year College Attendance: Evidence from Two Cohorts a Decade Apart." *American Journal of Education,* 1987, *96,* 57–80.

Alsalam, N., and Rogers, G. T. 1991. *The Condition of Education, 1991.* Vol. 2. Washington, D.C.: National Center for Education Statistics, 1991.

American Assembly of Collegiate Schools of Business. *Accreditation Council Policies, Procedures, and Standards: 1990–1992.* St. Louis, Mo.: American Assembly of Collegiate Schools of Business, 1989.

American Assembly of Collegiate Schools of Business. *Standards for Business and Accounting Accreditation.* St. Louis, Mo.: American Assembly of Collegiate Schools of Business, 1991. (Photocopied)

American College Testing Service. *National Collegiate Athletic Association Survey of Graduation Rates After Five Years for Males First Entering College in Fall 1975.* Iowa City, Iowa: American College Testing Service, 1981.

American Institutes for Research. *Report No. 1: Summary Results from the 1987–88 National Study of Intercollegiate Athletes.* Palo Alto, Calif.: American Institutes for Research, 1988a.

American Institutes for Research. *Report No. 2: Methodology of the*

1987–88 National Study of Intercollegiate Athletes. Palo Alto, Calif.: American Institutes for Research, 1988b.

American Institutes for Research. *Report No. 3: The Experiences of Black Intercollegiate Athletes at NCAA Division I Institutions.* Palo Alto, Calif.: American Institutes for Research, 1989a.

American Institutes for Research. *Report No. 5: Analysis of the Academic Transcripts of Intercollegiate Athletes at NCAA Division I Institutions.* Palo Alto, Calif.: American Institutes for Research, 1989b.

Anderson, K. L. "Post–High School Experiences and College Attrition." *Sociology of Education,* 1981, *54,* 1–15.

Anderson, R. C. "The Notion of Schema and the Educational Enterprise: General Discussion." In R. C. Anderson, J. R. Spiro, and W. E. Montague (eds.), *Schooling and the Acquisition of Knowledge.* Hillsdale, N.J.: Erlbaum, 1977.

Association of American Colleges. *Integrity in the College Curriculum.* Washington, D.C.: Association of American Colleges, 1985.

Astin, A. W. *Four Critical Years: Effects of College on Beliefs, Attitudes, and Knowledge.* San Francisco: Jossey-Bass, 1977.

Astin, A. W. *Minorities in American Higher Education: Recent Trends, Current Prospects, and Recommendations.* San Francisco: Jossey-Bass, 1982.

Astin, A. W. "Student Involvement: A Developmental Theory for Higher Education." *Journal of College Student Personnel,* 1984, *25,* 277–308.

Astin, A. W., Green, K. C., and Korn, W. S. *The American Freshman: Twenty Year Trends.* Los Angeles: Higher Education Research Institute, University of California, 1987.

Astin, H. S. "The Meaning of Work in Women's Lives." *Counseling Psychologist,* 1984, *12,* 117–126.

Astin, H. S., and Kent, L. "Gender Roles in Transition: Research and Policy Implications in Higher Education." *Journal of Higher Education,* 1983, *54*(3), 309–324.

Axthelm, P. "The Shame of College Sports." *Newsweek,* Sept. 22, 1980, pp. 54–59.

Axthelm, P. "Kareem: Taller Than Ever." *Newsweek,* Dec. 5, 1983, p. 129.

Becker, G. S. *The Economics of Discrimination.* Chicago: University of Chicago Press, 1957.

Becker, G. S. *Human Capital.* (2nd ed.) Chicago: University of Chicago Press, 1975.

Belenky, M. F., Clinchy, B. M., Goldberger, N. R., and Tarule, J. M. *Women's Ways of Knowing.* New York: Basic Books, 1986.

Bennett, W. J. *To Reclaim a Legacy.* Washington, D.C.: National Endowment for the Humanities, 1984.

Berg, H. M., and Ferber, M. A. "Men and Women Graduate Students: Who Succeeds and Why?" *Journal of Higher Education,* 1983, *54*(6), 629-648.

Berg, I., and Freedman, M. "The American Workplace: Illusions and Realities." *Change,* 1977, *9*(11), 24-30, 62.

Bloch, M. *The Historian's Craft.* (Peter Putnam, trans.) New York: Knopf, 1953.

Bloom, A. *The Closing of the American Mind.* New York: Simon & Schuster, 1987.

Booth, W. C. "The Common Aims That Divide Us." In R. I. Brod and D. Fisher (eds.), *Profession, 1981.* New York: Modern Language Association of America, 1981.

Booth, W. C. "Cultural Literacy and Liberal Learning: An Open Letter to E. D. Hirsch, Jr." *Change,* 1989, *20*(4), 10-21.

Borus, M. E. (ed.). *Youth and the Labor Market.* Kalamazoo, Mich.: W. E. Upjohn Institute for Employment Research, 1984.

Boyer, E. L. *College: The Undergraduate Experience in America.* New York: HarperCollins, 1987.

Brede, R. M., and Camp, H. J. "The Education of College Student-Athletes." *Sociology of Sport Journal,* 1987, *4,* 245-257.

Breneman, D. W., and Nelson, S. C. *Financing Community Colleges: An Economic Perspective.* Washington, D.C.: Brookings Institution, 1981.

Brint, S., and Karabel, J. *The Diverted Dream: Community Colleges and the Promise of Educational Opportunity in America, 1900-1985.* New York: Oxford University Press, 1989.

Brook, J. S., Whiteman, M., Peisach, E., and Deutsch, M. "Aspiration Levels of and for Children." *Journal of Genetic Psychology,* 1974, *124,* 3-16.

Burkheimer, G. J., and Novak, T. P. *A Capsule Description of*

Young Adults Seven and One-Half Years After High School. Washington, D.C.: National Center for Education Statistics, 1981.

Campbell, A. *The Sense of Well-Being in America: Recent Patterns and Trends.* New York: McGraw-Hill, 1981.

Campbell, A., Converse, P. E., and Rodgers, W. L. *The Quality of American Life.* New York: Russell Sage Foundation, 1976.

Carlisle, R.D.B. "Poor Reception for Broadcast Graduates." *Change,* 1976, *8*(3), 50–53.

Carnegie Commission on Higher Education. *New Students and New Places: Policies for the Future Growth and Development of American Higher Education.* New York: McGraw Hill, 1971.

Center for Human Resources Research, Ohio State University. *The National Longitudinal Surveys Handbook.* Columbus, Ohio: Center for Human Resources Research, Ohio State University, 1982.

Chall, J. S. *Stages of Reading Development.* New York: McGraw-Hill, 1983.

Chelimsky, E. "Review of Two Studies on College Athlete Graduation Rates." Memo to the Hon. James J. Howard. Report no. B-220175. Washington, D.C.: General Accounting Office, 1985.

Cheney, L. V. *50 Hours: A Core Curriculum for College Students.* Washington, D.C.: National Endowment for the Humanities, 1989.

Cheney, L. V. *Tyrannical Machines.* Washington, D.C.: National Endowment for the Humanities, 1990.

Clark, B. R. "The 'Cooling-Out' Function in Higher Education." *American Journal of Sociology,* 1960a, *65,* 560–576.

Clark, B. R. *The Open-Door College.* New York: McGraw-Hill, 1960b.

Clark, B. R. "The 'Cooling-Out' Function Revisited." In G. B. Vaughan (ed.), *Questioning the Community College Role.* San Francisco: Jossey-Bass, 1980.

Cohen, A. M. "Degree Achievement by Minorities in Community Colleges." *Review of Higher Education,* 1988, *11,* 383–402.

Cohen, A. M., and Brawer, F. B. *The American Community College.* (2nd ed.) San Francisco: Jossey-Bass, 1989.

Cohen, P. A. "College Grades and Adult Achievement: A Research Synthesis." *Research in Higher Education,* 1984, *20*(3), 281–293.

Collins, R. *The Credential Society.* New York: Academic Press, 1979.

Committee on Energy and Commerce, U.S. House of Representatives. *Hearings Before the Subcommittee on Commerce, Consumer Protection, and Competitiveness* (Intercollegiate Sports). Serial no. 102-70. Washington, D.C.: U.S. Government Printing Office, 1992.

Committee on Labor and Human Resources, U.S. Senate. *Hearing Before the Subcommittee on Employment and Productivity* (Women and the Workplace: Looking Toward the Future). Senate Hearing no. 102-227. Washington, D.C.: U.S. Government Printing Office, 1991.

Conaty, J., Alsalam, N., James, E., and To, D. L. "College Quality and Future Earnings: Where Should You Send Your Sons and Daughters to College?" Paper presented at the annual meeting of the American Sociological Association, San Francisco, Aug. 1989.

Connerton, P. *How Societies Remember.* Cambridge, England: Cambridge University Press, 1989.

Cullen, F. T., Latessa, E. J., and Byrne, J. P. "Scandal and Reform in Collegiate Athletics." *Journal of Higher Education,* 1990, *61*(1), 50–64.

Daniels, L. A. "Diversity, Correctness, and Campus Life." *Change,* 1991, *23*(5), 16–20.

Dean, E. "Introduction." In E. Dean (ed.), *Education and Economic Productivity.* New York: Ballinger, 1984.

Dean, J. "Rituals of the Herd." *Rolling Stone,* Oct. 7, 1976, pp. 38–58.

Dearman, N. B., and Plisko, V. W. *The Condition of Education: 1981 Edition.* Washington, D.C.: National Center for Education Statistics, 1981.

deArmas, C. P., and McDavis, R. J. "White, Black, and Hispanic Students' Perceptions of a Community College Environment." *Journal of College Student Personnel,* 1981, *22,* 337–341.

Department of Education and Science (United Kingdom). *Statistical Bulletin,* 1987, ISSN 0142-5013, Table 4, p. 8.

de Wolf, V. A. "High School Mathematics Preparation and Sex Differences in Quantitative Abilities." *Psychology of Women Quarterly*, 1981, *5*, 555–567.

Diamond, E. E., and Tittle, C. K. "Sex Equity in Testing." In S. Klein (ed.), *Handbook for Achieving Sex Equity Through Education*. Baltimore, Md.: Johns Hopkins University Press, 1985.

Dougherty, K. "The Effects of Community Colleges: Aid or Hindrance to Socioeconomic Attainment?" *Sociology of Education*, 1987, *60*, 86–103.

Dresch, S. P. "Demography, Technology, and Higher Education: Toward a Formal Model of Educational Adaptation." *Journal of Political Economy*, 1975, *83*(2), 535–569.

Dressel, P. L., and DeLisle, F. H. *Undergraduate Curriculum Trends*. Washington, D.C.: American Council on Education, 1969.

Duncan, G. J., and others. *Years of Poverty, Years of Plenty*. Ann Arbor, Mich.: Institute for Social Research, University of Michigan, 1984.

Educational Testing Service. *Performance at the Top: From Elementary Through Graduate School*. Princeton, N.J.: Educational Testing Service, 1991.

Edwards, H. "Educating Black Athletes." *Atlantic Monthly*, 1983, *252*(2), 31–38.

Edwards, H. "Beyond Symptoms: Unethical Behavior in American Collegiate Sport and the Problem of the Color Line." *Journal of Sport and Social Issues*, 1985, *9*, 3–11.

Eitzen, D. S., and Purdy, D. A. "The Academic Preparation and Achievement of Black and White Collegiate Athletes." *Journal of Sport and Social Issues*, 1986, *10*, 15–29.

England, P. "Explanation of Job Segregation and the Sex Gap in Pay." In *Comparable Worth: Issues for the 80s*. Washington, D.C.: U.S. Commission on Civil Rights, 1984.

European Round Table. *Education for European Competence*. Brussels, Belgium: European Round Table, 1989.

Feldman, K. A., and Newcomb, T. M. *The Impact of College on Students*. San Francisco: Jossey-Bass, 1969.

Feldman, S. D. *Escape from the Doll's House: Women in Graduate and Professional School Education*. New York: McGraw-Hill, 1974.

Fennema, E. "Girls, Women, and Mathematics." In E. Fennema and M. J. Ayer (eds.), *Women and Education: Equity or Equality?* Berkeley, Calif.: McCutchan, 1984.

Ferguson, C. A. "Language Development." In J. A. Fishman, C. A. Ferguson, and J. Das Gupta (eds.), *Language Problems of Developing Nations.* New York: Wiley, 1968.

Fetters, W. B., Stowe, P. S., and Owings, J. A. *Quality of Responses of High School Students to Questionnaire Items.* Washington, D.C.: National Center for Education Statistics, 1984.

Fishman, J. A. "The Impact of Nationalism on Language Planning." In J. Rubin and B. H. Jernud (eds.), *Can Language Be Planned?* Honolulu: University of Hawaii Press, 1971.

Fishman, J. A. *Bilingual Education: An International Sociological Perspective.* Rowley, Mass.: Newbury House, 1976.

Folger, J. K., Astin, H. S., and Bayer, A. E. *Human Resources and Higher Education.* New York: Russell Sage Foundation, 1970.

Forster, R. "Achievements of the *Annales* School." *Journal of Economic History,* 1978, *38,* 58–76.

Fox, M. F., and Hesse-Biber, S. *Women at Work.* Mountain View, Calif.: Mayfield, 1984.

Freeman, R. B. *Black Elite: The New Market for Highly Educated Black Americans.* New York: McGraw-Hill, 1976.

Freeman, R. B., and Hollomon, J. H. "The Declining Value of College Going." *Change,* 1975, *7*(7), 24–31, 62.

Gallup Organization. *A Survey of College Seniors: Knowledge of History and Literature.* Princeton, N.J.: Gallup Organization, 1989.

Gardner, E. "Some Aspects of the Use and Misuse of Standardized Aptitude and Achievement Tests." In A. K. Wigdor and W. R. Garner (eds.), *Ability Testing: Uses, Consequences, and Controversies.* Vol. 2. Washington: National Academy Press, 1982.

Geertz, C. "The Uses of Diversity." *Michigan Quarterly Review,* 1986, *25,* 105–123.

General Accounting Office. *Financial Assistance to Scholarship Athletes.* Briefing Report no. GAO/HRD-87-78BR. Washington, D.C.: General Accounting Office, 1987.

Gordon, M. "A Conversation with Peg Gordon." *Saturday Review of Education,* 1973, *1*(4), 38–40.

Grandy, J. *Profiles of Prospective Humanities Majors.* Final report for NEH grant no. OP-20119-83. Princeton, N.J.: Educational Testing Service, 1984.

Grant, G. "Universal BA?" *New Republic,* 1972, *166*(26), 13-16.

Grant, S. A. "Language Policy in the United States." *Association of Departments of Foreign Languages Bulletin,* 1978, *9*(4), 1-12.

Grubb, W. N. "Vocationalizing Higher Education: The Causes of Enrollment and Completion in Two-Year Colleges, 1970-1980." *Economics of Education Review,* 1988, 7, 301-319.

Grubb, W. N. "The Effects of Differentiation on Educational Attainment: The Case of Community Colleges." *Review of Higher Education,* 1989, *12*, 349-374.

Grubb, W. N. "The Decline of Community College Transfer Rates." *Journal of Higher Education,* 1991, *62*, 194-217.

Hafner, A. L. "The 'Traditional' Undergraduate Woman in the Mid-1980s: A Changing Profile." In C. S. Pearson, D. L. Shavlick, and J. G. Touchton (eds.), *Educating the Majority.* New York: American Council on Education/Macmillan, 1989.

Hanoch, G. "A Multivariate Model of Labor Supply: Methodology and Estimation." In J. P. Smith (ed.), *Female Labor Supply: Theory and Estimation.* Princeton, N.J.: Princeton University Press, 1980.

Harvey, G., and Noble, E. "Economic Considerations for Achieving Sex Equity Through Education." In S. Klein (ed.), *Handbook for Achieving Sex Equity Through Education.* Baltimore, Md.: Johns Hopkins University Press, 1985.

Haveman, R. H., and Wolfe, B. L. "Education, Productivity, and Well-Being: On Defining and Measuring the Economic Characteristics of Schooling." In E. Dean (ed.), *Education and Economic Productivity.* New York: Ballinger, 1984.

Hennessee, J. "Yogurt: Getting into the Culture." *New Times,* 1976, *7*(2), 45-55.

Hirsch, E. D., Jr. "Cultural Literacy." *American Scholar,* 1983, *52*, 159-169.

Hirsch, E. D., Jr. *Cultural Literacy: What Every American Needs to Know.* New York: Random House, 1988.

Holt, J. "The Little Red Prison." *Harper's,* 1972, *244*(1465), 80-82.

Holton G. "Scientific Research and Scholarship." *Daedalus,* 1962, *91,* 362–399.

Hunt, L. "French History in the Last Twenty Years: The Rise and Fall of the *Annales* Paradigm." *Journal of Contemporary History,* 1986, *21,* 209–224.

Hyman, H. H., Wright, C. R. and Reed, J. S. *The Enduring Effects of Education.* Chicago: University of Chicago Press, 1975.

International Financial Statistics Yearbook, 1992. Vol. 45. Washington, D.C.: International Monetary Fund, 1992.

James, E., Alsalam, N., Conaty, J., and To, D. L. "College Quality and Future Earnings." *American Economic Review,* 1989, *79*(2), 247–252.

Jencks, C. S. *Who Gets Ahead? The Determinants of Economic Success in America.* New York: Basic Books, 1979.

Jencks, C. S., Crouse, J., and Mueser, P. "The Wisconsin Model of Status Attainment: A National Replication with Improved Measures of Ability and Aspiration." *Sociology of Education,* 1983, *56,* 3–19.

Jencks, C. S., and others. *Inequality: A Reassessment of the Effect of Family and Schooling in America.* New York: Basic Books, 1979.

Juster, F. T. "Introduction and Summary." In T. J. Juster (ed.), *Education, Income, and Human Behavior.* New York: McGraw-Hill, 1975.

Kanter, R. M. *Men and Women of the Corporation.* New York: Basic Books, 1977.

Karabel, J. "Community Colleges and Social Stratification." *Harvard Educational Review,* 1972, *42,* 521–561.

Karabel, J. "Community Colleges and Social Stratification in the 1980s." In L. S. Zwerling (ed.), *The Community College and Its Critics.* New Directions for Community Colleges, no. 54. San Francisco: Jossey-Bass, 1986.

Karabel, J., and Astin, A. W. "Social Class, Academic Ability, and College 'Quality.'" *Social Forces,* 1975, *53,* 381–398.

Kaufman, D. R., and Richardson, B. L. *Achievement and Women: Challenging the Assumptions.* New York: Free Press, 1982.

Kennedy, D. "We Can't 'Reform' College Athletics." *Washington Post,* Oct. 27, 1990, p. A25.

Keyes, R. "CB: America's New Party Line." *New Times,* 1976, *6*(10), 45–51.

Knepper, P. *Student Progress in College: NLS-72 Postsecondary Education Transcript Study.* CS no. 89-411. Washington, D.C.: National Center for Education Statistics, 1989.

Knight Foundation Commission on Intercollegiate Athletics. *Keeping Faith with the Student-Athlete.* Charlotte, N.C.: Knight Foundation Commission on Intercollegiate Athletics, 1991.

Kohl, H. "The Primal Scene of Education: An Exchange." *New York Review of Books,* Apr. 13, 1989, p. 50.

Kolstad, A. *NLS-72/DMDC Military Records: Data File User's Manual.* CS no. 87-383. Washington, D.C.: National Center for Education Statistics, 1987.

Kriegel, L. "When Blue-Collar Students Go to College." *Saturday Review of Education,* 1972, *55*(30), 46–51.

Kuhn, T. *The Structure of Scientific Revolutions.* (2nd ed.) Chicago: University of Chicago Press, 1970.

Lapchick, R. Interview with T. Marchese. *AAHE Bulletin,* 1990, *42,* 6.

Lederman, D. "Forgoing Freshman Competition Seems to Help Academically At-Risk Athletes." *Chronicle of Higher Education,* Nov. 4, 1992, p. A31.

Leibowitz, A. "Education and the Allocation of Women's Time." In T. Juster (ed.), *Education, Income, and Human Behavior.* New York: McGraw-Hill, 1975.

Leonard, W. M. "The Sports Experience of the Black College Athlete: Exploitation in the Academy." *International Review for the Sociology of Sport,* 1986, *21,* 35–49.

Levin, B., and Clowes, D. "Realization of Educational Aspirations Among Blacks and Whites in Two- and Four-Year Colleges." *Community/Junior College Research Quarterly,* 1980, *4,* 185–193.

Levin, H. "Semantics of Culture." In G. Holton (ed.), *Science and Culture.* Boston: Beacon Press, 1967.

Levine, A. "The Meaning of Diversity." *Change,* 1991, *23*(5), 4–5.

Levine, A., and Cureton, J. "The Quiet Revolution: Eleven Facts About Multiculturalism and the Curriculum." *Change,* 1992, *24*(1), 24–29.

Lewis, L. L., and Farris, E. *Undergraduate General Education and Humanities Requirements.* Higher Education Surveys Report, Survey no. 7. Rockville, Md.: Westat, 1989.

London, H. B. *The Culture of a Community College.* New York: Praeger, 1978.

Long, J. E., and Caudill, S. B. "The Impact of Participation in Intercollegiate Athletics on Income and Graduation." *Review of Economics and Statistics,* 1991, *73*(3), 525–531.

Lyle, J. R., and Ross, J. L. *Women in Industry.* Lexington, Mass.: Heath, 1973.

Machlup, F. *The Production and Distribution of Knowledge in the United States.* Princeton, N.J.: Princeton University Press, 1962.

Machlup, F. *Knowledge: Its Creation, Distribution, and Economic Significance.* 2 vols. Princeton, N.J.: Princeton University Press, 1980.

Maline, M. B. *The National Longitudinal Study of the High School Class of 1972: Annotated Bibliography of Studies, 1980–1992.* Washington, D.C.: U.S. Department of Education, 1993.

Medsker, L. L., and Tillery, D. *Breaking the Access Barriers: A Profile of Two-Year Colleges.* New York: McGraw-Hill, 1971.

Mickelson, R. A. "Why Does Jane Read and Write So Well? The Anomaly of Women's Achievement." *Sociology of Education,* 1989, *62*(2), 47–63.

Miller, J. D. "Scientific Literacy: A Conceptual and Empirical Review." *Daedalus,* 1983, *112*(2), 29–48.

Mincer, J. "Human Capital and the Labor Market: A Review of Current Research." *Educational Researcher,* 1989, *18*(4), 27–34.

Minsky, M. "A Framework for Representing Knowledge." In P. H. Winston (ed.), *The Psychology of Computer Vision.* New York: McGraw-Hill, 1975.

Monk-Turner, E. "Sex, Educational Differentiation, and Occupational Status." *Sociological Quarterly,* 1983, *24*, 393–404.

Moore, S. J. *Introducing Chinese into High Schools: The Dodge Initiative.* Washington, D.C.: National Foreign Language Center, 1992.

Morgan, W. R. "Quality of Learning and Quality of Life for Public and Private High School Youth." In M. E. Borus (ed.), *Youth and the Labor Market.* Kalamazoo, Mich: W. E. Upjohn Institute for Employment Research, 1984.

Mueller, M. "Yellow Stripes and Dead Armadillos." In P. Franklin (ed.), *Profession, 1989.* New York: Modern Language Association of America, 1989.

Murphy, K., and Welch, F. "Wage Premiums for College Graduates: Recent Growth and Possible Explanations." *Educational Researcher,* 1989, *18*(4), 17-26.

Nakamura, A., and Nakamura, M. *The Second Paycheck: A Socioeconomic Analysis of Earnings.* San Diego, Calif.: Academic Press, 1989.

National Association of Schools of Music. *1991-1992 Handbook.* Reston, Va.: National Association of Schools of Music, 1991.

National Center for Education Statistics. *Data Base Documentation: 1987 Survey of 1985-86 College Graduates.* Washington, D.C.: National Center for Education Statistics, 1987.

National Collegiate Athletic Association. *1988 Division I Academic Reporting Compilation.* Mission, Kans: National Collegiate Athletic Association, 1989.

National Science Foundation. *Scientists, Engineers, and Technicians in Manufacturing and Nonmanufacturing Industries, 1980-81.* Washington, D.C.: National Science Foundation, 1984.

National Science Foundation. *Scientists, Engineers, and Technicians in Manufacturing Industries, 1989.* Washington, D.C.: National Science Foundation, 1992a.

National Science Foundation. *Scientists, Engineers, and Technicians in Nonmanufacturing Industries, 1990.* Washington, D.C.: National Science Foundation, 1992b.

Neumann, W., and Riesman, D. "The Community College Elite." In G. B. Vaughan (ed.), *Questioning the Community College Role.* San Francisco: Jossey-Bass, 1980.

Nunley, C. R., and Breneman, D. W. "Defining and Measuring Quality in Community College Education." In J. S. Eaton (ed.), *Colleges of Choice.* New York: American Council on Education/ Macmillan, 1988.

O'Toole, J. "The Reserve Army of the Underemployed." *Change,* 1975, *7*(4), 26-33, 63.

Pallas, A., and Alexander, K. "Sex Differences in Quantitative SAT

Performance: New Evidence on the Differential Course Work Hypothesis." *American Educational Research Journal,* 1983, *20*(2), 165–182.

Pascale, D. *Managing on the Edge.* New York: Simon & Schuster, 1990.

Pascarella, E. T., and others. "Long-Term Persistence of Two-Year College Students." Paper presented at the annual convention of the Association for the Study of Higher Education, Chicago, Oct. 1986. (ED 268-900)

Pascarella, E. T., and Smart, J. C. "Is the Effect of Grades on Early Career Income General or Conditional?" *Review of Higher Education,* 1990, *14*(1), 83–99.

Peterson, R. A. "Measuring Culture, Leisure, and Time Use." *Annals of the American Academy of Political and Social Science,* 1981, *453*, 169–179.

Pincus, F. L. "The False Promises of Community Colleges: Class Conflict and Vocational Education." *Harvard Educational Review,* 1980, *60*, 332–361.

Pincus, F. L. "Vocational Education: More False Promises." In L. S. Zwerling (ed.), *The Community College and Its Critics.* New Directions for Community Colleges, no. 54. San Francisco: Jossey-Bass, 1986.

Pincus, F. L., and Archer, E. *Bridges to Opportunity: Are Community Colleges Meeting the Transfer Needs of Minority Students?* New York: Academy for Educational Development, 1989.

Piore, M. F. "Notes for a Theory of Labor Market Stratification." In R. C. Edwards, M. Reich, and D. Gordon (eds.), *Labor Market Segmentation.* Lexington, Mass.: Heath, 1975.

Polachek, S. W. "Women in the Economy: Perspectives on Gender Inequality." In *Comparable Worth: Issues for the 80s.* Washington, D.C.: U.S. Commission on Civil Rights, 1984.

Purdy, D. A., Eitzen, D. S., and Hufnagel, R. "Are Athletes Also Students? The Educational Attainment of College Athletes." *Social Problems,* 1982, *29*, 439–448.

Ratcliff, J., and Associates. *Determining the Effect of Different Coursework Patterns on the General Learned Abilities of College Students.* OR Working Paper no. 90-524. Washington, D.C.: Office of Research, U.S. Department of Education, 1990.

Resnick, L. "Comprehending and Learning: Implications for a Cognitive Theory of Instruction." In H. Mandl, N. L. Stein, and T. Trabasso (eds.), *Learning and Comprehension of Text.* Hillsdale, N.J.: Erlbaum, 1984.

Richardson, R. C., Jr. "The Presence of Access and the Pursuit of Achievement." In J. S. Eaton (ed.), *Colleges of Choice.* New York: American Council on Education/Macmillan, 1988.

Ries, P., and Thurgood, D. H. *Summary Report 1991: Doctorate Recipients from United States Universities.* Washington, D.C.: National Academy Press, 1993.

Robinson, J. P. " 'Massification' and Democratization of the Leisure Class." *Annals of the American Academy of Political and Social Science,* 1978, *435,* 206-225.

Rosenbaum, J. E. "Track Misperceptions and Frustrated College Plans." *Sociology of Education,* 1980, *53,* 74-88.

Ross, E. W. "Social Studies and the Ruse of Cultural Literacy." *Social Science Record,* 1989, *26,* 13-15.

Rosser, P. *The SAT Gender Gap.* Washington, D.C.: Center for Women's Policy Studies, 1989.

Roueche, J., and Baker, G. *Access and Excellence: The Open Door Colleges.* Washington, D.C.: Community College Press, 1987.

Rudman, W. J. "The Sport Mystique in Black Culture." *Sociology of Sport Journal,* 1986, *3,* 305-319.

Rumberger, R. W., and Daymont, T. N. "The Economic Value of Academic and Vocational Training in High School." In M. E. Borus (ed.), *Youth and the Labor Market.* Kalamazoo, Mich.: W. E. Upjohn Institute for Employment Research, 1984.

Rumelhart, D. E. "Schemata: The Building Blocks of Cognition." In R. J. Spiro, B. C. Bruce, and W. F. Brewer (eds.), *Theoretical Issues in Reading Comprehension.* Hillsdale, N.J.: Erlbaum, 1980.

Sack, A. L., and Thiel, R. "College Football and Social Mobility: A Case Study of Notre Dame Football Players." *Sociology of Education,* 1979, *52,* 60-66.

"School Helping Athletes Return to the Classroom." *New York Times,* Oct. 20, 1991, p. 35.

Sears, K., and Gilley, J. W. "History of Intercollegiate Athletics." In J. W. Gilley (ed.), *Administration of University Athletic Pro-*

grams: Internal Control and Excellence. Washington, D.C.: American Council on Education, 1986.

Sells, L. W. *High School Math as the Critical Filter in the Job Market,* 1973. (ED 080-351)

Sewell, W. H., and Hauser, R. M. *Occupation and Earnings: Achievement Early in the Career.* New York: Academic Press, 1975.

Sewell, W. H., and Hauser, R. M. "Causes and Consequences of Higher Education: Models of the Status Attainment Process." In W. H. Sewell, R. M. Hauser, and D. L. Featherman (eds.), *Schooling and Achievement in American Society.* New York: Academic Press, 1976.

Sewell, W. H., Hauser, R. M., and Wolf, W. "Sex, Schooling, and Occupational Status." *American Journal of Sociology,* 1980, *86*(3), 551–583.

Simon, K. A., and Frankel, M. M. *Projections of Education Statistics to 1981-82.* Washington, D.C.: U.S. Office of Education, 1972.

Simonson, R., and Walker, S. *The Graywolf Annual 5: Multicultural Literacy.* St. Paul, Minn.: Graywolf Press, 1988.

Sivart, W. A. "Ethnic Studies: Vanishing or Not?" *Saturday Review of Education,* 1973, *1*(1), 54.

Smart, J. C., and Pascarella, E. T. "Socioeconomic Achievements of Former College Students." *Journal of Higher Education,* 1986, *57*(5), 529–549.

Smith, J. P., and Ward, M. P. *Women's Wages and Work in the Twentieth Century.* Santa Monica: Calif.: Rand, 1984.

Snyder, T. D. *Digest of Education Statistics, 1990.* Washington, D.C.: National Center for Education Statistics, 1990.

Snyder, T. D. *Digest of Education Statistics, 1992.* Washington, D.C.: National Center for Education Statistics, 1992.

Snyder, T. D. *Digest of Education Statistics, 1993.* Washington, D.C.: National Center for Education Statistics, 1993.

Sperber, M. A. "The College Coach as Entrepreneur." *Academe,* 1987, *73*(4), 30–33.

Sperber, M. A. *College Sports Inc.: The Athletic Department Vs the University.* Troy, Mo.: Holt, Rinehart & Winston, 1990.

Stage, F. "Student Typologies and the Study of College Outcomes." *Review of Higher Education,* 1988, *11,* 247–258.

Steele, S. "The Recoloring of Campus Life." *Harper's, 278* (1665), 47–55.

Steinberg, R. J. "Identifying Wage Discrimination and Implementing Pay Equity Adjustments." In *Comparable Worth: Issues for the 80s.* Washington, D.C.: U.S. Commission on Civil Rights, 1984.

Stern, J. D., and Chandler, M. O. *The Condition of Education, 1988.* Vol. 2: *Postsecondary Education.* Washington, D.C.: National Center for Education Statistics, 1988.

Stockard, J., and Wood, J. W. "The Myth of Female Underachievement." *American Educational Research Journal,* 1984, *21*(4), 825–838.

Study Group on the Conditions of Excellence in American Higher Education. *Involvement in Learning.* Washington, D.C.: National Institute of Education, 1984.

"Study Now, Pay Never." *Newsweek,* Mar. 7, 1977, p. 95.

Suter, L. E., and Miller, H. P. "Income Differences Between Men and Career Women." *American Journal of Sociology,* 1973, *59,* 962–974.

Taubman, P., and Wales, T. "Education as an Investment and a Screening Device." In F. T. Juster (ed.), *Education, Income, and Human Behavior.* New York: McGraw-Hill, 1975.

Taylor, M. E., Stafford, C. E., and Place, C. *National Longitudinal Study of the High School Class of 1972: Study Reports and Update: Review and Annotation.* Washington, D.C.: National Center for Education Statistics, 1981.

Thelin, J. R., and Wiseman, L. L. *The Old College Try: Balancing Academics and Athletics in Higher Education.* ASHE-ERIC Higher Education Report no. 4. Washington, D.C.: George Washington University, 1989.

Tinto, V. *Leaving College: Rethinking the Causes and Cures of Student Attrition.* Chicago: University of Chicago Press, 1987.

Todorov, T. "Crimes Against Humanities." *New Republic,* July 3, 1989, pp. 26–30.

Toombs, W., Fairweather, J., Chen, A., and Amey, M. *Open to View: Practice and Purpose in General Education, 1988.* University Park, Pa.: Center for the Study of Higher Education, Pennsylvania State University, 1989.

Tourangeau, R., and others. *The National Longitudinal Study of the High School Class of 1972: Fifth (1986) Follow-Up Data User's Manual.* Washington, D.C.: National Center for Education Statistics, 1987.

Treiman, D. W., and Hartmann, H. *Women, Wages, and Work: Equal Pay for Equal Value.* Washington, D.C.: National Academy Press, 1981.

Tribe, D., and Tribe, A. "Assessing Law Students: Lecturers' Attitudes and Practices." *Assessment and Evaluation in Higher Education,* 1988, *13,* 195–211.

"The Turned-Off Voter." *Newsweek,* Sept. 13, 1976, p. 16.

U.S. Bureau of the Census. *Social Indicators III.* Washington, D.C.: U.S. Bureau of the Census, 1980.

Velez, W. "Finishing College: The Effects of College Type." *Sociology of Education,* 1985, *58,* 191–200.

Velez, W., and Javalgi, R. G. "Two-Year College to Four-Year College: The Likelihood of Transfer." *American Journal of Education,* 1987, *96*(1), 81–94.

Warren, J. R. "A Model for Assessing Undergraduate Learning in Mechanical Engineering." In C. Adelman (ed.), *Signs and Traces: Model Indicators of College Student Learning in the Disciplines.* Washington, D.C.: U.S. Government Printing Office, 1989.

Webb, J., Campbell, D. T., Schwartz, R. D., and Sechrest, L. *Unobtrusive Measures.* Chicago: University of Chicago Press, 1966.

Weintraub, K. *Visions of Culture.* Chicago: University of Chicago Press, 1966.

Weistart, J. C. "College Sports Reform: Where Are the Faculty?" *Academe,* 1987, *73*(4), 12–17.

Wentworth, E. "No Silver Spoon for Higher Education." *Saturday Review,* 1972, *55*(30), 38–39.

Whiteley, M. A., and Fenske, R. H. "The College Mathematics Experience and Changes in Majors: A Structural Model Analysis." *Review of Higher Education,* 1990, *13*(3), 357–386.

Whitner, P. A., and Myers, R. C. "Academics and an Athlete: A Case Study." *Journal of Higher Education,* 1986, *57*(6), 659–672.

Wilson, K. M. *The Relationship of GRE General Test Item–Type Part Scores to Undergraduate Grades.* Report no. GREB-81-22P. Princeton, N.J.: Educational Testing Service, 1985.

Wilson, S. R., and Wise, L. L. *The American Citizen: 11 Years After High School.* Palo Alto, Calif.: American Institutes for Research, 1975.

Winkler, H. "The Importance of Being Fonzie." "My Turn" essay. *Newsweek,* Sept. 21, 1976, p. 11.

Wise, L., McLaughlin, D. H., and Steel, L. *The Project TALENT Data Bank Handbook.* Palo Alto, Calif.: American Institutes for Research, 1977.

Wright, F. L. *The Living City.* New York: Dutton, 1970.

Zwerling, L. S. *Second Best: The Crisis of the Community College.* New York: McGraw-Hill, 1976.

Zwerling, L. S. "Lifelong Learning: A New Form of Tracking." In L. S. Zwerling (ed.), *The Community College and Its Critics.* San Francisco: Jossey-Bass, 1986.

Index

Stage, F., 127
Standard deviation units (SDUs), 40–41
Statistical significance, 20–21
Statistics: information from, 19–20, 21–27; statistical versus historical significance with, 20–21; study of, and gender, 46–47. *See also* Mathematics; Numbers
Steel, L., 277
Steele, S., 205
Steinberg, R. J., 59
Stern, J. D., 193
Stockard, J., 73
Stowe, P. S., 11
Student Athlete Right-to-Know Act (S.580), 113, 117n1
Student Right-to-Know and Campus Security Act (P.L. 101–542), 20–21, 30, 113, 114, 117n1, 119n5
Students: high-academic resource, 143–144, 145; nontraditional, 248, 249; proprietary/vocational school, 233, 260n2. *See also* Community college students; Performing arts students
Study Group on the Conditions of Excellence in American Higher Education, 259
"Study Now, Pay Never," 233
Support services, for athletes, 102–103
Supradialects, 180–182, 184, 202, 217
Survey of Earned Doctorates, 75n4
Surveys, 7, 8; data from, 9–14; of deans, 190–191; enrollment, 191–192; response rates for, 7–8; versus tests, 218n3. *See also* Longitudinal studies
Suter, L. E., 57–58
Syllabi, as information source, 192

T

Tarule, J. M., 67
Taubman, P., 56
Taylor, M. W., 15
Test scores, 7, 19; by degree earned

and general postsecondary attendance pattern, 143; and high school curriculum, 40–42; high school seniors' aspirations versus plans by, 139–140, 172–173; of varsity athletes, 95–97; versus survey data, 9
Tests: de facto national, 192–194; versus surveys, 218n3
Thelin, J. R., 84
Thiel, R., 109
Thorndike, R., 275
Thurgood, D. H., 75n4
Tillery, D., 155
Tinto, V., 127
Title, C. K., 41
To, D. L., 55, 57, 165
Todorov, T., 176
Toombs, W., 189
Total Quality Management (TQM), 236
Tourangeau, R., 7
Tragash, H., 68
Transcripts, 8; information on community college students from, 126–128, 168n1; as source of information, 194–196; for student classification, 156–157, 169n5; versus survey data, 9–11, 12–13. *See also* Post-secondary education transcript sample (NLS-PETS or PETS)
Transfer: calculation of rates of, 131; and community college entrance time, 138; definition of, 128–129, 130–131
Treiman, D. W., 59, 70
Tribe, A., 192
Tribe, D., 192

U

Unemployment: of performing arts students, 111; and postsecondary attendance patterns, 164; of varsity athletes, 109–110; women's experience with, 54–55
Universes: and answers to questions, 21–24, 25–26; and infor-